HENRY T. NORTHEN, Ph.D., University of California, is Professor of Botany at the University of Wyoming, where he has been a member of the faculty since 1936. He is a Fellow of the American Association for the Advancement of Science and a member of the Botanical Society of America and the American Society of Plant Physiologists. Dr. Northen is the author of *Introductory Plant Science*, published by The Ronald Press Company.

REBECCA T. NORTHEN, M.A., Mount Holyoke College, specializes in orchid culture and has worked with her husband on research problems in plant physiology. She is a trustee of the American Orchid Society and a member of several other orchid societies. Mrs. Northen has written widely on orchids as well as subjects of general interest, and is co-author with her husband of *The Secret of the Green Thumb*, published by The Ronald Press Company.

GREENHOUSE GARDENING

HENRY T. NORTHEN

REBECCA T. NORTHEN

SECOND EDITION

THE RONALD PRESS COMPANY · NEW YORK

Library of Congress Catalog Card Number: 75–190208
PRINTED IN THE UNITED STATES OF AMERICA

Preface

There has been a tremendous surge of interest in greenhouse gardening in the years since the first edition of this book was published. More people have greenhouses now, and many others plan to incorporate a greenhouse in a new home. Gardening under glass has always had a special appeal. It is a fascinating and wonderfully satisfying hobby, with endless possibilities. Schools, from the junior high to the university levels, are building greenhouses, not only for courses in horticulture, but also to give biology students experience with living plants and a means for experimentation. The therapeutic effect of growing things has proven of such value that many hospitals and institutions are building greenhouses for their patients. For everyone, the relaxation from stressful living that gardening brings is, of course, one of the great joys of a greenhouse.

A greenhouse is most successful and gives most pleasure when it is well built and well managed. And success with plants is best assured when their needs are understood. A true grower wants information he can use, whether he is an amateur, a professional, an amateur who wants to make his greenhouse a profitable hobby, or a teacher. It is our aim to give the practical and necessary information on selecting, building, equipping, and managing a greenhouse, and modern methods for growing familiar as well as unusual and exotic plants. No amateur is content to remain static; he is naturally adventuresome and wants to try new things, to advance from the simpler to the specialized, both in techniques and kinds of plants. We have, therefore, strived to make this new edition even more comprehensive and detailed so as to carry the grower along as his interests expand, to introduce him to new possibilities, new ways to make the most of his space, and new techniques that he, as well as the professional, can use.

Many styles of greenhouses are presented. The standard types have been improved in construction and interesting new ones have been designed to add a decorative note to a garden. Methods of glazing have been improved and new glazing materials have been produced. Along with practical consideration of these we also discuss modern methods of heating, cooling, and ventilating a greenhouse, and new ways to water plants. Not everyone will want to adopt all of the new systems, but we present them for the grower to make his own choices.

As in the first edition, we have tried to make the book enjoyable reading. Material has been expanded and reorganized for easier reference. There are an increased number and diversity of illustrations. We have continued the important "how-to" pictures, giving step-by-step handling of plants from seed to bloom. These illustrations show how to repot, divide, make cuttings, control shape and flower production, and control blooming time.

Each plant is introduced with both its scientific name and its common name, if it possesses one. For each plant or group of related plants, we give the country of origin and something about the native habitat—what the forests, plains, or deserts are like, how the plants have adapted themselves to these environments, and how all this affects their requirements in cultivation. Fascinating bits of lore are added—plant history, the meaning of names, and peculiarities of habit, as for example how insectivorous plants operate. We have included a great many more kinds in this edition—new varieties, miniatures, delightfully decorative things to add spice to a greenhouse collection.

Plants are grouped according to temperature and light requirements, as well as their method of culture. Instead of giving the type of growing medium for each kind, we simplify matters by giving a medium suitable for all those in one chapter, or one group within a chapter. This makes for ease in selecting what to grow as well as what to grow them in. Because gardening soil is not always available, especially in many urban areas, we also give mixes containing no soil that can successfully be used in its place.

Many advances in culture have occurred in the past fifteen years. We describe new types of fertilizers and new methods of applying them. For pest and disease control we avoid the chemicals most hazardous to man and the environment, centering our attention on those that are biodegradable and less toxic to man and to animal life, some of which are new and more effective.

We extend our gratitude to all of those whose work has contributed to the development of greenhouse gardening, to those who have furnished information personally, and to those who have so kindly loaned us pictures for publication.

HENRY T. NORTHEN
REBECCA T. NORTHEN

Laramie, Wyoming
November, 1972

Contents

CONTENTS

GREENHOUSE
GARDENING

1

Gardening Under Glass

A haven of warmth and color, where the smell of damp earth mingles with the perfume of flowers—this is a greenhouse. A place where the cares of the day ease out through your fingertips as you dig and pot and water and handle green growing things—this also is a greenhouse.

And it is more. With a greenhouse you need no longer retire to the house when frost comes, to spend evenings yearning over seed catalogues, but can garden the year around. Its controlled environment frees you from dependence on hardy or seasonal things and allows you endless choices, for even in the coldest climate you can bring into it the most tender exotics. Sheltered from the elements and with pest control made easy, plants can be grown to greater perfection than outdoors. In a greenhouse you have an intimate relationship with plants and an opportunity to explore their mysteries as you follow the germination of seeds, the development of roots, and the formation of flower buds. If you are a camera enthusiast you will never lack for subjects, for there is fascination in every part of a plant or flower.

A greenhouse hobby can lead you in many directions with only your imagination to limit you—in fact a greenhouse will almost of itself lead you from one delightful phase to another.

With planning you can have a succession of blooms throughout the year—for example, chrysanthemums in the fall, followed in winter and spring by snapdragons, carnations, stock, calendulas, pansies, schizanthus, and a host of others, many quite spectacular and

3

unusual, such as gerberas and blue lace flower. This is perhaps the easiest and most economical group, for they can be grown in benches of soil at a night temperature of 50 degrees (kind to the fuel bill), and in full sun. Along with them you can raise pot plants such as geraniums in infinite variety, primrose and cyclamen, and have spring in winter with tulips, daffodils, and hyacinths.

Desert plants hold a special fascination. You can create a landscape with cacti from Mexico and our Southwest, using tree-like forms with columnar shapes and those which have branching pad-like structure, little ground-hugging kinds, and a host of others weird or beautiful, often humorous in aspect. For contrast you can place among them some of the more gentle and graceful succulents. Also, there are the sometimes incredible plants from African deserts such as living rocks, euphorbias, and aloes. Along with these can be grown the epiphytic night-blooming cereus and its relatives, whose midnight shows of ethereal blooms become a highlight of each year.

Many plant lovers are specialists at heart, and for them there are bromeliads with leaves brilliantly colored and patterned and spikes of flowers in striking color combinations; thousands of species of orchids never seen in florist shops, boldly showy or serenely beautiful, tiny or large, and with fascinating habits and forms; gesneriads such as African violets and their glowing velvety- or waxy-flowered relatives episcia, gloxinia, achimenes, columnea and many others; bog plants, among which the carnivorous kinds are a specialty unto themselves—the graceful or lurid pitcher plants, venus fly trap whose hinged leaves snap shut when touched, and sundews whose tiny leaves sparkle with mucilage-tipped hairs.

One could go wild over ferns alone, some of which are so un-fern-like that they can fool the uninitiated. There are birdnest ferns, walking ferns, holly, maidenhair and Creton brake ferns, water ferns, endless ruffled varieties of Boston fern, and the great epiphytic staghorns. One needs color to accompany their greenery, so ferns are usually interspersed with flowering plants.

A specialist in one group can often spare affection for plants from other groups. One kind may be his chief love, but interest and variety can be added by combining it with a few from other families. Orchids can be accentuated by bromeliads; gesneriads grow happily with either or both of these, and cacti form a pleasing contrast to all. (Cacti, incidentally, seem to thrive with a humidity above that of their native habitat.) Among these specialty plants

Fig. 1–1. You can have foliage and flowers from your own greenhouse the year around. Here begonias and ivy have been used by Myra J. Brooks. (Roche)

Fig. 1–2. The magenta-flowered hybrid *Epiphyllum* Prof. Ebert at the left is suitable for small pots. (Ladislaus Cutak) Right, succulents from several families grow side by side to make a delightful array in a greenhouse bench.

there are kinds that come from both high and low elevations and which can be grown in either the 50-degree greenhouse already mentioned, or in one where the nights are kept at 60 degrees. Individual light requirements can be managed by shading. Part of the fun with a greenhouse comes from inventing ways to grow plants with different needs together, understanding fully that the basic requirement of temperature must be met.

Your enthusiasm for a hobby plant and its relatives may lead to a fine collection, to a breeding program, and to expert knowledge of the group. It also leads to friendship with people who share your interests, often to correspondence with those in other countries. Societies exist for fanciers of African violets, begonias, gloxinias, cacti and succulents, orchids, camellias, lilies, and primroses, to name only a few. There is a special fascination in sharing problems and triumphs with others who understand and appreciate your efforts. Out of an initial interest in having flowers both for their own sake and to bring into the house can arise a hobby for some members of the family in flower arranging and corsage making. This leads to study of arranging in foreign lands and to a deeper study of the philosophy and culture of the people.

Not the least of the joys comes in expanding your knowledge of the native habitats of the plants and the history of their discovery. We owe a debt of gratitude to the early botanical explorers and to the geographical explorers who had a deep interest in nature. Many of them spent years in unexplored tropics discovering the plants that are so familiar and so readily available to us today. They endured great physical hardship while hacking paths through spiny vegetation, climbing tall trees to reach epiphytes high overhead, traveling rivers in dugout canoes to penetrate regions accessible in no other way, suffering from mountain sickness and bitter cold in high elevations, and from malaria and yellow fever in low lands, not to mention the bites of venomous snakes and insects and dangers from large cats. They had to live off the land and often became ill from malnutrition. Some had a gift for making friends with isolated tribes but some suffered at their hands, a few even met death among them. The disappearances of some explorers have never been solved. How these people managed under such circumstances to bring out their beautifully prepared herbarium specimens and collections of living plants is difficult for us to comprehend. Our travel is so easy compared to theirs.

Explorers are still finding new species, and searching for them even now is not always easy. Exploding population in tropical countries is causing destruction of native forests so that exploration now assumes the aspect of saving species from extinction. Remnants of virgin forest can sometimes be found only in canyons too steep to be logged over or farmed, but it is amazing to us to see what steep land *is* cut over and farmed by people faced with starvation. The problem is twofold—to try to bring out rare species before their habitat is destroyed, and at the same time not to strip areas that might remain intact. Commercial collecting today often causes severe destruction, but so also does collecting by native peoples who can sell plants for a few cents in the market places. Many countries now forbid collecting by foreigners and allow exporters to ship out only plants they have grown and propagated. If you approach it with care and understanding, with concern for the perpetuation of plants in their native habitats, you can have a collecting experience yourself in countries where it is permitted. Even better, in areas where species are threatened, hunting with a camera is wiser than actually gathering plants, and bringing home seeds of course does no harm.

Most of the kinds of plants grown in greenhouses are from the

Fig. 1–3. The magnificent cape primrose is a relative of the African violet. (Antonelli Brothers)

tropics. It will be a revelation to you to find out what a variety of climates exists in these tropics. We ordinarily associate the word with heat and humidity, and it is true that at low elevations the tropics are often hot and damp, but they often include deserts. In the mountains, however, temperatures become cooler as the altitude increases. Thus, at an elevation of 9,000 the temperature is around 54 degrees. Above that it decreases to freezing at timberline, and becomes even colder where the summits are clothed with perpetual snow. The belt between 3,000 and 6,000 feet offers the richest number of species, and plants from here thrive in a greenhouse night temperature of 60 degrees. The cooler elevations give plants that grow well with nights of 50 degrees. On the other hand, those that occur naturally from 3,000 feet down to sea level may accept a night temperature of 65 degrees even though they may have somewhat warmer conditions in their native habitats.

If you do bring home plants, they must be inspected and fumigated at a port of entry in this country to eliminate pests they may harbor. For a permit to import and for information about quarantine stations, write to Plant Quarantine Division, USDA, 209 River Street, Hoboken, N. J. 07030. The shipping labels they furnish bear your permit number and must accompany all plants sent through the mail. Plants you bring with you must be deposited at the USDA quarantine center at the port by which you return, to be retrieved after they have been treated.

A greenhouse does not spring full blown from a dream. It requires planning and understanding as well as some cost. However, a small greenhouse is not as expensive as you might think. If you have to sacrifice something in order to own one, you will be pleasantly surprised to find that it may come to no more than a paved terrace or patio, an elaborate outdoor fireplace, or a two-week vacation. And constructing it will give as much pleasure as the latter! Maintaining it involves increased fuel bills, which will depend on its size and your climate, and something for supplies such as pots and insecticides, all of which, measured in terms of recreation, will seem small.

Most hobbyists operate their greenhouses for fun rather than for profit. But at times a surplus of plants or flowers can be sold to help it pay its way. Potted plants at Christmas, Easter, and other holidays can be sold by yourself or through local stores. Seedlings, both for flower beds and vegetable gardens, can be raised and sold in the spring. Growing your own bedding plants, whether annuals

Fig. 1–4. Bromeliads, upper, and orchids, lower, are wonderful hobby plants.

or perennials, can be not only fun, but also can save you money, and you can raise kinds not ordinarily available from commercial growers. You can even raise trees and shrubs as seedlings or cuttings for yourself or for sale. It should be said that you cannot make a living from a small greenhouse—for that you need greater space and must devote more time to it. Amateurs have, however, frequently expanded a hobby into a business or a profitable sideline, sometimes after retirement. This should not be undertaken unless you know there is a demand for what you will raise.

Anything seems strange until we can give it a name. People sometimes think scientific plant names are horrible, and indeed some of them are. Of course, for some plants the scientific name is the common one since no one has ever come up with a nickname. For example, *Delphinium, Camellia, Chrysanthemum, Dahlia, Begonia,* which are generic names, are easy to say because we're used to them. The naming of plants is systematic. The taxonomists see to it that no two different plants have the same name. To keep things clear, a double name is used. The first name is that of the genus (plural, genera) to which a plant belongs, and the second is its specific or species name ("species" is both singular and plural). Some genera have few members, others have hundreds. You could liken a *genus* to a *suit* in a deck of cards—cards in the same suit are related by the characters, hearts or spades, for example, on their faces. An *individual card* in the suit is distinguished from the others by its number, and could be likened to a *species*, which differs from other members of the genus by one particular characteristic. As suits together form a deck, having in common the decoration on the back of the cards, so do a group of related genera form a *family.* An example would be the African violet. It belongs to the family *Gesneriaceae.* The genus to which it belongs is distinguished from other genera of this family by the name *Saintpaulia.* Each member of the genus is given its own specific name, that of the African violet being *ionantha.* No other species in the plant kingdom has that pair of names—*Saintpaulia ionantha.* Some of the other genera in the family Gesneriaceae are *Gloxinia, Episcia,* and *Columnea.* In this book, in order to help establish family relationships and see what less well known kinds belong with the more familiar ones, we'll give the family name along with genus and species. But we'll give the common name where there is one, just to put the acquaintance on an easier plane.

2

Selecting and Building Your Greenhouse

Selecting and building a greenhouse is truly an adventure. You will be more satisfied with the end result if you consider carefully the variety of greenhouses available before making a choice. Visit the greenhouses in your community. Talk with the owners and get their opinions of the kinds they have. Study the various types of greenhouse and learn how easy or how difficult they are to build. Look at the foundations, the walks, the arrangement and construction of the benches, and make notes about the desirable and undesirable features of each. In each greenhouse you visit, inspect the heating system and inquire about cost, operating expenses, reliability, and other features.

Write to greenhouse companies for literature. (A number of greenhouse companies advertise in gardening magazines which are available at newsstands or at your library; from these ads you can secure addresses.) Greenhouse manufacturers are featuring small greenhouses of excellent design, which are more attractive, less expensive, and more serviceable than those available a few years ago. The modern aluminum greenhouses have many desirable features. They do not require painting and there is nothing to rust or rot. Of course, aluminum greenhouses are more expensive than wooden ones. If your budget is limited, a good redwood greenhouse will give you many years of satisfaction. There are also greenhouses that have a supporting structure of steel but sash bars of redwood. These, too, are very satisfactory.

If wooden greenhouses are protected with paint they will last a lifetime. The woodwork should be given a primary coat at the factory. As soon as the framework is erected, and before glazing, paint the framework inside and outside. Apply another coat after the greenhouse has been glazed. The outside of a greenhouse should be repainted every other year, the inside every four or five years.

Types and Styles

Several types and styles of greenhouse are available. You can select a breezeway type, a lean-to model, a free-standing even-span greenhouse, or an even-span greenhouse to be attached to a building. Even-span greenhouses are symmetrical, with the two sides of the roof equal in length from the ridge to the eaves; they are adaptable to almost any location. In addition to conventional styles there are A-shapes, Gothic arch forms, or circular or octagonal forms resembling a carrousel. Many are designed to rest on a foundation which is 24 to 30 inches high, but others, the glass-to-ground type, are supported on a foundation only 8 inches high. With the glass-to-ground greenhouse, plants may be grown both on benches and

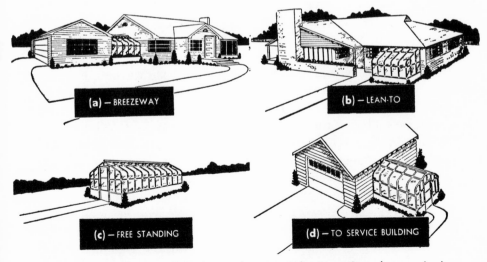

Fig. 2–1. Different styles of greenhouses. (Aluminum Greenhouses, Inc.)

under them, provided watering is managed so as not to keep the lower ones too wet.

The greenhouse may have vertical sides or slanting ones, and the eaves may be curved or straight. The straight-eaved greenhouse is the usual type, and is more economical from the point of view of glass replacement. Various kinds of greenhouses are prefabricated. All the parts are cut to fit, and you need only assemble them according to the directions furnished. All the fastenings are supplied, down to the last nut and bolt. Glass, putty if necessary, glass clips, and other items come with the order, as do foundation plans and assembly plans.

Obtain a greenhouse of a size that will fit your budget, your plans for growing plants, and the amount of time you want to spend caring for plants. One danger is that even a very small greenhouse will seem large at first. Nearly all greenhouse hobbyists soon find their greenhouses overflowing and wish that they had built larger ones in the beginning. Plan your first greenhouse of generous dimensions, preferably of a type that can be added onto in the future. In addition to lack of space, a very small greenhouse has the disadvantage of making temperature control difficult. It heats rapidly when the sun shines and cools off quickly when the sun goes down, which causes sudden rise and fall of temperature. Just as a spoonful of hot coffee cools more rapidly than a cupful, so does a small volume of air. Furthermore, a small volume of air will heat up more rapidly than a large one.

Location

Whether the greenhouse is to be planned with a new home or is to be built at an already existing residence, locate it where it will receive an abundance of light through the day. Ideally, the location should be such that the south, east, and west rays of the sun are not cut off. Don't build the greenhouse under or too close to trees, even small ones. Remember that the trees will grow large and that you will be using the greenhouse for many years.

It is best to have the floor of the greenhouse at ground level. If the floor is much below ground level drainage may be poor, and if rains are heavy the greenhouse may be flooded. If the floor of the greenhouse is several feet below ground level, the greenhouse may be too damp, and it may be difficult to heat it uniformly. Further-

Fig. 2–2. The greenhouse at the top, an Everlite aluminum curved eave greenhouse, was erected on the roof of a high school. Installed in this house is a hot water heating system consisting of a gas heater vented to the outside, fin tube radiators and thermostat, and transite benches. (Aluminum Greenhouses, Inc.) Below, a free-standing aluminum Orlyt greenhouse. (Lord and Burnham)

more, nearby buildings, trees, and shrubs may shade the greenhouse excessively.

If your home is on the south side of the street, you should not have any problem in locating the greenhouse in an open place in the back yard. If your residence is on the north side, place the greenhouse toward the very back of the yard, out of the winter shadow of the house. If you want an attached greenhouse, it is better to locate it on the south or east side of the residence than on the north or west side. The great benefit of a south exposure is that it affords more sun in the winter. A greenhouse on the east should be placed to take advantage of the sun from the south in winter. In a greenhouse that receives sun for only half a day, shade-loving plants thrive, but sun-loving plants might not do their best. A *small* greenhouse on the west side can become very hot in the summer and must often have heavier shade than is good for the plants. The point to keep in mind is to locate a greenhouse where it will receive the most hours of light each day, and plan to use seasonal shading on the glass when necessary.

If possible, locate the greenhouse where it will harmonize with the garden and architectural features. If you are planning to build a new home, have the architect incorporate the greenhouse in the plans. Supply him with the plans and the information that you have obtained from the greenhouse manufacturer, and insist that the greenhouse be situated where there is good light. In general, a greenhouse fabricated by a reliable company is better than a homemade one.

Foundations

As with any permanent building, a good foundation is important and determines to a large extent the durability of the structure. Generally you will have to construct the foundation for the greenhouse; that is, the foundation does not come with the greenhouse. But don't start until you receive detailed specifications from the greenhouse manufacturer. Never rely on the pictures which illustrate the manufacturer's advertisement, for these do not show such things as sill structure and bolts to fasten the framework to the sill.

Before you start on the foundation, lay out the walks and plan the footings for the benches. If you intend to use gravel under the benches, haul it to the proper place before the foundation goes up.

Fig. 2–3. A small greenhouse can be a decorative addition to a garden. Above, an A-frame, the Sun-Glory model. Below, the Sun-Bon, especially suitable for a garden with an oriental flavor. (Sturdi-Built Manufacturing Company)

Fig. 2–4. The Everlite curved eave lean-to has been neatly fitted to the residence. (Aluminum Greenhouses, Inc.)

Also plan the water supply. We will have more to say about paths, benches, and water later.

Many large greenhouses are supported by metal posts that rest on concrete footings. The posts and columns, not the walls, support this type of greenhouse. The footings should extend below the frost line, generally about 2½ feet below ground level in the northern states, and should be on solid ground. The walls may be of concrete, 4 inches thick and extending about 4 inches below ground level, or may be constructed of bricks, cut stone, concrete blocks, cinder blocks, or stuccoed tile, resting on a concrete footing.

Many of the hobby-size greenhouses do not have posts and columns for support. The weight rests on the foundation wall, which must therefore be sturdy. A greenhouse sill of special design is fastened to the top of the wall, and to this sill the greenhouse is secured. Concrete walls 8 inches thick and extending below frost level are strong and durable. If you prefer brick or concrete blocks,

Fig. 2–5. The REX Gothic Arch greenhouse has a frame entirely of red-wood. The pipes seen within are purely for supporting hanging plants and controls. (Trans Sphere Corporation)

lay them on a base of poured concrete. If you plan to move from your residence in five years or so and do not want a permanent greenhouse, you can build the foundation of wood. However, for a permanent greenhouse, we do not recommend a wood foundation, because in a few years the posts will rot and the greenhouse will sag.

Glazing

Up until a decade or two ago, glass was the universal glazing material. It has stood the test of time and has the advantage of greatest light transmission and ease of care that make it still the favorite today. Double-strength glass is preferred over single-strength and although it costs more is well worth it.

In certain types of wooden and aluminum greenhouses the panes of glass are overlapped about an eighth of an inch, and the edges of the glass rest on a bed of putty or some other glazing compound. If the sash bars are made of aluminum, the glass is held securely in place by specially designed clips. These clips facilitate assembly and glass replacement. If the sash bars are made of wood, glazing nails are used to keep the glass in place, one directly below the lower edge of the glass on each side to keep the pane from sliding down, one on each side 2 inches from the lower end of the pane, and one on each side at about the middle.

Some greenhouses come with large panes of glass, the edges of which rest in a channel lined with rubber or plastic. The glass is held in place by pressure of an aluminum barcap fastened to the sash bars on the outside. No putty is necessary.

Fiberglass is becoming quite popular as a substitute for glass. It is a product made of glass fibers embedded in a plastic resin. It comes in either corrugated or flat panels, clear or translucent, colorless or slightly tinted. The clear or translucent panels are preferable. Of the colors only a faint peach or pink is acceptable from the point of view of light quality; blue and green cut out the red end of the spectrum which is necessary for flowering. Be sure to get a type that is fire-resistant; check this with your local building authority. Fiberglass is easy to install. When new the clear or translucent panels transmit about 80 per cent of the incident light, which in regions with bright winters is ample for good growth. In regions where the winter months are extremely cloudy or dull, fiberglass may not be as satisfactory for plants requiring bright light, although it would be ample for such shade plants as begonias, gesneriads, ferns, anthuriums, philodendrons, and some orchids.

The first fiberglass on the market weathered badly; the glass fibers became exposed and collected dust, with a consequent reduction of light. It was necessary to scrape the surface and apply an acrylic coat to partially restore its clarity. Newer types are factory-coated with surface resins to improve durability, and these promise longer life although they remain to be tested in use. Advantages of fiberglass include ease of installation and resistance to breakage by hail, rocks, and falling tree limbs and from stress due to movement of the greenhouse frame during high winds. Many growers are enthusiastic about its soft, shadow-free light transmission.

The least expensive greenhouse covering is plastic film, of which there are several types, polyethylene film, Mylar (a polyester film), and polyvinyl fluoride film (PVF). All are nonrigid, of course, and none is permanent. They can be stretched over a homemade frame of wood or pipe (some growers have ingeniously made frames of electrical conduit), or a prefabricated one available from greenhouse companies, complete with door and precut film.

Polyethylene film is available in various thicknesses; 6-mil and 4-mil are the weights generally used. Just to give an idea of cost, at present a 14 × 14-foot frame plus precut 6-mil polyethylene film costs about $125.00. Some growers use a double layer with a dead air space in between for insulation, 6-mil (.006 inches thick) on the outside and 4-mil on the inside. Polyethylene film has high light transmission but lacks durability. It will last a year at the most and then must be replaced.

Mylar is a stiffer material and is more durable than polyethylene, lasting about four years on the roof and up to seven on vertical sides. Its light transmission is equal to that of glass. It costs a bit more—a prefabricated frame with 5-mil Mylar comes to about $220.00 for a 14 × 14-foot greenhouse.

Polyvinyl fluoride (PVF), called Tedlar, is new. Preliminary studies indicate that it may be more durable than Mylar, but it has not been tested long enough to be certain.

The greenhouse building itself is only part of the initial cost. Heating and ventilating systems, benches, walks, water pipes, electric lights, and operating costs are the same whether the covering is of glass, fiberglass, or plastic film. Glass and fiberglass long outlast the films, and replacement of the latter soon bring the eventual cost up to that of the former.

Ventilation

Ventilation is necessary both to bring fresh air to the plants and to provide air exchange for controlling summer heat. A greenhouse can become an oven if it is left closed when the sun is shining. There are numerous ways to provide ventilation. The simplest is by means of sections on both sides of the ridge that can be opened and closed by hand. Side ventilators are also helpful, allowing a flow of cooler air from near ground level up and out through the top. These can be automated by motors that respond to a thermostat, a great help for those who have to be away from home during the day. (Shading, either by painting the glass with whitewash or by installing various kinds of sun screens is necessary in summer to reduce the heat and will be described in the next chapter.)

In recent years alternate methods have been developed. An exhaust fan may be installed above plant level at one end of the greenhouse and a jalousie (a shutter with horizontal slats that swing open freely) at a lower level at the opposite end. With automatic controls the fan goes on when the temperature in the greenhouse exceeds the thermostat setting, and the vanes of the jalousie open as the fan reduces the inside pressure. Thus, the hot air is pulled out and replaced with cooler air from outdoors.

A modification of this exhaust system is especially helpful for bringing in fresh air during cool or cold weather. Called convection tube ventilation, it is rather a new development but is by now quite generally used in commercial greenhouses. A large flexible perforated plastic tube is suspended just below the ridge, with one end closed and the other end open and connected to a jalousie. No air moves through it until an exhaust fan is turned on. The exhaust fan can be located anywhere in the greenhouse, but ordinarily is at the end opposite the jalousie. It can be installed especially for the purpose, or can be the fan already installed as described above or used with the pad-and-fan cooling system described below. In essence, the exhaust fan lowers the air pressure within the greenhouse, and air is drawn in from outdoors to equalize it. As the air moves in through the jalousie it fills the plastic tube and is forced out through the perforations. The gentle movement allows the cool fresh air to mix with the warm air in the upper part of the greenhouse, and thus provides ventilation without cold drafts. A more elaborate arrangement makes use of a motorized fan between the jalousie and the tube to draw in outside air and force it through the tube. This convection tube system is more readily adaptable to greenhouses of fair size than to quite small ones. Another use of the perforated tubing is to distribute warm air evenly from a unit heater.

Even with shading and ventilation, the summer temperatures may still be too high for best growth of greenhouse plants. Inexpensive evaporative cooling systems solve the problem. It's best if one is included in the original plans for your greenhouse, but you can install one later. These are of two types—unit coolers, and pad and fan arrangements. If you already have an exhaust fan at one end of the greenhouse, the latter can be used. If not, a unit cooler may be the simpler method.

Unit coolers are those made for homes and are controlled by a cooling thermostat. Three sides consist of pads of aspen wood fiber (superior to the aluminum or paper pads) which are kept wet by water circulated over them by a small pump. A squirrel cage blower draws air through the wet pads and blows it into the greenhouse, and the air is cooled as the water evaporates. Such a cooler is placed in an opening at one end of the greenhouse so that outside air is pulled through it and blown into the greenhouse. A ventilator must be kept slightly open at the other end (or a jalousie installed) so that the air can move on through it, maintaining a constant current of cooled air. This system is called "positive pressure" since air is forced into the greenhouse.

The pad-and-fan system works on the same principle but involves use of an exhaust fan at one end and aspen pads at the other. The pads are installed in place of a section of glass. Troughs are placed both below and above the pads and a pump circulates water from the lower one to the one above, from which it trickles down through the pads. When the temperature rises, a cooling thermostat turns on the fan and the pump. Air is pulled out of the greenhouse, and outside air is drawn through the wet pads at the other end. This is called a "negative pressure" system.

Walks

The walks may be of concrete, flagstone, or brick. The concrete may be colored if desired. Flagstones or bricks laid on a cement base and pointed up with mortar are attractive and serviceable. The width of the walk depends on a number of factors—the types of plants grown, the width of the greenhouse, the size and arrangement of the benches, and the owner's desires. Two feet is a good average width. The walks should be higher than the floor; this makes it easy to hose them clean without leaving puddles of water or mud to soil the shoes. The atmosphere will be more moist if sand, soil, or gravel is used under the benches instead of concrete. However, if it is necessary to have a concrete floor, for instance if the greenhouse is on the roof of another building, be sure to have a floor drain and sufficient slope to carry off excess water.

Benches

The greenhouse company will suggest bench arrangements and types; some sell prefabricated benches. The usual height of benches is 30 inches, but it can vary between 24 and 36 inches according to your preference. One that suits a tall person may be uncomfortable for a short one. The height of the greenhouse to the eaves should also be considered, as should the kinds of plants to be grown. Snapdragons, roses, and carnations, for example, need a lot of head room, while African violets, gloxinias, and others of similar habit require only a small amount. If the benches are high and the roof low, the former may touch the glass, whereas the latter would not. You may wish to use stepped-up benches to display the plants better. The basic height might be 2 feet, with two shelves on each side and one running down the middle, each about 8 inches above the other.

The supports for the bed of the bench may be constructed of concrete, angle iron, pipe, or wood. The pipe or wood should rest on concrete footings or on bricks or concrete blocks.

The bench itself may be made of sheet aluminum, either flat or corrugated, wood, concrete, transite (an asbestos and concrete mixture), various metal mesh products such as hardware cloth and Expand-X, or rigid plastic material such as used under large light fixtures. For wooden benches, pecky cypress and redwood are preferred because they long outlast other kinds and do not have to be treated against rot. If other kinds are used, they should be treated with preservatives such as Cuprinol or Kopex. Never use creosote, which is injurious to plants. Growers of orchids and other pot plants often prefer open mesh materials as they provide perfect drainage and air circulation, and give few places for slugs and insects to breed. If wood, aluminum, transite, or concrete is used, make sure there is good drainage—leave spaces between boards or pieces of transite, punch holes in aluminum, or use molds for the concrete which leave holes in the finished piece. Even with such

---

Fig. 2–6. Systems for cooling and ventilation. Upper, details for installing a convection tube system; left, with motor-driven fan; right, without fan. (Acme Engineering and Manufacturing Corp.) Center, convection tube system in operation. Note here also the pads at the end, which operate in conjunction with an exhaust fan in hot weather—the wet "pad- and fan system." Lower left, diagram of convection tube ventilation, with intake louvers at end of tube and exhaust fan at opposite end. (National Greenhouse Company) Lower right, a unit cooler (International Metal Div., McGraw-Edison Company)

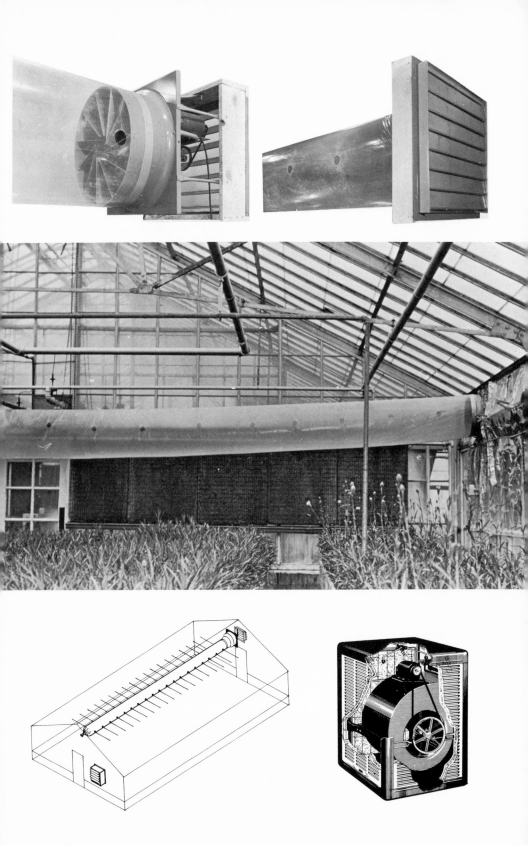

precautions it is wise to cover the bench with a layer of gravel to improve drainage. Benches that are to be filled with soil must have sides 6 inches or so high, and in these a layer of gravel should be laid before the soil is added.

Benches to be used for soilless culture (see page 62) must be waterproof and preferably have a V-shaped bottom. They may be constructed of concrete, steel, or wood lined with vinyl plastic. Concrete and steel should be painted on the inside with horticultural asphalt to prevent possible injury to plants from toxic substances dissolved from these materials.

Heating

Although plants require a lower temperature at night than during the day, they do best when it remains even during both periods. Hence, any heating system should be controlled by a sensitive thermostat. To guard against dangerous extremes caused by power or fuel failure, or pilots extinguished by wind, a temperature alarm should be installed. This is an alarm, run by battery, that rings a bell in the house when the temperature goes below or above the desired levels set on the dial. All heaters or boilers operating within a greenhouse should be vented to the outside. Products of combustion often include gases that are injurious to plants and can cause blasting of flowers.

For your own safety, and for a dependable supply of heat, secure plans for a heating system from a reliable firm. Greenhouse companies usually sell systems for their own greenhouses. You may choose the type, depending on what kind of fuel is least expensive in your locality and for your climate. The capacity of a heater should always be based on the temperature at which you wish to run your greenhouse, and the lowest temperature expected in your area. Artificial gas should never be used in a greenhouse; it is extremely poisonous to plant life.

The average greenhouse with glass or fiberglass requires 12,000 BTUs of heat input for each 1,000 square feet of exposed surface (glass plus foundation) for each 10-degree difference between inside and outside temperature. For example, if the lowest temperature in your region is zero degrees and you wish to maintain the greenhouse at 60 degrees during the night, the BTU output of the heater should be 6 × 12,000 = 72,000 BTU for each 1,000 square feet of exposed surface. If the surface is only 500 square feet, the output should be 36,000 BTU.

The least expensive heaters are those that circulate warm air, and they are quite satisfactory. The fuel may be natural or bottled gas or oil. The heaters are designed to be set in the foundation, with air for combustion drawn from outside and products of combustion vented to the outside. Others may be installed inside the greenhouse, either at the end of a walk or under a bench, and these must have vent pipes to the outside. We have found that horizontal heaters for use in homes can also be used in a greenhouse.

Most warm air heaters are equipped with a fan to circulate the heated air. It is best if the fan runs continuously, and not just when the heat is on, so as to keep the air constantly in motion. This brings the cooled air back to the heater so that there is less lag in its operation and keeps the temperature throughout the greenhouse more uniform. If a heater is designed so that the fan runs only when the heat is on, an electrician may be able to bypass the control. Otherwise, a separate fan should be installed to circulate the air. It is best to set the flame low enough so that the heater runs more or less continuously, that is, without sudden bursts of great

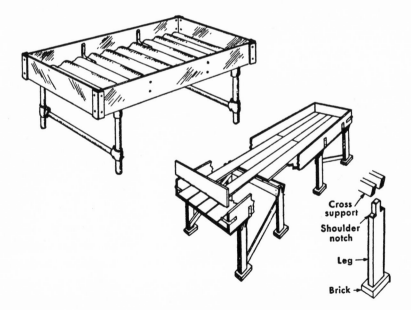

Fig. 2–7. Above, a transite bench. (Aluminum Greenhouses, Inc.) Below, detail for the construction of a bench from wood. (Lord and Burnham)

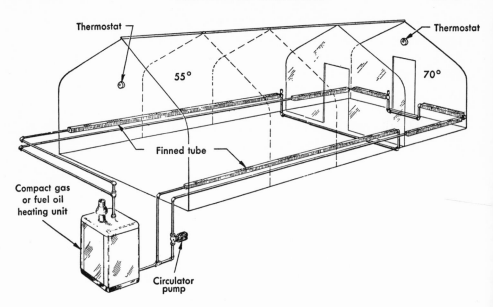

Fig. 2–8. Zone control heating system. (Aluminum Greenhouses, Inc.)

heat followed by long periods of cooling. All should be equipped with safety controls and an automatic shutoff valve.

A hot water system with forced flow and finned tubing is perhaps the ideal heating method, but is more expensive than warm air. It is safe; it furnishes a gentle heat, and it tends to provide more uniform temperatures because the tubing remains warm for some time after the fire is out. For a small greenhouse the finned tubes should be set around the inside base of the foundation, two or three inches from the wall and a similar distance above the floor. For a larger one, it may be necessary to have tubes running down the center as well. The flow of hot water can be accelerated by installing a circulator propeller, or a pump, in the system. If a circulator is used, less radiating surface will be needed. The fuel for the boiler may be coal, oil, or gas. A coal-burning boiler or one using artificial gas should never be set in a greenhouse but rather should be in a separate building, because fumes from these fuels are injurious to plant life. Properly constructed and vented boilers using natural gas or oil may be placed inside the greenhouse. Oil heaters or boilers must have a high flue or an induced draft fan and vent pipe. A gas heater requires a vent pipe with a top only slightly higher than the greenhouse ridge. A heating specialist or the greenhouse manufacturer will help you determine the size of boiler, the amount of finned tubing, and the best placement for both.

If your home has a hot-water heating system, a heating engineer can devise a means to run hot water to the greenhouse, provided, of course, that the boiler can carry the extra load. He will plan separate thermostatic controls and a circulating pump. If you have a steam boiler of ample capacity, he can plan a dual system, with steam for your residence and circulating hot water for the greenhouse.

Electric heaters may be feasible where winters are mild or electricity very inexpensive. They, too, must be equipped with thermostats and with fans to circulate the air. They require a separate line from the fuse box and should be installed by an electrician. Electric heat is often too costly for cold regions.

Fuel costs change from year to year, but just as an indication let us say that what it would cost in the area of Corpus Christi, Texas would be trebled in New York or Ohio, and multiplied by five in Anchorage, Alaska. In general, it costs about twice as much to maintain a greenhouse night temperature of 60 degrees as it does to maintain one of 50 degrees. The difference is due partly to the difference in temperature itself, and partly to the shorter heating season necessary for "cool" crops.

Fuel costs may be reduced 20 per cent to 40 per cent by installing polyethylene film inside the greenhouse to provide a dead air space of 1 to 2 inches between the film and the glass. The film need not be heavy—a 2-mil gauge is enough. A product called AirCap manufactured as a shipping material is becoming popular for the same purpose. It consists of two layers of plastic film between which air bubbles have been sealed. One side is smooth, and the bubbles project on the other. While it is quite expensive, its ease of installation makes it desirable. It is necessary only to press the smooth side onto wet glass and it adheres until pulled off.

A greenhouse of fair length, 20 feet or more, can be divided into two sections by a partition to give an area for cool-loving plants and another for warmth-loving kinds. Heat can be provided by separate hot-water lines from the boiler, a warm-air heater in each section, or by a duct system with motorized dampers from a single heater. If one section is maintained with 50-degree nights and the other with 60-degree nights, a great variety of kinds can be grown successfully.

Water

Water should be piped into the greenhouse and faucets located at convenient places. It is desirable to have both hot and cold water. Ideally, the water should be at about 60 degrees. Water softened by systems that add sodium are not suitable for plants because the excess sodium accumulates in the soil to harmful levels. Therefore, water for the greenhouse should be taken from the main pipeline before it is treated by such softeners. Methods that remove salts from the water are safe, but these are somewhat expensive and are needed only where the local water is really too high in salt content. This is a matter for advice from other greenhouse operators in your area, for not all "hard" water is bad, and in fact is rarely so.

Humidity

Most plants grow best in moist air with a relative humidity of about 65 per cent. In dry areas and in any area during the season of artificial heat, moisture should be added to the greenhouse atmosphere. You may wish to install mist sprayers under the bench, operated manually or by a humidistat, or buy a unit humidifier with automatic controls. The humidistat should be sensitive enough to turn the sprayers or the humidifer on and off when the relative humidity varies from the value for which you set it. However, many amateur growers and practically all commercial greenhousemen get along without humidifiers. They keep the air moist by wetting down the walks and the ground under the benches, and at times spraying water on the plants and between the pots.

Electricity

Electricity is needed for the operation of any automatic controls, for heaters particularly and for humidifiers and vent motors if you have them. Light in the greenhouse is also necessary for checking conditions at night. It also makes it possible to work in the evenings and to show your plants to friends who drop in. By artificially lengthening the days the growth of some plants can be speeded up and the flowering time of certain kinds can be controlled (with care not to upset the flowering of those that need short days to bloom).

Outlets conveniently placed are, therefore, a great boon. You can even plug in a radio or portable television set in order to enjoy a game or a symphony while working.

Controls

Controls for small greenhouses usually consist of thermostats for heaters, coolers, and ventilators, and humidistats for humidifiers, each operating separately and specifically. The science of electronics is now being put to use for complete automation. There are greenhouse engineering specialists who can set up interacting controls to enable the grower to "program" his greenhouse. All the equipment is operated by electronic sensors and controls, which blend the action of heaters, ventilators, humidifiers, and coolers to create the desired atmosphere for any season or for any particular crop. Automatic watering can be included.

Such systems are being installed in some commercial and institutional greenhouses, the cost being balanced by savings in labor. They are as yet too expensive for most hobbyists, but in the future may come within the reach of the backyard grower.

3

Managing Your Greenhouse

Creation of the congenial environment in which greenhouse plants prosper means gently balancing their various requirements. They need water, minerals from the soil, light, warmth, a moist atmosphere, and clean air. Not all kinds of plants want the same degree of heat, wetness, or light, however, so it is necessary to understand the particular requirements of those you wish to grow. Kinds native to a dry climate will resent too much water, and those from a wet one will shrivel if the air is too dry. Kinds from a cool, high elevation may suffer from heat in a greenhouse attuned to the needs of those from a warm climate, and the latter may turn sodden and yellow if it is too cold for them.

Each aspect of the environment affects other factors. There is a subtle interplay between light, heat, and humidity, for example, and between temperature and frequency of watering, and the latter is in turn related to the type of soil. Rapport with your plants and development of skill in handling them will come about more readily if you understand their basic needs. It is easier to grow kinds that all have the same requirements, but with a bit of intuition and experimentation you can modify the treatment of this or that group and have a wide variety.

Watering

The physiological activities of all living things take place in the presence of water. Minerals in the soil must be in solution before roots can absorb them. The chemical reactions in the cells themselves, such as food making and the manufacture of myriad products, and the movement of these materials from cell to cell, all go on in water solutions. Thus, when water is lacking, food manufacture ceases, cells cannot divide or increase in size, growth ceases, and plants cannot develop, flower, or fruit and they may shed their leaves or drop their buds. With most plants, wilting is a sign of lack of water, and it goes without saying that they should be watered before they wilt. However, there are kinds that do not immediately wilt when water is deficient, such as orchids, bromeliads, some geraniums, kalanchoë, Christmas cactus, and others. These are built to resist drought, and at first they just cease to grow and make food, though if the drought continues over a long period they will eventually shrivel.

When water is lacking, part of the root system may die. If this happens it may take some time for the roots to regenerate and the plant to resume vigorous growth. One result may be development of thin woody stems that cannot conduct water quickly. Such plants seldom become lush specimens, even though they may later be given good care. For most plants there should be no check in development up to maturity. Some kinds, of course, have dormant periods that must be recognized with lessened water or periods of complete dryness.

Overwatering results in literal drowning. Air must be present in the soil along with water, for plants need oxygen at the roots. If the spaces in the soil are continually filled with water to the exclusion of air, oxygen will be deficient and the roots will be unable to carry on respiration. They will cease to carry on their normal function of absorbing water and minerals. Root death will follow if the condition goes on too long, evidenced in nature when artificial lakes flood trees that originally stood above the water line. When water is applied, it fills the air spaces momentarily, and then as some drains away and as the plants use it, the air spaces open up and draw in fresh air. For this reason, it is best to let the soil dry somewhat before watering again.

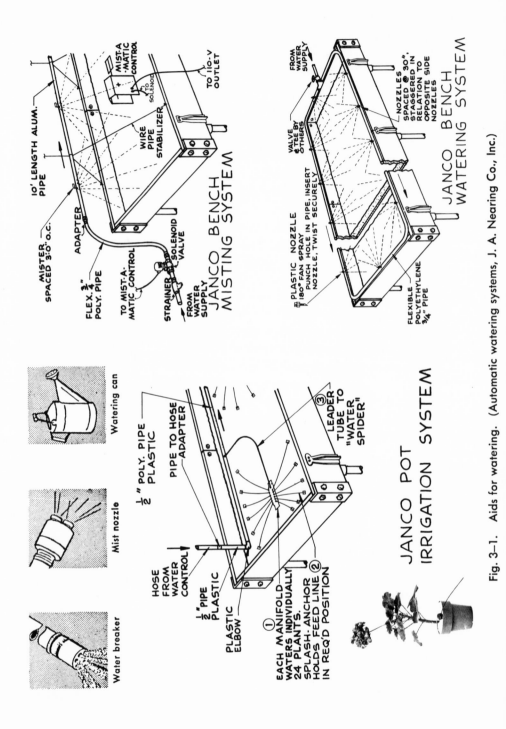

Watering can

Mist nozzle

Water breaker

MIST-A-MATIC CONTROL

TO SOLENOID

TO 110-V OUTLET

10' LENGTH ALUM. PIPE

WIRE PIPE STABILIZER

MISTER SPACED 3:0" o.c.

ADAPTER

FLEX. ½" POLY. PIPE

TO MIST-A-MATIC CONTROL

STRAINER

SOLENOID VALVE

FROM WATER SUPPLY

JANCO BENCH MISTING SYSTEM

FROM WATER SUPPLY

NOZZLES SPACED 30", STAGGERED IN RELATION TO OPPOSITE SIDE NOZZLES

VALVE & TEE BY OTHERS

PLASTIC NOZZLE 180° FAN SPRAY PUNCH HOLE IN PIPE, INSERT NOZZLE, TWIST SECURELY

FLEXIBLE POLYETHYLENE ¾" PIPE

JANCO BENCH WATERING SYSTEM

½" POLY. PIPE PLASTIC

PIPE TO HOSE ADAPTER

LEADER TUBE TO "WATER SPIDER" ③

HOSE FROM WATER CONTROL

½" PIPE PLASTIC

PLASTIC ELBOW

EACH MANIFOLD WATERS INDIVIDUALLY 24 PLANTS. SPLASH-ANCHOR HOLDS FEED LINE ② IN REQ'D POSITION ①

JANCO POT IRRIGATION SYSTEM

Fig. 3–1. Aids for watering. (Automatic watering systems, J. A. Nearing Co., Inc.)

For most kinds it is best to apply water directly into the pots or in the bench rather than to spray overhead. Give enough each time to moisten the soil from top to bottom, but be careful not to use such force as to wash away the soil or expose the roots. A water breaker attached to the hose will lessen the force, as will breaking the flow with your fingers held over the end. The old-fashioned watering can, while seldom used now, can be a help when you wish to water only a plant or two here and there.

Frequency of watering is related to the type of soil, the size and nature of the container, and the needs of the plants. Kinds such as cinerarias, hydrangeas, and acalypha use large amounts of water and, therefore, require frequent watering, whereas cattleya orchids and cyclamen use it sparingly and require less frequent applications. Sandy soils hold less water than loam and accordingly plants in a sandy mix must be watered more often. Small pots dry more rapidly than large ones, and clay pots faster than plastic. During the warm months of the year, and also during the season when artificial heat is used, many kinds require water daily; but during cool or cloudy weather several days may elapse between waterings. There are a number of ways to tell whether plants need watering. If you tap a clay pot (not a plastic one) and hear a dull sound, the soil is moist; if it gives a ringing sound, water it. You can often tell by the weight of the pot whether the soil has dried, and if you have a large number of the same kind of plant in the same size pot, you can decide whether to water by lifting sample pots here and there. If the soil is dark it probably still has available moisture, if light it is dry.

Determining when to water a bench is not so simple. During winter when the heat is going, soil may dry from the bottom of the bench upward. Push a clean trowel or other instrument down through the soil to the bottom boards; if it is hard to insert, makes a grating sound, and comes out clean and free of particles, the soil is dry and should be watered. If the surface itself is dry, the bench is certainly in need of water.

Plants just potted or transplanted should always be watered thoroughly immediately after the job is done. Bulbs and tubers should also be given a good watering after they are planted. However, after this first watering you should keep the bulbs and tubers on the dry side until roots develop, after which water them as you would other actively growing plants. If unrooted bulbs or tubers are maintained in soggy soil, they may rot. Remember, too, that until roots develop the water in the soil is not readily absorbed and it will stay wet longer, so care should be exercised with newly transplanted things until they become re-established.

You will have to water seeds and seedlings carefully, or you may wash them out of the soil. These may be watered with a can equipped with a fine rose (a nozzle with many small openings at the end), or you may place the flat or pot in a tray of water and let the soil take up water from below, removing it when it is entirely damp.

Some plants have alternating periods of activity and rest. The resting period is often during the winter, and at this stage of development the plants use less water than when they are actively growing. Soon after the turn of the year, poinsettias, for example, will enter their rest period. No matter how much you water the plants, the leaves will fall off. In the autumn tuberous begonias and gloxinias generally enter their rest period. You will notice a gradual dying and shriveling of the foliage. This is a sign they are entering their rest period, and water should be withheld. During the resting period several days, or even weeks or months, depending on the species, may elapse between waterings. When active growth begins again, the plants will require water more frequently.

If possible, use water which is the same temperature as that of the greenhouse. Very cold water may check the growth of some plants and may cause spotting of the foliage if splashed on the leaves; African violets, begonias, cape primroses, and gloxinias are especially sensitive to spotting by cold water.

Because many greenhouse plants make their best growth when the soil is neutral or slightly acid, it is best to use water that is not strongly alkaline, that is, not over pH 8. Continued use of alkaline water may make the soil too alkaline and the leaves may turn yellow, a result of the iron in the soil becoming insoluble and, therefore, not available to the plants. If this happens, you may correct the iron deficiency by watering every other week with a solution made up of one ounce of iron sulfate to two gallons of water, or by using an iron chelate. Continued use of "hard" water (this is different from alkaline water, as hard water may in fact have a satisfactory pH) may allow salts to concentrate in the soil to the detriment of the plants. By always watering from the top and giving enough to drain out the bottom, excess salts will be flushed out.

Rain water is ideal; some growers collect it for regular use or for certain plants, but this is not always practical. Certain water conditioners are on the market for correcting the alkalinity of tap water, and for removing excess salts. Never use sodium-softened water on plants; the additional sodium is harmful and interferes with normal growth.

What to do about watering when one is away on vacation or business presents a real problem. Many greenhouse owners call on their neighbors or hire someone. Another possibility is use of an automatic system. In general automatic systems are not as good as careful hand-watering because, of course, they lack judgment. One that waters everything at the same time will furnish the same amount of water to all plants, large and small, newly potted and well-established, resting and nonresting, and may also give too much water during rainy weather. One that is carefully regulated to the needs of groups of plants may be worth the expense for those who have to be away frequently or for long periods, or who can work in the greenhouse only on weekends. Equipment is available from greenhouse manufacturers.

For plants grown in benches, nozzles can be placed at intervals along the periphery to spray water on the soil surface. Separate lines, each controlled by a time clock connected to an electric water valve, can be installed for plants with different needs. For pot plants, water can be supplied directly to each pot through plastic tubes. The individual tubes, about the diameter of spaghetti, lead from a larger one laid along the bench, which in turn leads back to the water connection. You can buy the tubes and a tool for inserting the small ones into the larger one, from supply houses. The small tubes that go to the pots curve around on the soil and are held in place by a weighted bulb at the end. They can be perforated in several places to allow water to flow evenly over the surface. In order to water different groups at different times, each set of tubes can be connected to its own electrically controlled valve. You will have to do some experimenting to find out how long the water should be allowed to run, and how often it needs to be turned on. Then you can set the timer accordingly.

Gadgets are fine and have their place, but to grow plants to perfection nothing takes the place of human skill, care, and judgment. The raising of plants then becomes an art, an opportunity for one to develop his own skill.

Humidity

The amount of moisture in the air plays an important role in the growth of plants. Many plants grow poorly in the home because the air is too dry. When moved into a humid greenhouse these plants thrive. When the air is dry—that is, when the relative humidity is low—plants lose water rapidly through their foliage and stems. This loss of water as vapor we call *transpiration*. Transpiration is high when the air is dry, the temperature warm, the day bright, and when the air is moving. When the relative humidity is high, transpiration is decreased. Hence, try to keep the air humid in the greenhouse. The ideal relative humidity is between 50 and 70 per cent. (At higher relative humidities plants grow well, but there is greater danger of disease getting started.) You can increase the humidity by spraying water on the walks and under the benches. Mist nozzles may be attached to pipes installed under the benches, or perhaps you will want a motor-operated humidifier. The latter can cost from $50 to $150, depending on the make and capacity, and can be operated with automatic controls.

Syringing

Many plants, among them orchids, carnations, snapdragons, cyclamen, and chrysanthemums, benefit from being syringed with a mist of water during the hotter hours of bright days. The spray reduces leaf temperatures and transpiration. Furthermore, forceful syringing washes insects off the foliage. Red spider, a common greenhouse pest, can be partially controlled in this manner. There are a number of nozzles on the market which break water from the hose into a fine mist suitable for syringing. Syringing is not a substitute for watering. When syringing, wet the foliage but do not apply enough water to fill the pots or benches.

Plants just moved into flats or pots should be syringed until they become established, as should cuttings. Spraying with water at frequent intervals will keep the leaves from wilting too much. Syringing sometimes encourages buds to develop. For example, newly potted dormant roses will develop faster if the stems and dormant buds are sprayed with water.

Certain plants, such as ferns, gloxinias, African violets, and tuberous begonias may be injured if syringed with cold water. These plants should not be sprayed with water, or, if sprayed, the water should be at greenhouse temperature.

Atmosphere

We are more comfortable in a well-ventilated room than in a stuffy, hot one. Opening the windows brings in fresh air and often lowers the temperature of the room. In a greenhouse in summer, the day temperatures become unbearably hot if the ventilators remain closed. Even in winter, the greenhouse needs some ventilation to furnish the plants fresh air. Also desirable is a fan to keep the air within the greenhouse in constant motion. Moving air promotes good growth and lessens the incidence of disease.

Fresh air contains both oxygen and carbon dioxide, which are essential for plant development. Plants use oxygen much as we do, to combine with sugars, to oxidize them. As the sugar is oxidized, energy is released and made available for the plants' activities. Roots, stems, leaves, flowers, and fruits all require a continuous supply of oxygen.

The carbon dioxide in the air is used by the plant to make sugar. In the leaves and other green parts of the plant, the carbon dioxide of the air is combined with water during the day to form sugar and to release oxygen, a process called photosynthesis. Light furnishes the energy for the process.

The plant makes many substances from the sugar. Sugar is changed into starch, cellulose, and fats, and with the addition of nitrogen, sulfur, and phosphorous, into proteins. These substances are combined in various ways to form additional tissues, and thereby the plant grows. They are also used to form flowers, fruits, and seeds and to make hormones, vitamins, chlorophyll, and red, blue, and orange pigments. Hence if plants are to thrive they must make an abundance of food, and for this process carbon dioxide is essential.

As previously mentioned, a greenhouse may be ventilated by thermostatically controlled fans with suitable inlets for air, or by ventilators. If ventilators are used they should be on both sides of the ridge. Side ventilators at the eaves or below the benches are desirable but not absolutely essential. With ventilators on both sides of the ridge, drafts can be avoided by opening them on the lee side. On quiet, hot days, they can all be opened. During the summer in many regions the ventilators may be kept open both day and night. In winter it may be possible to have them open for only a short time, and then only occasionally, although the plants will benefit from fresh air whenever this can be done. Closing them before the temperature drops toward late afternoon will make for more equable temperature and will reduce the fuel bill. Ventilation is one way to minimize the incidence of disease. Without ventilation on a cloudy day the relative humidity may become excessive, thereby favoring the development of disease-causing organisms.

When the weather is changeable, the sun out one hour and behind the clouds the next, the temperature may fluctuate widely unless you open and close the ventilators with the vagaries of the weather. Many amateurs, especially those who are away from the greenhouse during most of the day, find automatic ventilation very desirable. Greenhouse companies sell motors to attach to the ventilators. The motor is controlled by a thermostat. When the temperature in the greenhouse reaches the setting, the motor opens the ventilators. When the temperature drops below the setting, the motor closes them.

During the summer you may have to screen the ventilators to keep out wasps, bees, and other undesirable visitors, especially if your plants are in flower. Fasten ordinary window screen to the frame of the ventilator. When flowers are pollinated, their life is much reduced. For example, orchids may last several weeks if the blossoms are not pollinated, but only about a day if pollinated.

Carbon Dioxide Enrichment

The normal amount of carbon dioxide in the atmosphere is 300 ppm (parts per million). Experiments carried out at several experiment stations here and abroad demonstrate that when other environmental conditions are optimal, enriching the air with additional carbon dioxide improves the growth of some kinds, increases the quality and number of flowers, and often hastens plants into bloom. The amount that gives best results is about four times normal, that is, about 1200 ppm. Many commercial growers in this country are now using the technique for such things as carnations, geraniums, roses, chrysanthemums, snapdragons, Easter lilies, calla lilies, gloxinias, African violets, hyacinths, bedding plants and greenhouse vegetables such as tomatoes and cucumbers. With orchids the results are not as clear-cut—some growers feel that seedlings are improved, but the results are difficult to assess with mature plants. More data are needed on other kinds of plants; some may respond and some may not.

Various methods of adding carbon dioxide have been tried. Best so far are special propane or natural gas burners with precision-made parts of stainless steel and a vitreous enamel coating that give absolutely complete combustion. (It is not safe to use ordinary open flame gas burners of the old-fashioned heater type, as fumes from these may injure the flowers.) The units made to date are for large greenhouses. It is hoped that smaller models will be available in the future.

Growing techniques must be much more precise with added carbon dioxide. The schedule of fertilizing must be increased in proportion to the amount of carbon dioxide given, and it must be said that nutrition is not yet fully worked out for all plants. Daytime temperature can be run 10 degrees higher in the winter (night temperature should remain as usual). Enrichment is most effective during the winter or at least in cool weather when the vents can remain closed. Opening them even one or two inches allows the carbon dioxide to escape. The units give off some heat, which must be taken into account. Plants cannot make use of the added carbon dioxide unless they have optimal light, hence the units should be operated only on bright, sunny days. Fans should be operated to circulate the enriched air evenly.

When crop improvement can mean the difference between profit and loss for a commercial grower, the extra expense and care necessary with carbon dioxide enrichment can pay off. An amateur grower, especially one with a mixed collection, may not be able to see sufficient improvement to justify the costs.

Light

Some plants—carnations, calendulas, snapdragons, and others—make their best growth and flower profusely with full sun. Others —African violets, gloxinias, philodendron, and begonias—prefer shade. Carnations and other sun plants make more food at high light intensity than in shade.

In African violets and other shade plants the amount of food made increases as the light intensity increases up to one-tenth to one-fifth full sunlight, or between 1,000 and 2,000 foot-candles.

Higher light intensities do not increase the amount of food made or the rate of growth. As a matter of fact, higher light intensities may be detrimental, resulting in burning the foliage. Shade-loving plants, therefore, must have the light intensity reduced when grown in a greenhouse.

Even plants which do best in full sun out of doors will usually require shade in a greenhouse during the summer months. During summer the full glare of the sun would result in temperatures so high that the growth of the plants would be retarded, or the plants might even be killed by the heat. Furthermore, when the temperatures soar, insects thrive and become a serious menace. Hence, in most parts of the country, it is necessary to shade the greenhouse from early May to late September. Of course, regional differences in climate may make it necessary to have a longer or shorter shading period, or to shade at some other season.

As we have said before, the light requirement for different plants varies; some thrive with full sun, others in moderate shade, and still different species with heavier shade. The appearance of your plants and their behavior will indicate whether or not they are re-

Fig. 3–2. Light must be in a certain range if plants are to thrive. They become tall and spindly when grown in weak light, and often do not flower. The gloxinia on the left was grown in deep shade, the one on the right with good light.

ceiving the proper amount of light. If the plants are leggy, deep green, and flower sparingly, the light intensity is too low. If the foliage becomes a pronounced yellow green (or sometimes red) and is hard and small, the plants are getting too much light, as they also are if burned spots appear on the leaves.

You can raise both sun-loving and shade-loving plants in the same greenhouse by shading one part of the greenhouse and not the other. Also, you will find the shaded part a good place to keep cuttings until they are rooted and newly potted plants until they recover from the shock of transplanting.

There are a number of ways to shade a greenhouse: painting the glass or using roller blinds, fixed lath frames (of wood or aluminum), or cloth. A popular paint type is Garland White Shading Compound, mixed with water. If you find that the shading compound is too easily washed off by rains, you can add a small amount of linseed oil or a special binding compound to the mixture. The mixture may be sprayed on or may be put on with a paint roller on a long handle. Shading compound without a binder may be scrubbed off fairly easily in the autumn using a stiff brush and plenty of water. If a binder has been added it may have to be scraped off with a sharpened putty knife.

Greenhouses that are shaded with roller blinds or fixed lath frames are neater in appearance than those that are painted. Wooden roll-up shades and plastic ones are available. They may be rolled up during cloudy weather and let down on bright days. Some are made of aluminum color fiberglass screening material, made to reduce the light to 65 to 70 per cent. The various types are available from greenhouse companies, and come complete with rope, pulleys, and hardware. Lath shading can be made to furnish whatever degree of shade you desire by adjusting the space between the strips. Saran cloth, a plastic screen-like material, comes in a number of grades designed to transmit various amounts of light. It can be fastened up inside the greenhouse, or preferably fastened to an outside framework 12 to 18 inches above the glass.

Temperature

The plants we grow in greenhouses have come from all parts of the world. Some have been introduced from warm regions, others from temperate zones, different ones from cooler regions or high

Fig. 3–3. Column stock grows well and flowers profusely at a night temperature of 50 degrees. (Bodger Seeds, Ltd.) The poinsettia, right, thrives at a night temperature of 60 degrees. (Roche)

elevations. Plants from diverse climatic regions cannot all be grown at the same temperature. Both the day and night temperatures must be suitable for the variety. Night temperatures are especially critical. If they are too high or too low for the species the plants will not thrive and flower. African violets, tuberous begonias, cattleya orchids, and many foliage plants thrive and flower well when the night temperature is 60 degrees, but do poorly at 50 degrees. Carnations, snapdragons, stocks, and cymbidium orchids make their best growth and flowers at a night temperature of 50 degrees, but may fail to flower at 60 degrees. In later chapters when only one temperature is given for culture, we mean the night temperature.

Day temperatures are also significant. In general, they should run about 10 or 15 degrees higher than the nights. If the plants you want to grow are adaptable to a house maintained at 50 degrees at night, the ideal day temperature would be 60 or 65 degrees. If you raise those kinds that do best with nights at 60 degrees, plan to keep the days at 70 to 75 degrees. These day temperatures are easier to control in winter than in summer, but with the longer days of summer and the greater amount of sunshine, the plants can take and even benefit from somewhat higher temperatures. Shading, ventilation, syringing, and cooling equipment must, however, be used to modify excessive temperatures.

If you place thermometers in different parts of your greenhouse, you will probably find that the temperature is not uniform throughout. In a greenhouse where the thermostat is set for 60-degree nights, one corner may have a temperature of 55 degrees, and here can be grown plants that prefer cooler conditions. Often the temperature near the roof will be several degrees warmer than on the bench, and plants that need a bit more warmth can be hung or placed on shelves. Ideally, if you want to raise both warm and cool kinds in any large number, the greenhouse should be partitioned as described in Chapter 2.

During the winter, leaves which touch the glass may become frozen. Keep them away from the glass or put up insulating material. Polyethylene film fastened an inch away from the glass not only protects the leaves but forms an air space that saves on heating bills. A packaging product called AirCap has been ingeniously put to use as an insulating material. It consists of two sheets of Saran-coated polyethylene film, one flat and the other sealed to it and enclosing air bubbles. The bubbles range in size from three-eighths of an inch to 1¼ inches in diameter. The type with larger bubbles gives better insulation, but this is more expensive than that with smaller bubbles, and the latter is also useful. AirCap is applied by pressing it with your hands onto clean, wet glass, to which it adheres until it is pulled off. Either side can be placed toward the glass; the bubble side adheres just as well as the flat side, and gives additional air pockets for insulation. It can be used on both the roof and sides of the greenhouse, in which case it helps to cut down the fuel bill, or on the sides only, where it prevents contact between the leaves and the cold glass. It cuts out little light, if any.

Temperature affects many processes in a plant: food making, food using, growth, and flowering. As the day temperature increases, up to about 85 degrees, the rate of food manufacture also increases. But 85 degrees is not an ideal day temperature for most plants. As the temperature goes up, so also does the rate of food using, the process called *respiration*. In respiration, food and oxygen are used and carbon dioxide and water are formed, and energy for carrying on the manifold activities of a plant is released. At temperatures of 85 or 90 degrees the rate of respiration may be so great that there is little food left for growth and flower production. At a temperature of 70 degrees much more food is made than is used, and plants thrive. During the night, food manufacture does not go on, but respiration continues. If night temperatures are too high, too great an amount of food will be respired and little or none will be available for growth. Hence, we see the reason for keeping the night temperature about 10 degrees lower than the day. During the day the temperature should offer a favorable balance between food making and food using, and during the night a temperature that gives a balance between food using and growth.

Sanitation

If your greenhouse is kept clean, you will take greater pride in it and the plants will grow better. Remove dead leaves and shriveled flowers. Don't permit mosses and algae to cover the outside of pots. They may be washed off easily with water and a rag or brush. The addition of an agent such as Consan-20 to the wash water will help in controlling algae, fungi, and surface bacteria. Walks and wood surfaces may also be washed with such an agent and will stay clean longer. Remove weeds from pots, benches, and the ground, and rake the latter occasionally. Such practices will cut down the population of slugs, insects, and disease organisms.

A yearly scrubbing of the woodwork in the greenhouse, and painting about every four years, will make it more attractive and create better growing conditions. In many regions some plants, such as carnations, stocks, snapdragons, and others, require all the light they can get during the winter months. Glass covered with dirt and the remains of shading gives markedly reduced light intensity. Hence in the autumn a scrubbing of the glass is beneficial for these plants. A stiff brush fastened to a long handle and plenty of water can be used to clean the glass.

There is a great temptation to crowd too much into a small greenhouse. The plants get larger, we divide some and acquire

Fig. 3–4. Lath frames, above, provide shade and are quite attractive. (Lord and Burnham) Right, a temperature alarm is indispensable. Here you see one set to ring when the temperature drops to 45 degrees or rises to 80. Below, used for orchid growing, this greenhouse is shaded with Alumalath, which is long lasting and neat. Notice that the benches are constructed of hardware cloth. (Horto Corp.)

others. We hesitate to throw things away. Finally, the greenhouse almost bulges. Overcrowding is common in most greenhouses, but it does not pay. It is far better to have fewer plants, given better care and space. Crowding allows the plants to shade each other, cutting down the amount of light per plant, and the plants become spindly and flower poorly. Crowding makes it very difficult to water properly. Some plants become waterlogged, others remain dry. Diseases and insect pests thrive where plants are crowded, and it is difficult to keep them under control because sprays do not adequately cover the plants.

Hail Protection

Let the experiences of local people with similar greenhouses help you decide whether or not protection from hail is necessary. Small panels of glass seem to be more readily broken by hail than large ones. Greenhouses are protected from hail by fastening hardware cloth to a metal or wooden frame about 6 inches above the glass. Generally it is only necessary to protect the glass on the roof.

Fiberglass is impervious to hail, which is one of its advantages. Panels of fiberglass can be used over the roof of a glass greenhouse to give protection from hail, and incidentally also to furnish shade.

Keeping Records

It would be wonderful if we could always remember when and how we did certain things, when certain plants flowered, and the number and quality of the flowers. But most of us are forgetful. When we have had remarkable success with a certain plant we try to think back about the culture we used, but too often the details are missing. If we had kept a daily diary, or even a weekly one, we might be able to duplicate in another year the conditions which resulted in such success.

You will find that it pays to keep records about the soil and the fertilizer program, the light intensity, and the temperature. Further, you will want to record the time seeds were sown, when cuttings were made, when the plants were pinched, and when they flowered. If you grow bulbs, keep records of when they were potted, where they were stored and for how long, as well as when they were brought into the greenhouse and when they flowered. If you keep records about when plants bloom with the cultural conditions you use, you will be better able to plan a desirable sequence of blooms.

If you have valuable plants that live for many years, such as African violets, amaryllis, camellias, hibiscus, gardenias, orchids, and others, you may want to keep a card for each plant. Record when the plant was purchased and from whom. On the card write the common and scientific names of the plant, the variety, and, if known, the pedigree. Record the native habitat of the plant and the conditions in its native home. Write down when the plant was potted or divided, the soil used, the fertilizer program. Record its flowering time, and the number of flowers produced and their quality. This will help you sort out the better plants from those that are not so rewarding and also help improve your cultural practices.

4

Soils and Nutrition

We have seen that plants need light, air, water, and a proper temperature if they are to thrive. In addition, they require certain minerals, which we often call *plant food*, for their development and flowering. Plants secure the minerals from soil. If the soil is lacking in one or more nutrients the plants will not grow, even though all other conditions are favorable. But minerals alone are not enough. In addition to a proper ratio of minerals, a soil should also be of good texture, hold plenty of water, be well aerated, and have the proper degree of acidity. These requirements can be met by mixing various ingredients normally present in soil, but in proportions that give an optimal balance, or, when the ingredients are hard to obtain, a situation becoming more common today, by making an imitation soil or soilless mixture that serves just as well and in fact is often easier to mix and is more uniform.

Planting Mixtures

To make the various soil mixtures you will need a supply of loam soil; organic matter in the form of peat moss, leaf mold, compost, or manure; and builders' sand (not ocean-beach sand), vermiculite, or perlite. You will find it convenient to store the ingredients in plastic garbage pails in the potting shed where they will be available for use in cold or wet weather.

Organic matter such as manure, leaf mold, or peat moss increases the water-holding capacity and the aeration of the soil, keeping it open and preventing compaction. These materials also tend to increase the soil's acidity, and, as they decay, essential minerals are gradually made available to plants. Neither peat moss nor leaf mold is as rich in nitrogen, phosphorous, and potassium as is manure. You can purchase leaf mold by the sack, or you can make your own by gathering leaves and placing them in a crib. If they are dry, moisten them and place boards on top to compact them. Maple leaves will generally be sufficiently decayed in a year's time; oak leaves will require two years.

Peat moss of the Canadian, German, or other sphagnum types, can be purchased at a reasonable cost from many supply companies. It is soft, spongy, and brown-colored, retains moisture well, and has a fairly high nitrogen content—about 1 to 3 per cent—but it is low in phosphorus and potassium. Peat moss is an important ingredient of many soil mixtures, and in many instances it can take the place of leaf mold, which may be difficult to obtain. It is also valuable for mulching plants which are growing in benches. A 1-inch mulch of peat moss over the soil makes for more vigorous growth of some crops.

It has been rather traditional in the past to make special mixtures for each kind of plant. However, experiments conducted in England, Germany, and the United States indicate that a variety of plants will grow equally well with the same mixture—a happy discovery that will make life easier for the small grower who has a few each of many kinds. Even a variety of proportions of the same ingredients makes little difference. Scientists used soil, peat, and perlite; soil and peat; and soil and perlite in different ratios, and with proper watering and fertilizers produced plants of equal vigor.

Among the soil mixes suitable for most plants are the following:

1. Two parts of soil; one part peat moss; one part perlite (a medium grade—$\frac{1}{8}$ to $\frac{1}{4}$ inch), vermiculite, or coarse sand; and 8 ounces of MagAmp fertilizer per bushel of the mixture. (One bushel equals 1.24 cubic feet.) MagAmp is a new slow-release fertilizer whose constituents are magnesium ammonium phosphate and magnesium potassium phosphate. Nitrogen, phosphorus, and potassium occur in the ratio of 7–40–7. The minerals are slowly made available to the roots and they are not readily leached out. Instead of MagAmp you can use 4 ounces of a complete garden fertilizer with a ratio of 5–10–5 to each bushel. The original application of MagAmp will last for six months at least, and is automatically re-

newed when plants are moved into larger pots or are put into benches. The garden fertilizer does not last as long, and when it is used plants must be given regular applications.

2. One part loam, one part peat moss, and one part sand or perlite, to which fertilizer has been added in the amounts given for the previous mix. Instead of the fertilizers previously mentioned some growers use one tablespoon of rock phosphate and one table-spoon of limestone to each gallon of soil mixture.

3. Two parts loam, one part leaf mold or peat moss, one-half part dehydrated cow manure, and one-half part coarse builders' sand or perlite. With this mixture no fertilizer need be added.

Soilless mixtures include the following:

1. One part peat moss, one part perlite, and one part vermiculite. To each bushel add 10 ounces of MagAmp and 16 ounces of agricultural limestone.

2. Sixteen quarts shredded peat moss and 16 quarts vermiculite (number 4) or perlite. To the mixture add 4 level tablespoons of 5–10–5 fertilizer and 4 level tablespoons of ground limestone (dolomite limestone is preferred). A mixture similar to this is available at garden stores under such trade names as Jiffy-Mix and Peat-Lite. The commercial mixtures are relatively inexpensive in large quantities; a 3-cubic-foot bag sells for about $4.00 and will fill about 600 2¼ inch pots.

These two mixes suit plants with a wide range of acid-alkaline preferences, making pH checks unnecessary. Moreover, they are sterile, eliminating the danger of infections by soil fungi and bacteria and the danger of introducing plant pests.

Planting mixtures are most conveniently made on the potting bench. Supposing a mixture of two parts loam, one part peat moss, and one part coarse sand is desired. Pass the soil through a half-inch mesh screen and the peat moss through a quarter-inch mesh. Make a flat pile of loam, say 6 inches high. Then add a 3-inch layer of peat moss, followed with a 3-inch layer of sand. Sprinkle the fertilizer over the top. Using a spade, start at one end of the pile and turn it over. Repeat twice. If the mixture is dry, dish the top of the pile and add water. In a day or two the water will have been uniformly absorbed and the mixture will be moist throughout. Turn it again to loosen it, and it will be ready for use. For potting, soil should not be too wet or too dry; it should be damp enough to adhere to itself and not crumble when a handful is gently squeezed, but not so moist that it drips.

Soil Acidity

Even though the soil is well supplied with air, water, and the essential minerals, plants will not thrive unless the *acidity* or *alkalinity* of the soil is suitable. Most plants thrive best in a neutral or slightly acid soil, but some, such as rhododendrons, azaleas, African violets, oranges, and orchids, prefer a more acid soil.

The *p*H *scale* is used to designate the degree of acidity or alkalinity of soil. A soil with a *p*H of 7 is neutral. Soils with *p*H values below 7 are acid, and the lower the figure the more acid the soil. A soil of *p*H 5 is more acid than one with a *p*H of 6. Because *p*H values are logarithms, a soil with a *p*H of 5 is ten times as acid as one with a *p*H of 6. Soils with *p*H values above 7 are alkaline and the higher the number, the more alkaline the soil. It is easy to determine the *p*H of soil. Various companies sell kits which measure *p*H. Generally, a colored solution of an indicator dye is made to flow through a soil sample. The color of the solution as it drains through is then compared to a standard chart from which the *p*H value is read. Another method is even simpler. All one needs is a spoon and a specially prepared paper. (The paper, with complete directions and *p*H preferences of various plants, sells for about a dollar.) A small amount of soil is placed in the bowl of a spoon close to the handle. Water is added to the front of the bowl and the spoon is then set on a level surface. The water will then flow into the soil. Next, a piece of the test paper is placed in the front of the bowl and the spoon is tilted so that the water from the soil runs on to the paper. The color of the paper is compared with colors printed on a chart that gives the *p*H value for each color.

Most plants thrive when the soil is in the range of about *p*H 6 or 7, for instance carnations, chrysanthemums, roses, calendulas, snapdragons, stocks, asters, clarkias, marigolds, pansies, and most primroses. Other plants grow best when the soil is more acid, in a range of *p*H 5 to *p*H 6, among them ageratum, amaryllis, begonia, cyclamen, fuchsia, gloxinia, lily, palm, and many orchids. Plants which prefer a very acid soil, *p*H 4 to *p*H 5, are azaleas, bromeliads, callas, camellias, and hydrangeas. If the soil in your region is too acid, the acidity may be diminished by the application of lime. The amount needed varies with the type of soil, the original *p*H of the soil, and the desired *p*H. Three ounces of limestone per cubic foot of soil will raise the *p*H of certain soils one unit, from *p*H 5 to 6, or from *p*H 6 to 7.

If soils are too alkaline, as they are in parts of the West, they may be made neutral or acid by the addition of sulfur. One and one-half ounces of sulfur per cubic foot of soil will lower the pH one unit, from pH 8 to 7, or from pH 7 to 6.

Iron salts are usually present in the soil but they may be insoluble unless the soil is of proper acidity. Iron chelate (pronounced "key-late") has generally supplanted compounds used in the past to correct the situation. Before applying it, moisten the soil. Follow the manufacturer's directions in making up and applying the solution. Iron sulfate, used before iron chelate became available, may still be used. Azaleas, camellias, gardenias, and hydrangeas benefit from application of iron sulfate, one pound per 100 square feet of bench area, or biweekly watering with a solution of one ounce of iron sulfate to two gallons of water, or from application of iron chelate. When peat moss and leaf mold decay, organic acids are produced and the soil becomes more acid. Alkaline soils can thus be made neutral or acid by the addition of organic matter, and neutral and slightly acid soils can be made more acid. A mixture of one part soil and one part peat moss will bring soil into the range of pH 5.5 to 6.5, which is ideal for gardenias, begonias, and gloxinias. Azaleas do well in peat moss alone, which has a pH of 4.5 to 5.5, provided they are given applications of fertilizer at intervals to make up for the lack of minerals in the peat.

Mineral Nutrition of Plants

Plants, like animals, need certain elements in their diet to make normal growth. If any one or two of these is deficient, growth veers from normal in some way. Iron is necessary to the formation of hemoglobin in human beings, and we know that an iron deficiency is one cause of anemia. A calcium or phosphorus deficiency results in poor teeth or poor bones. Plants show definite symptoms when some essential element is unavailable to them. An iron deficiency denies them one of the elements necessary in the formation of chlorophyll, so that the leaves become yellow, or *chlorotic*. When nitrogen is deficient, growth is stunted.

There are sixteen essential elements, some of which are necessary in large amounts, called *macronutrients*, and others in small amounts, called *micronutrients* or *trace elements*. The latter group is peculiar in that, while extremely small quantities are required for normal growth, concentrations over the beneficial amounts are injurious. The role of the trace elements was not suspected for a long time, partly because the quantities required by plants are so small, and partly because most soils contain them. By the use of a technique called, variously, *nutriculture, hydroponics,* or *water culture,* scientists were able to give plants arbitrary diets and watch their reactions. They learned what elements the plants used in growth, and how various concentrations affected them. They were able to chart the symptoms when some element was omitted from the diet, or present in too great amount. With their knowledge and their chart of symptoms, they were able to diagnose ailments and prescribe a cure.

Plants obtain three of the sixteen essential elements from air and water: *oxygen, carbon,* and *hydrogen.* The rest they obtain from the soil as dissolved mineral salts; these are *nitrogen, phosphorus, potassium, calcium, magnesium, iron, sulfur,* and the trace elements, *chlorine, manganese, boron, copper, zinc,* and *molybdenum.* Plants require large amounts of nitrogen, phosphorus, and potassium, and the soil reserves of these are limited. It is, therefore, often necessary to add fertilizers containing compounds of these three to soils. Manufacturers give symbols like 5–10–5, 4–12–4, and so on, on the labels; these signify the percentages of nitrogen (N), as the pure element, phosphorus (P), as P_2O_5, and potassium (K), as K_2O, respectively. Certain greenhouse plants may suffer from lack of iron. Except for iron, nitrogen, phosphorus, and potassium, the reserves of the other elements are generally great enough to meet the needs of the plants.

A deficiency of nitrogen results in stunted growth and a yellowing of the foliage, but the leaves do not fall off. When the supply of nitrogen is ample, the leaves have a good green color. An excessive amount of nitrogen encourages the development of leaves and stems at the expense of flowers, and makes a soft growth which is susceptible to disease. Nitrogen can be added to the soil in organic form or as certain salts. Dried blood and manure are rich in nitrogen. Sodium nitrate, calcium nitrate, ammonium sulfate, and ammonium nitrate are salts which furnish available nitrogen to plants.

When phosphorus is deficient the plants are stunted and the foliage is dark green. Phosphorus hastens the ripening of fruits and seeds. Bone meal and superphosphate are excellent sources of phosphorus. A moderate excess of phosphorus is not likely to injure most plants. However, gardenias and azaleas are especially susceptible to an overdose of phosphorus. Too great amounts of phosphorus may make iron insoluble and not available to plants.

A deficiency of potassium is shown by dwarfness, and by the death of the tips and edges of the leaves. Wood ashes and potassium chloride are sources of potassium. Slight excesses of potassium are not injurious, but large overdoses may cause a yellowing of the foliage, wilting, and even death of the plant.

The symptoms exhibited by a deficiency of nitrogen, phosphorus, potassium, and other essential elements are summarized in this table:

KEY TO NUTRIENT DEFICIENT SYMPTOMS *

I. Effects general on whole plant or localized on older, lower leaves.

    A. Effects usually general on whole plant, although often manifested by yellowing and dying of older leaves.

        1. Foliage light green. Growth stunted, stalks slender, and few new breaks. Leaves small, lower ones lighter yellow than upper. Yellowing followed by a drying to a light brown color, usually little dropping. *Minus nitrogen.*

        2. Foliage dark green. Retarded growth. Lower leaves sometimes yellow between veins but more often purplish, particularly on petiole. Leaves dropping early. *Minus phosphorus.*

    B. Effects usually local on older, lower leaves.

        1. Lower leaves mottled, usually with dead areas near tip and margins. Yellowing beginning at margin and continuing toward center. Margins later becoming brown and curving under, and older leaves drooping. *Minus potassium.*

        2. Lower leaves yellow, with dead areas in late stages. Chlorosis (yellowing of leaves) between the veins, veins normal green. Leaf margins curling upward or downward or developing a puckering effect. Necrosis (dead areas) developing between the veins very suddenly, usually within 24 hours. *Minus magnesium.*

II. Effects localized on new leaves.

    A. Terminal bud remaining alive.

* Ohio Agricultural Experiment Station.

1. Leaves chlorotic (yellowish) between the veins; veins remaining green.

   a. Necrotic spots (dead spots) usually absent. In extreme cases necrosis of margins and tip of leaf, sometimes extending inward, developing large areas. Only larger veins remaining green. *Minus iron.*

   NOTE: Certain cultural factors, such as high *p*H, overwatering, low temperature, and nematodes on roots, may cause identical symptoms. However, the symptoms are still probably of iron deficiency in the plant due to unavailability of iron caused by these factors.

   b. Necrotic spots usually present and scattered over the leaf surface. Checkered or finely netted effect produced by even the smallest veins remaining green. Poor bloom, both size and color. *Minus manganese.*

2. Leaves light green, veins lighter than adjoining interveinal areas. Some necrotic spots. Little or no drying of older leaves. *Minus sulfur.*

B. Terminal bud usually dead.

   1. Necrosis at tips and margins of young leaves. Young leaves often definitely hooked at tip. Death of roots actually preceding all the above symptoms. *Minus calcium.*

   2. Breakdown at base of young leaves. Stems and petioles brittle. Death of roots, particularly the meristematic tips. *Minus boron.*

Feeding Plants

For some time after young plants are potted or moved into flats or benches, fertilizer need not be added. However, after they have been placed in their final pots or permanent places in the bench, a regular schedule for fertilizer application should be set up, unless, of course, MagAmp has been used. Soils may become deficient in nitrogen, phosphorus, or potassium, or in all three. If all are lacking, you should use a complete fertilizer.

Water-soluble fertilizers may be applied as a solution to the bench or to the pots every 2 or 3 weeks. If only a few plants need feeding, a watering can may be used, with the recommended amount dissolved in a gallon of water. It is always best to have the soil moist before the solution is applied, and then to give the same amount of solution as you would if you were giving a regular watering. If many plants require feeding, there are various kinds of equipment that will make the job easier. Shown in the accompanying figure is a simple siphon attachment that draws the solution out of a bucket and adds it to the water flowing through the hose. It delivers approximately one part solution to 16 parts of water; the solution in the bucket is, therefore, made up 16 times as strong as the final dilution should be. There are various jar-type containers with siphons, and injector-type mixers that become more expensive as they become larger and more elaborate. Many growers prefer the latter type, and certainly one would be worth the cost for a large greenhouse.

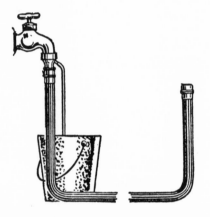

Fig. 4–1. A Hozon or similar gadget enables you to fertilize plants with a hose. The fertilizer solution is sucked from the bucket and mixed with water. (Hozon Co.)

In many instances only one element need be added to the soil in which established plants are growing. For example, nitrogen may become deficient, but phosphorus and potassium may be abundant in the soil. Sodium nitrate and ammonium sulfate are good sources of nitrogen. Sodium nitrate is the preferred form for sweet peas, but for most other plants ammonium sulfate is desirable. The former tends to make the soil more alkaline, the latter to make it more acid. Ammonium sulfate and sodium nitrate are applied at a rate of one pound to 100 square feet of bench area. Nitrogen fertilizers are best applied to pot plants in liquid form. Dissolve one ounce of ammonium sulfate or sodium nitrate in two gallons of water, and water the plants with this solution, making sure that the soil is moist before the solution is added. In general, large established plants will benefit from applications of ammonium sulfate, once every two weeks, when growth is active.

If phosphorus deficiences become evident in the plants, add superphosphate to the soil or give a complete fertilizer. Superphosphate is not readily soluble; it can be sprinkled on the surface and will dissolve slowly over a period of time. A potassium deficiency can be rectified by applying a solution of one ounce of potassium chloride in two gallons of water.

Some growers prefer to fertilize with each watering. They use a very dilute fertilizer solution, prepared by adding one-twentieth the amount recommended on the label.

Excess of Nutrients

Too much fertilizer may be more harmful than too little. When nutrients are in excess plants grow poorly, flower sparsely if at all, and may die. When plants are actively growing they can benefit from periodic applications of fertilizer, but when growth is slow, as it is during the winter months, plants won't benefit and can be injured. Don't make the mistake of believing that adding fertilizer will always speed growth. Growth may be slow because the days are short, as they are in the winter months, or because they are cloudy, or because the temperatures are not right for the species. Too much or too little water makes for poor growth, as does improper pH. Furthermore, plants may have inherent rest periods.

Periodic applications of fertilizer to soil in a bench may result in such an excess of salts in the soil that plants will not grow. The excess salts may be removed by *leaching* them out. Apply an abundance of water to the soil, at least one gallon per square foot, and let the surplus drain through the soil and out the drainage cracks. Repeat this procedure three times, at half-hour intervals. It is best to use warm water (65 to 75 degrees). Leaching takes out beneficial nutrients as well as harmful and useless ones. After leaching, add fertilizer to bring the soil to the proper nutritional level. If the soil in the bench is not changed at the end of one year, be sure to leach out the excess salts. Salts also build up in pots and they should be leached in the same manner.

Soil Sterilization

If plants are to thrive the soil must be free of such harmful agents as nematodes, pathogenic fungi, and insects. Perhaps you have had young seedlings topple over and die. They were attacked by a fungus which lives in the soil and causes a disease known as *damping-off.* Small roundworms known as nematodes attack the roots of many plants, producing galls on the roots and lowering the vitality of the plants. Cutworms and certain aphids may be present in the soil. Certain chemicals are now available which will kill the destructive organisms in the soil as well as weed seeds. Such chemicals must be used cautiously, however, because they may be injurious to man.

One soil sterilant is Vapam, which should be used in a greenhouse empty of plants or out-of-doors. The fumes of Vapam are poisonous to plants and irritating to eyes, nasal passages, and skin. You should wear goggles, rubber footwear, and gloves when handling Vapam. The recommended amount of Vapam is mixed with water and the soil is watered with the solution. The soil must be aerated for two weeks before using it, taking care to prevent contamination in the interval.

If only a small amount of sterilized soil is necessary the moist soil may be heated in an oven in a shallow pan at 200 to 250 degrees for 60 minutes. Aerate the soil for several hours before using it.

Steam sterilization of greenhouse soil is ideal and is widely practiced by large commercial growers using special equipment. The soil is exposed to steam for about an hour and a half.

Nutriculture

Growing plants without soil can be an interesting hobby and a great deal of fun. But the interest in it waxes and wanes and has at times been almost ruined by grossly exaggerated claims and even misrepresentations. Plants will not grow better in water than in the best soil culture.

Growing plants without soil is called nutriculture, hydroponics, or soilless culture. The necessary minerals are furnished in a solution of water and dissolved inorganic chemicals. The solution should contain the essential minerals in the proper proportions, because the diet of the plants depends entirely on what is added to the water. The minerals can be purchased ready-mixed under various trade names, and the amount specified in the directions should be added to a given unit of water.

Two methods which can be used for the soilless culture of plants are "liquid culture" and "gravel culture."

In liquid culture the roots of plants grow in a culture solution held in a tank or other container. An ivy growing in a bottle of water is a kind of liquid culture. Some plants, tomato for example, may be supported above the surface of the solution by wire netting or by a board with holes drilled in it. A wire netting support can be made from chicken wire fashioned to form a shallow basket. The basket is filled with a layer of straw or excelsior, and the young plants are set in the basket just as you would put them in a flat. Their roots extend through the basket down into the culture solution held in a tank below. The level of the culture solution should be one inch below the basket.

As the roots develop in the culture solution, the composition of the solution changes, because some minerals are absorbed faster than others. Not only do the amounts of minerals change with time but so also do the proportions of one to another. To maintain the proper mineral environment for roots it is necessary to change the solution at weekly or biweekly intervals. The used solution is poured off and a fresh solution poured in.

Plants make better growth in liquid culture when the solution and roots are periodically aerated. Air should be bubbled through the solution at intervals during each day.

Silica gravel and lightweight aggregate of one-fourth to one-half inch diameter are ideal for the gravel culture of plants. Plants may be grown in well drained pots, boxes, or specially constructed benches. The plants are irrigated with a nutrient solution one to three times a day, depending on the crop and the weather. The irrigations must be frequent because the coarse aggregate retains only a small volume of the solution. The culture solution may be applied by surface irrigations, or, better, by subirrigation.

Gravel culture with subirrigation is an excellent technique for raising many greenhouse crops such as roses, carnations, chrysanthemums, snapdragons, gardenias, asters, and stocks. For large-scale production the plants are grown in watertight benches of concrete or steel which have been painted with horticultural asphalt emulsion. The bench is 6 inches deep at the edge and about 8 inches deep in the center. A V-shaped bottom is necessary for proper subirrigation and drainage. The bench should have a fall of one inch for each 100 feet in length. Half-round 4-inch drainage tile is run down the center of the bench to conduct the culture solution and drain it off. A reservoir for the storage of the nutrient solution is located under the bench. A centrifugal pump is installed to pump the solution from the reservoir into the bench. The reservoir should have a capacity of 40 per cent of the cubic feet in the bench.

The bench is filled with silica gravel, or, better, with a light weight aggregate, in which the plants are then placed. The nutrient

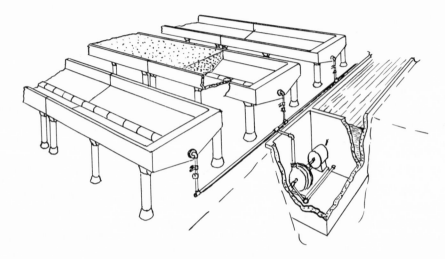

Fig. 4–2. An installation for the gravel culture of plants. A half-round tile extends the length of the concrete bench, which has a V-shaped bottom. The nutrient solution is pumped from the reservoir into the bench once to four times a day. After each filling, the solution must drain back into the reservoir. (Purdue University Agricultural Experiment Station)

solution is pumped into the beds one to four times a day, depending on weather and the crop. As soon as the solution reaches the surface of the gravel, it is allowed to drain out again, back into the reservoir. The solution can be used over and over again for about two weeks. However, if facilities are available for testing the nutrient solution and adjusting the mineral supply the solution may be used for two months.

The nutrient solution used for subirrigation and liquid culture can be purchased ready-mixed.. The ready-mixed culture solution is prepared by adding the appropriate amount of a mixture of minerals to a certain amount of water; the manufacturers specify on the labels the amount to add to a certain quantity of water. Many mixtures of essential nutrients are on the market. Usually the mixture of salts that is used for liquid feeding is also suitable for a culture solution.

5

Growing Plants from Seeds

Greenhouse plants, like those in your garden, may be started in a number of ways—from seeds, bulbs, corms, tubers, and cuttings. Some favorites that are usually started from seed are aster, calendula, cineraria, cyclamen, marigold, pansy, primrose, schizanthus, snapdragon, and sweet pea. In addition, many that are familiarly started from leaf cuttings, such as begonia, gloxinia, streptocarpus, and African violet, may also be grown from seed.

When you make a cutting from a plant which you have seen in flower you know that the plant which develops will be identical. The characteristics of many plants that develop from seed cannot be known for certain until they flower. The plant-to-be is already established in the seed, as a fully formed embryo. Its growth habit and the color, size, and shape of the flowers are already determined by its inheritance. Good culture will allow its inherited characteristics to express themselves to the fullest degree, but no amount of care will produce desirable flowers from an embryo plant with poor inheritance. It is, therefore, important to buy seed only from experienced and reputable growers, who use the best stock as breeding plants. Some seed is produced by pure strains of plants, others by crossing pure strains to obtain a given type. Some seed you buy will be of mixed hybrid ancestry, and from it you will get a variety of colors. When you make a hybrid cross of your own, such as a cross between two varieties of African violet, the seed produced may give a wide variety of types. Some will resemble one or the other parent, some will be like various ancestors of the parents, and

63

some will be new combinations of characteristics of the parents. From such a hybrid cross new varieties may spring.

The germination of seeds depends on their being planted at the proper depth and having the proper conditions of water, air, and temperature. Depth of planting is related to the size of seeds. Generally, seeds are planted at a depth of three or four times their diameter. However, very small seeds, such as those of begonias and gloxinias, and seeds which require light for germination, should not be covered, but instead they should be merely scattered over the soil surface.

Sowing Seeds

You will probably want to start most seeds in flats, pots, or pans (shallow pots) filled with soil. A good general soil mixture consists of equal parts of finely screened soil, sand, and peat moss. This mixture or any other one should be moist, not too wet or dry, before it is used. Cover the drainage holes of the flat (or pot) with pieces of broken pot (called *crock*) or gravel, and then fill with soil, making certain that at least the uppermost layer consists of finely screened soil. With your hands, firm the soil around the edges, make smooth, and then, for many seeds, firm moderately with a board or block.

Fig. 5–1. Left, covering marigold seeds with vermiculite after they were sown on soil. An even stand of seedlings two weeks later is shown to the right.

Seeds of begonias, gloxinias, and other plants with tiny seeds germinate best when sown on a leveled but not firmed surface. The small roots cannot penetrate packed soil. The seeds may be sown broadcast or preferably in rows. Small seeds may be mixed with fine sand and then scattered over the surface. After sowing, cover relatively large seeds with soil, sand, or, better, with vermiculite. Water by placing the pot or flat in a pan of water so that the water is taken up from below, or use a fine spray. If the former method is used, remove the pot or flat when the soil is moist; never let it remain in the water for a long period. Cover the flat or pot with a pane of glass or with polyethylene film, or enclose the container in a polyethylene bag, to retard evaporation.

Seeds of many species germinate equally well in the dark or light; for these place a sheet of paper over the glass or film and then place the container in a warm, shaded place in the greenhouse.

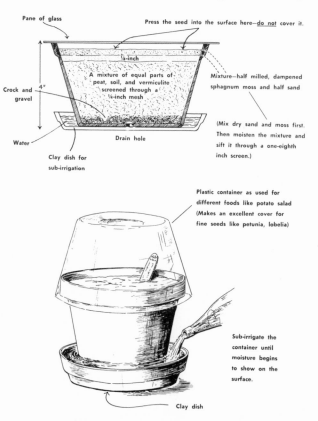

Fig. 5–2. Helpful hints for sowing small seeds. (Otto Dahl)

Seeds of some species require light for a high percentage of germination, among them African violet, begonia, gloxinia, kalanchoë, petunia, primrose, snapdragon, and streptocarpus. After sowing and covering with glass or film, place the containers in a shaded place where the light intensity is less than one-tenth of full sunlight. Higher light intensities may inhibit growth and should be avoided. In contrast to those which germinate best when light is present are those whose germination is promoted by darkness, among them calendula, mesembryanthemum, and schizanthus. For such seeds light should be excluded until germination occurs.

To prevent damping-off, a fungus disease that attacks the seedlings at the ground line with consequent rotting of the stem, use sterilized soil or Jiffy-Mix, or cover the soil with a sterile material. For the latter, nearly fill a pot or other container with a mixture of one part each of sifted loam, sifted peat moss, and coarse builder's sand, then gently firm it. Place over this a half-inch layer of moist sphagnum moss that has been passed through a quarter-inch screen, or moist vermiculite, or fine perlite, or an even mixture of sphagnum moss and sand. Firm the top layer gently and then sow the seed.

Sow fine seed such as petunia, snapdragon, African violet, and begonia directly on top of the medium without covering it. Larger seed such as zinnia and aster should be covered just enough to hide the seed from view.

A uniformly moist seed bed may be attained by sowing seed on soil in a glass jar. Place the jar on its side and make a layer of sand over which place a layer of whatever soil mix you plan to use. Firm it, plant the seed, and give it a fine mist spray of water. Then cover the open end with a sheet of polyethylene film. Use only polyethylene, which retains moisture but allows oxygen and carbon dioxide to pass in and out.

The preferred temperature for germination is about 70 degrees day and night, at which most species will sprout in one to three weeks. A few species require a lower temperature, about 60 degrees, for prompt germination, among them cyclamen and freezia. Never let the soil become dry during the germination period; shading the containers help reduce evaporation. Also avoid waterlogging the soil. Too little or too much water may be fatal.

As soon as the seeds have sprouted, remove the paper shade but leave the glass or film on for the first week or so. If moisture condenses on it wipe it off, and prop it open a little to allow air to circulate. If the atmosphere is too close the seedlings may damp off. If damping-off occurs, or, better, to prevent it, water the young plants with a fungicide. After the glass is removed, give them good light or they will become tall and spindly.

Time to Sow

If you are going to raise a variety of plants in your greenhouse you will probably want something in flower during all months of the year. Perhaps the fall chrysanthemums can be followed by carnations, snapdragons, calendulas, or some other flower crop. It will take some planning on your part to have plants of another kind ready to put in the bench when the plants which are through flowering have been removed. The following table will help you plan a year-round sequence of blooms. You will notice that the time of flowering is determined by the date on which the seeds are sown. For instance, if you sow seeds of snapdragons in March you can expect flowers from July on. A July sowing will enable you to cut the first flowers at Christmas, and one in November will give you flowers in March and later. Of course, various cultural practices, which we will discuss later, may modify the dates of flowering.

FLOWERING SCHEDULE

Seeds planted in January	*Plants bloom in*
Begonias	August–December
Clarkia	April–May
Gloxinias	August–September
Petunias	April–June
Snapdragons	April–June
Stocks	May–June
Sweet peas	April–June

Seeds planted in February	*Plants bloom in*
Asters	June–July
Marigolds	May
Stocks	May–June
Sweet peas	April–June

Seeds planted in March	*Plants bloom in*
Asters	July
Gerbera	December and later

FLOWERING SCHEDULE (*Cont.*)

Primula obconica	December
Primula sinensis	April the following year
Snapdragons	July–later
Zinnias	Late May–June

Seeds planted in April	*Plants bloom in*
Annual Gypsophyla	June–July
Asters	July
Lupines	June

Seeds planted in May	*Plants bloom in*
Cinerarias	January and later
Lupines	January–February
Snapdragons	December
Sweet peas	September on

Seeds planted in June	*Plants bloom in*
Cinerarias	Early January on
Lupines	January–February
Sweet peas	September–December

Seeds planted in July	*Plants bloom in*
Calceolaria	April–May
Calendula	November
Pansies	November on
Primula obconica	April on
Primula sinensis	April on
Snapdragons	Christmas on
Stocks	January–February
Sweet peas	October–February

Seeds planted in August	*Plants bloom in*
Calceolaria	Late May
Calendula	December on
Cineraria	February–March
Cyclamen	November–February of following year
Marigolds (winter flowering)	November–January
Nemesia	October–February
Pansies	December–March
Primula malacoides	March and later
Schizanthus	Late December
Snapdragons	February–April
Stocks	January–February

FLOWERING SCHEDULE (*Cont.*)

Seeds planted in September	*Plants bloom in*
Calendula	February–March
Cineraria	April–May
Larkspur	April–May
Lupines	January–February
Stocks	February
Sweet peas	December–March

Seeds planted in October	*Plants bloom in*
Calendula	March and later
Larkspur	Late May
Stocks	April on
Sweet peas	February–May

Seeds planted in November	*Plants bloom in*
Calendula	April–May
Larkspur	April–May
Snapdragons	March–June
Stocks	April–May
Sweet peas	March–May

Seeds planted in December	*Plants bloom in*
Calendula	April–May
Clarkia	May
Gloxinia	August
Godetia	June
Nemesia	May
Phlox	February and later
Salpiglossis	May–June
Scabiosa	June
Stocks	Late May
Sweet peas	March–May

From Seedling to Mature Plant

After the seedlings have made their first set of true leaves they are ready for transplanting; generally first into flats (transplant flats) and later into the bench or pots. (The first leaves to appear on certain seedlings are modified leaves, called *cotyledons*. These generally remain small and soon drop off. The true leaves appear somewhat later and will develop into full-sized ones.)

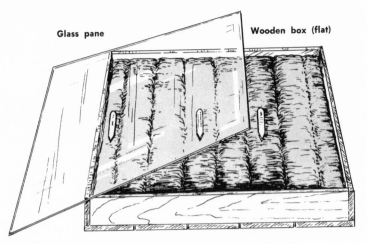

Fig. 5–3. A flat prepared for seed sowing. The seeds will be planted in rows thereby giving the seedlings more space and better air circulation. (Otto Dahl)

Fig. 5–4. Here streptocarpus seedlings that are crowded are removed in groups with a spatula prior to pricking off.

The general sequence for moving plants along may be diagrammed as follows:

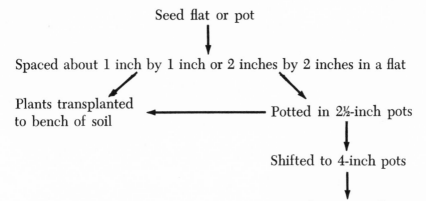

If the plants are to be grown in a bench they may be planted in the bench from the transplant flats or from 2½-inch pots.

"Pricking off" is a gardener's term for the first transplanting of seedlings. They may be put into wooden or plastic flats, or pots of clay, plastic, or compressed peat. Flats or large shallow pots (called seed pans) should have a layer of gravel or crock over the bottom for drainage, and then be filled to within a half-inch of the rim with a mixture of one part each of loam, peat moss, and either vermiculite, coarse sand, or fine perlite. Level this and firm it moderately.

Carefully remove the seedlings by lifting them up with a putty knife or similar tool. Avoid breaking roots. A spotting board speeds up transplanting. This tool is used to make regularly spaced holes in the soil. Place the root system of a seedling in a hole, and then with your fingers firm the soil about the roots. The dibble technique is also suitable for pricking off seedlings. First, make rows in the soil at regular intervals. Then, with a dibble—a pointed stick—make a hole. Insert the root system, and then firm the soil by pressing with the dibble on the soil near the seedling. When the flat is planted, water it thoroughly. Shade the flat with newspaper or cloth stretched over wires above the plants for the first few days, until the seedlings have recovered from the shock of transplanting.

When seedlings are to go into round or square peat pots instead of into a transplant flat, arrange the pots in a flat or other container so that they rest against each other and fill with soil. Firm the soil,

Fig. 5–5. Pricking off. A flat is filled with soil, firmed, and marked for planting (below, left). Below, right, part of the flat after seedlings have been set in. In the larger pictures, the root system is inserted into the hole made with the dibble, then the soil is firmed.

then dibble the seedlings in, one to a pot. A new innovation is the Jiffy-7 peat wafer, which is compressed to one-quarter inch by 1½ inches. When water is added it swells up within minutes to the equivalent of a 1½-inch pot, already filled with a fertilized soil and ready for planting. Make a hole in the top, insert the roots of a seedling and firm the soil about them. When further transplanting is necessary, the peat pot and the Jiffy-7 are set directly into the bench or into a regular pot without disturbing the young plant.

To remove flat-grown seedlings to the bench or into pots, lift the flat and, holding it at an angle, tap one end on the potting bench. This will compact the soil and leave about an inch of space between the soil and the end. Then with a knife cut through the soil between the rows and then between the plants so that each can be lifted out in a block of soil.

Pot plants are shifted to increasingly larger pots until they are in about a 6-inch size, when they should be large enough to flower. Some kinds flower nicely in 4- or 5-inch pots. Generally the shift is made from 2½-inch to 4-inch and then to 6-inch, or with vigorous plants from 2½ directly to 5- or 6-inch ones.

Pots come in a variety of shapes and sizes. They increase in diameter by the half inch from 2 to 7 inches, and by the inch from 7 to 12 inches. There are also 14-, 16-, and 18-inch pots. The sizes are the inner diameters at the rim. With regard to depth, there are the usual standard pots and kinds that are more shallow. Azalea pots are only three-quarters as high as standard ones, and are more attractive and have more stability. They are preferable for ferns, azaleas, bulbs, and many other plants. Bulb or seed pans are even more shallow.

Only clean pots should be used. If they are dirty or have been used before, the roots will stick to the inside and be injured when the plant is removed. Used pots should be scrubbed with plain water and rinsed. Clay pots should be soaked in water for about an hour and then allowed to drain so that the surface water evaporates, leaving the pores filled with water. If this is not done, the dry pot will draw water from the soil within.

Potting soil should be neither too wet nor too dry. If, after squeezing a handful, you can see the impression of your fingers and several cracks in the soil, it is right for potting. If it won't hold its form it is too dry, and if it feels like a gob of mud it is too wet.

When a plant is ready for a larger pot, it is usually moved along without disturbing the roots. This is called "shifting." An experienced grower can look at a plant and tell when it needs shifting. If you are in doubt as to whether a plant is ready, knock it out of the pot and note the extent of the roots. If they form a fairly dense network around the ball of soil, it needs to be moved into a larger pot; if few roots are seen it is best to wait for a while.

The removal of a plant from its pot is called "knocking out." Hold the pot by the rim and spread the fingers over the soil, the stem of the plant between them. Hold the bottom of the pot with the other hand, turn it upside down, and tap the rim sharply against the bench to dislodge the ball of soil. Generally only one tap is necessary. The plant will fall down into the hand that is spread across the surface to receive it. After the plant is removed, it is "shouldered," that is, part of the surface soil is rubbed off so that fresh soil may take its place in the larger pot.

The illustrations on pages 76–77 show the steps in potting. For sizes 4 inches and over, place two or three pieces of crock (broken pot) or of gravel over the drainage hole (not necessary in smaller sizes). Scoop enough soil into the pot so that when the ball of the plant is placed on it the top will be the proper distance

Peat Pots for Transplanting

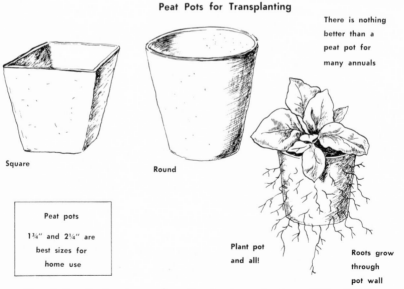

There is nothing better than a peat pot for many annuals

Square

Round

Peat pots

1¾" and 2¼" are best sizes for home use

Plant pot and all!

Roots grow through pot wall

Fig. 5–6. Peat pots are favorites for transplanting. (Otto Dahl)

Fig. 5–7.   Left, a snapdragon plant has been removed from the transplant flat and placed in a pot
partially filled with soil. Right, the pot is filled with
soil and then the soil is firmed.

below the rim—about a half-inch for pots of 4-inch diameter and
smaller, an inch for larger ones. Then fill the pot somewhat above
the rim, firm the soil with your thumbs (or with a potting stick for
large pots), and tap the pot on the bench to settle it. Water it
thoroughly. The space from soil to rim is planned so that it will
hold enough water to moisten the soil from top to bottom.

Wilting of newly potted plants may be reduced by syringing them
several times a day and providing them with shade. After the first
thorough watering keep the soil somewhat on the dry side until root
action is good.

The techniques of sowing seed, transplanting, potting, and shifting which we have just described apply to plants which grow in soil.
Orchids and bromeliads require special techniques.

Containers

The variety of containers increases with each passing year. Plastic pots, either square or round, have become quite popular. They
are inexpensive, light in weight, durable, and easy to clean, and
they require less frequent watering than clay ones.

Hanging baskets of wire, or plastic strips, or redwood slats add
decorative charm to a greenhouse, and are particularly necessary

Fig. 5–8. Above, a plant is removed from a pot by tapping the rim of the pot on the bench. Below, adding crock to a 4-inch pot.

Fig. 5–8 (Cont.).　Above, in potting, cover crock with soil, place plant in position, and fill with soil.　Below, firm the soil with the thumbs.

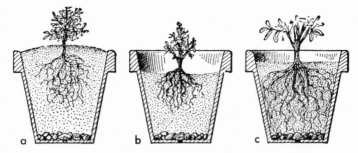

Fig. 5–9. Examples of poor (a and b) and good (c) potting. In a, the pot is too full, with no space left for water. In b, it does not contain enough soil. (From *Propagation of Plants*, by M. G. Kains and L. M. McQueston; Orange Judd Co.)

Fig. 5–10. Driftwood or wind timber of intriguing shape can be made into jungle trees for plants that grow in nature on trees.

for plants that have pendant leaves or flower stems. Among the kinds that thrive in hanging containers are certain varieties of begonias, episcias, fuchsias, geraniums, and ferns. For orchids, the basket is filled with osmunda fiber.

Driftwood of intriguing shapes can be made into "jungle trees" for plants that grow in nature on trees, plants called epiphytes or "air plants." Natural or excavated pockets are filled with soil for certain begonias and gesneriads, or with osmunda fiber or other material for ferns, bromeliads, and orchids. Small orchid plants can be grown on pieces of bark (cork, hardwood, or redwood) or tree fern trunk, and then hung like Christmas tree ornaments on the branches of driftwood or wind blasted timber. Tree fern logs or artificial logs stuffed with sphagnum moss can be used as climbing poles for vines or plants that attach themselves by aerial roots.

6

Propagating Plants

Plants do not always come true from seed. This is particularly true of hybrids, whose seeds contain various combinations of characteristics inherited from their progenitors. Not all may be desirable, but among them may be new and unusual combinations of color and form that are beautiful and appealing. Sometimes through extensive further breeding it is possible to get a hybrid to come true, but the exact one sought may never show up again if the cross is repeated. Therefore, the best and sometimes only way to duplicate it and increase its numbers is by propagating it vegetatively. It can be divided year after year, a rather slow method. Or it can be increased more rapidly by means of cuttings—of stem, leaf, or root according to the kind. Those which form bulbs, corms, or tubers allow propagation by the offsets that grow from the main bulb or corm, or by extension of the tuber. Nurserymen take great care in selecting the most desirable types originated from seed, and in then multiplying them vegetatively until they have a sufficient quantity to put on the market. Thus, often a named variety we buy has come from a single plant chosen among many.

Not only will plants grown from vegetative propagations be exactly like the parents, but by this means you can grow larger plants in a shorter time. The techniques are easy to apply, and the experience valuable and fascinating. You can increase the numbers of your favorites both for the greenhouse and the yard, even multiply trees and shrubs.

Cuttings

There are three major types of cuttings (sometimes called slips): *leaf* cuttings, *stem* cuttings, and *root* cuttings. Only a few plants, such as *Anemone japonica*, cottonwood, horseradish, oriental poppy, and raspberry, may be reproduced by root cuttings, but many kinds can be propagated by leaf and stem cuttings. Among the choice plants which can be increased by leaf cuttings are begonias, gloxinias, African violets, and kalanchoë. Practically all plants can be increased by stem cuttings.

If you plan to make many cuttings, it would pay to set aside a portion of a bench just for propagation. Because cuttings root best at 70 degrees Fahrenheit you may wish to use supplemental heat provided by a heating cable or a thermostatically controlled prop-

Fig. 6–1. Practically all plants may be propagated by stem cuttings. Left, making a stem cutting of chrysanthemum. Right, a rooted cutting ready for potting or benching.

agation mat. The latter is perhaps the better. Roll it out, plug it in, and then fill the area with the rooting medium, which may be sand or a mixture of sand and peat moss, or simply vermiculite or fine perlite alone, media which encourage rooting by allowing good aeration as well as holding water.

Many gardeners do not have a propagating bench; they simply fill a pot or flat with the rooting medium and keep it in a shaded spot. Such containers may be placed directly on an electric propagation mat spread out on a bench.

A high humidity prevents wilting and favors rooting. Actually, rooting is delayed if the cuttings wilt. An enclosure of polyethylene film may be used, or the cuttings may be covered with plastic plant domes or glass or plastic bowls. The method favored by professionals is frequent misting—bathing the cuttings with a fine fog. This can be accomplished by use of an inexpensive mist humidifier, such as those sold for use in the home, similar models of which are also made for small greenhouses. For fairly large areas mist nozzles can be mounted about a foot above the cuttings. All of these should be controlled to go on and off for five or six seconds each minute. A simple control makes use of a time clock but a more complex device is available that turns the fogger off when the leaves are moist and on when they become dry.

Stem Cuttings

Among the plants which are usually propagated by stem cuttings are carnations, chrysanthemums, geraniums, poinsettias, and gardenias. Examine the plants carefully and take cuttings only from desirable varieties and healthy plants. Never take cuttings from a diseased plant with the expectation that they will recover. You will merely be asking for trouble. The best stem cuttings are obtained from stems that are moderately hard, not soft and flabby. If the stem cracks as you bend it, it is about right. Cut off the top four or five inches of the stem, generally making the cut just below a joint. Remove the lower leaf or two and dip the basal end into a hormone powder, such as Rootone or Hormodin. (The use of a rooting hormone is optional; most cuttings of herbaceous greenhouse plants root nearly as well without hormones.) Insert the cuttings in the rooting medium. If sand or a mixture of sand and peat is used, insert the cuttings in holes made with a dibble or in

Fig. 6–2. Rooting hormones hasten root formation in some plants. On the right are camellia cuttings that were dipped in a rooting hormone. Those at the left were not dipped. (Boyce Thompson Institute)

a groove made by drawing a knife through the medium. If one of the lighter, looser materials is used, simply push the basal end of the cutting into it to a depth of one or two inches. In either case, firm the medium after the cuttings are planted, and then water them.

When the cuttings are rooted they should be potted without delay. The cuttings are ready for potting when the roots are between half an inch and an inch long. If they are allowed to remain in the rooting medium too long they become stunted, and may remain so even though they are subsequently given good care.

Cuttings are often potted in 2½-inch pots. Partially fill the pot with soil. Hold the plant so that the roots spread over the soil. Then fill the pot and firm the soil. Water the plants and place them in a shaded spot for a few days. From the 2½-inch pots they may be planted in the bench or shifted into larger pots, according to the method described previously.

Air Layerage

When they become old, aphelandra, dieffenbachia, dracaena, philodendrons, and the rubber plant lose their lower leaves, leaving

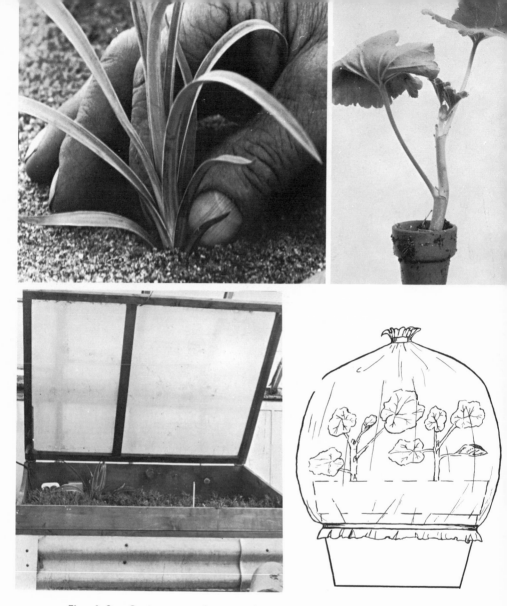

Fig. 6–3. Cuttings may be rooted in sand contained in a bench, upper left, or in a pot, upper right. A propagating case, lower left, provides ideal conditions for the rooting of cuttings, as does a pot covered with polyethylene film, lower right.

an unattractive, naked stem. The leafy top part may be rooted by air layerage, as illustrated in the figure on page 86. A cut is made halfway through the stem a short distance below the lowest leaf. Then the stem is slit up the middle for a distance of an inch or two. The cut surface is then dusted with a rooting hormone and a small

Fig. 6–4. Potting a rooted geranium cutting. The cutting is held in position in a pot partly filled with soil and then more soil is added and firmed.

amount of sphagnum moss is inserted in the slit stem. Next, sphagnum moss is placed around the area and covered with polyethylene film. When roots have formed, the rooted top portion is separated and potted. The basal portion may be cut back, leaving one or two nodes from which new shoots will develop. Or the barren cane can be cut into segments, each with a node. Place the segments on damp rooting medium and barely cover; from each portion a new plant may develop.

Air layerage may also be used to propagate trees and shrubs outdoors. The rooted twig is severed from the parent plant after leaf fall. In cold regions it is best to pot the new plant and carry it over the first winter in a cold frame or a greenhouse.

Leaf Cuttings

You can increase your favorite gloxinias, African violets, Rex begonias, streptocarpus, and kalanchoë plants by leaf cuttings.

Fig. 6–5. Upper, steps in air layerage. Right, the stem is cut halfway through and then slit up the middle. Moist sphagnum is inserted in the slit and wrapped around the area. Left, the sphagnum is covered with polyethylene film. After roots form the new plant will be potted. Lower, the leafless basal portion of stems of dracenas and similar plants are placed on moist sand. After shoots develop they may be removed and potted.

Kalanchoë can be increased by placing a leaf flat on sand. New plants will develop from notches along the margin of the leaf. Sometimes young plants even develop on leaves which remain on the plant.

The Rex begonia is increased by removing a leaf, cutting through the main veins just below the point at which two large branch veins come together, and then placing the leaf flat on moist sand or on a half-and-half mixture of sand and peat which is in a box or other container. A few small pebbles may be placed on the leaf to keep it in contact with the medium, or staples made of wire may be used.

Fig. 6–6. Upper, Rex begonia may be propagated by laying a leaf on sand, left, or by inserting V-shaped pieces of a leaf, right, in a rooting medium. Lower left, a small tuber develops at the end of the vein of a leaf cutting of gloxinia after it has been grown vertically in sand. The cutting should be left in place until the tuber makes roots and a shoot. Lower right, sansevieria is propagated by inserting leaf segments in sand.

The container should then be covered with a pane of glass and provided with shade. In time a young plant will develop at each cut. Another method of increasing Rex begonias is to cut the leaf into triangular pieces 2 inches across, making certain that each piece has a major vein. The pieces are inserted to a depth of half an inch in the rooting medium. This method can also be used for gloxinias.

Fig. 6–7. African violets are easily propagated from leaf cuttings. Remove a leaf from a plant, left, and insert the petiole in the rooting medium. In time young plants will develop from the petiole, right. Remove the young plants and pot them individually.

New plants develop at the base of leaf stalks (petioles) of African violets, *Begonia melior,* streptocarpus, and gloxinias. Remove a mature leaf with its stalk from the base of the plant. Insert the leaf stalk in moist rooting medium to a depth of 1 to 2 inches. If you do not have a propagating case, use a fish bowl, a large glass jar, a box covered with glass, or a terrarium as the container. Or you may use a small pot covered with a glass jar. The moist atmosphere in such containers keeps the leaf from wilting and hastens the formation of new plants. In due time, one to several young plants will form at the base of the leaf stalk. These are removed to flats or small pots.

Time to Start Cuttings

Cuttings should be made at the appropriate season. June is a good time to propagate shrubs for outdoor use. The young shoots of lilac, forsythia, spirea, rose, elaeagnus, clematis, and other shrubs are in the proper state of maturity in June. Cuttings of these shrubs root readily at this time. Cuttings of evergreens are best made in November.

The time for making leaf or stem cuttings of greenhouse plants will depend to some extent on the time you want the plants to flower and how large you want them to be when they flower.

The following table shows the time at which many commercial growers start cuttings of a variety of plants, and the time at which the plants flower. Of course, if the plants are to flower at the indicated times, they must be cultivated in a precise way. Methods of culture are given in subsequent chapters.

Plant	Take cuttings	Flower
Begonias, Rex	November	Plants in 4" pots by fall
Bouvardia	February–March	November–January
Carnations	December–February	Fall on
Chrysanthemums	May–June	October–December
Coleus	September	Large plants by spring
Fuchsia	March	June–July
Gardenia	December–February	December
Geraniums	August	May
Hydrangea	February	Following year
Lantana	August–September	May on
Philodendron	October	May–June for plants of fair size
Poinsettias	June–September	Christmas
Saintpaulia (African violet)	December–February	November on

Division of Plants

Some greenhouse plants can be divided, among them orchids, African violets, aspidistra, and some ferns. The division of an orchid plant is described later. Large African violet plants generally have several crowns, each with its own tuft of leaves, and these can be separated. Knock a plant out of the pot, loosen the soil ball, and separate the crowns with the least possible injury to the roots. Pot each piece separately.

Bulbs, Corms, and Tubers

Many desirable greenhouse plants are started from bulbs, corms, and tubers, among them daffodils, tulips, amaryllis, tuberous begonias, and gloxinias. We will have more to say about the propagation of these plants in subsequent chapters, but let us here consider their structure. The *bulb* of a tulip or daffodil consists of fleshy scales surrounding immature leaves and flower parts. The bulbs of these plants which you receive in the fall should have the flower parts already formed in miniature. You may see them by slicing through a bulb vertically and examining it with a hand lens. You will see an immature flower surrounded by leaves in the center of the bulb. Because the flowers are already formed you need only give the bulbs the proper conditions for their development. Until the shoots of tulips and daffodils are two or three inches high the plants should be kept at a temperature of about 48 degrees. To meet this requirement place the potted bulbs in a room at 48 degrees, or place the pots in a cold frame and cover them with straw, or bury the pots in a trench and cover them with soil.

At a temperature of 48 degrees, the leaves, stems, and flower buds of tulips and daffodils elongate most rapidly and in proper balance with one another. Furthermore, root growth is most rapid at this temperature. When the shoots are 2 or 3 inches long and the roots well developed, the best temperature for growing the plants shifts from 48 degrees to 60 degrees. Hence when the shoots are 2 to 3 inches long, the pots can be moved into the greenhouse.

Flower buds are not present in bulbs of all plants. Inside the scaly leaves of a lily bulb a short stem bearing small leaves is present, but no flowers. In lilies the flowers form after the plant has made considerable growth.

Corms, such as those of the crocus and gladiolus, are often called bulbs, but from a structural standpoint a corm is very different from a bulb. In corms, the bulk of the tissue is fleshy stem tissue, whereas in bulbs it consists of fleshy scalelike leaves. Each ring that you see when you cut an onion or tulip bulb is a fleshy scalelike leaf. You will not see such modified leaves if you cut a section through a corm of gladiolus or crocus. A corm is solid, not scaly.

The tuberous begonia has a modified underground stem known as a *tuber*, which is a thickened stem and bears eyes. The entire tuber of a tuberous begonia is generally planted, but if you wish you can cut it into pieces, each with an eye, and plant the pieces separately.

7

Controlling Shape, Size, and Flowering Time

We can control to some extent the shape of a plant and the time at which it will flower. We may want some plants to be bushy specimens, producing a multitude of blossoms; others we may want to grow to a single stem, bearing one large exhibition bloom. An understanding of where leaves, stems, and flowers are produced will enable you to control, at least to some extent, the shape, stature, and flowering of your plants.

The tip of the stem, both of the main and branch stems, is the region where new stem tissue, additional leaves, and flowers are formed. During the growing period the stem tips form leaves. Then, when conditions are just right they form flowers instead of leaves. Later in this chapter we will consider the conditions which bring about this remarkable change in behavior.

Pinching

If we remove the very tip of a stem, that stem cannot grow longer and no new leaves can form on it. If you will examine any stem you will notice that a lateral bud is present at every joint of the stem, just above the point at which each leaf is attached. These lateral buds, like the very tip of the stem, have the capacity to develop stem tissue and new leaves, and, under certain conditions,

Fig. 7–1. Pinching is used to promote branching and to time a crop. The left figure illustrates a soft pinch; only the very soft tip of the stem with immature leaves is removed. When several upper leaves and a considerable part of the stem is removed, right, the pinch is known as a a hard pinch.

flowers. When the tip of the stem is present and producing leaves it forms a hormone that moves down the main stem and prevents these lateral buds from growing. When the stem tip is forming flowers, this hormone is no longer produced and the side buds grow into branches.

If we want the lateral buds to develop into branches before flowering time we simply remove the tip of the stem. Generally we remove the tip with our thumb and first finger, and hence call the process *pinching*. If we remove only the extreme tip we call such removal a soft pinch. If we remove a length of the stem with several leaves we call it a hard pinch. Never remove all the leaves from a plant when you pinch it, even though buds are present where leaves have fallen; but instead, leave enough foliage to support the plant. Remember the leaves are the foodmaking organs of the plant.

Suppose we want a bushy plant and that we now have a plant with just one stem. After we pinch the tip of the stem several lateral buds will develop into branches. When these are about 4 inches long we can remove the stem tip of each. Then several lateral buds on each branch will develop, and the resulting plant will be a bushy one.

With some plants we can delay flowering by pinching off the tip of the stem. Suppose the tip of a snapdragon stem is just about to produce flowers. If we let the plant alone it will flower in a short time. If we pinch off the stem tip, flowering will be delayed, because the lateral buds must first grow into branches bearing leaves before they can produce flowers. Only after the branches have reached a certain size will they form blooms.

Hence we can delay the flowering of a plant and time the crop by removing the tip of the stem. If we pinch plants at a certain time we can have flowers on a predictable date. For example, if young snapdragon plants started from seed in July are pinched in August, they will flower at Christmas. On the other hand, unpinched snapdragon plants started from seed at the same time will flower in late October and early November.

Pinching standard chrysanthemums—those which are to bear just one large flower on a stem—on a certain date makes for higher quality flowers. After the plants are pinched, several branches will develop. One or two are allowed to develop; the others are removed. When side branches develop on the remaining stems, they are removed. Furthermore, the stems are disbudded. The date for pinching varies with the variety, as listed in the chapter on cut flowers.

Disbudding

If only one flower develops on a stem it will be a large one. For instance, to secure large flowers of calendulas, carnations, and certain chrysanthemums, remove all but one of the flower buds on each stem. The removal of unwanted flower buds is called *disbudding*. We will have more to say about this when we discuss the culture of various greenhouse plants.

Plant Supports

A number of greenhouse plants need support to keep their stems straight, and to enhance their beauty and symmetry. Furthermore, properly staked plants occupy less bench space than sprawling, un-

Fig. 7–2. Disbudding chrysanthemums. With the thumb and index finger, remove all flower buds except the terminal one. When you are through, the plant will appear as in the middle photograph. One large flower develops on each stem.

staked ones. Don't wait until the stem becomes crooked or falls over before staking a plant. If you stake a plant before the need is apparent, the stem will be straight and the stake will be quite inconspicuous when the plant is in flower. Wooden, bamboo, or metal stakes made of #4 wire are suitable for pot plants. Sink the stake firmly in the pot. Fasten a piece of raffia or soft string to the stake, and after passing it around the stem tie it somewhat firmly to the stake, but not so tightly that it interferes with the growth of the stem. Hyacinths and some other plants may be supported with wire pushed into the soil and bent at the top to form a horizontal loop around the stem of the plant. Certain plants can be supported by an encircling string or wire attached at the proper height to three or more upright stakes.

Plants growing in benches may also be supported by stakes. If the stakes are many feet tall they should be fastened at their tops to an overhead wire running the length of the bench, above the row. Wires running lengthwise some distance above the soil and between the rows of plants with crosswire strings at intervals furnish good support for carnations, pompon chrysanthemums, and snapdragons. These plants may also be supported by welded wire fabric that can be raised progressively higher as the plants grow.

Controlling Height

Easter lilies, poinsettias, and chrysanthemums are generally more attractive when they are compact with short internodes. The simplest way to obtain such plants is to select dwarf varieties. However, some naturally tall varieties may have desirable features that are lacking in the dwarf kinds. These tall plants may be dwarfed by chemicals which should be used according to the manufacturer's directions. If Cycocel is added to the soil prior to October 15, poinsettias will be compact plants with darker green foliage and deeper red bracts. Phosphon is used as a height-retardant for forced Easter lilies and pot chrysanthemums; when added to the soil it gives more compact plants with stronger stems and deeper green leaves.

Flowering

To get the greatest pleasure from a greenhouse there should be some plants in flower during all months of the year. When one kind is through flowering, something else should take its place.

We have seen that the time certain plants are started determines when they blossom, and that flowering of some kinds can be delayed by pinching. Furthermore, some plants flower over a long period once they have reached a certain size, for example African violets, carnations, snapdragons, pansies, roses, sweetpeas, and calendulas.

Other plants flower only at certain seasons—chrysanthemums in the fall, poinsettias at Christmas, the China aster in the summer. Length of day and temperature markedly influence the season when these nonperpetual flowering plants bloom. These, as well as many others, will not flower unless the day length is within a certain range. We call chrysanthemums and poinsettias short-day plants; the China aster a long-day plant. Plants which flower when the days are either long or short are called day-neutral plants. The discussion which follows gives the general principles for the control of flowering. More detailed directions are given for certain plants when their culture is discussed in later chapters.

The short-day plants in general flower when the days are less than 13 hours long, that is, 13 hours of light and 11 hours of darkness each day. Among these are some species that will flower only when the day is less than 12 hours, and others for which 14 hours represents a short day. The long-day plants produce flower buds when the days are longer than 13 or 14 hours. It is possible to get earlier flowering of short- and long-day plants by giving them the day length they require to set flower buds. It is possible to delay their flowering by artificially imitating the day length that prevents flower bud formation.

Short-day plants. Short-day plants normally flower in autumn, winter, or early spring. Chrysanthemums, Christmas cactus, *Euphorbia fulgens*, kalanchoë, stevia, and poinsettia are typical short-day plants. They may be brought into flower earlier than usual by artificially shortening the day to the number of hours conducive to flower-bud formation. A framework of wood or wire should be constructed around the plants. Black sateen cloth that is light proof, or heavy black paper, is then arranged so that it can be conveniently drawn over the framework each afternoon and removed each morning. All light must be excluded, else the project will fail. The usual schedule is to cover the plants at 5 P.M. and uncover them at 7 A.M., thus giving them 10 hours of daylight, and 14 hours of darkness. (In the trade this is loosely called *shading.* You should not confuse this type of shading with lessening the light intensity by painting the glass or using cheesecloth.)

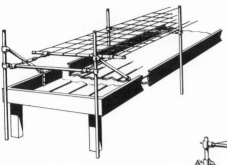

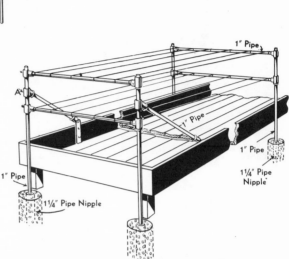

Fig. 7–3. Flowers may be supported by welded wire fabric, raised progressively higher as the plants grow, upper left, or by wires running lengthwise of the bench and strings crosswise, upper right and lower. (Upper figures, National Greenhouse Co.)

Fig. 7-4. The season of flowering of some plants may be controlled by regulating the day length. Upper, the day length may be shortened by covering plants with light-proof black sateen cloth for part of each day. Lower, the day length may be increased by turning on hundred-watt incandescent lamps from just before sundown and letting them burn until 10 p.m. (Kenneth Post and Cornell University)

Treatment must be started before the buds form, otherwise nothing is gained. It is well to know the normal time for bud formation, to be able to plan how long in advance to begin treatment. The periods of bud formation for some short-day plants are:

Plant	Normal bud-formation period
Chrysanthemum	August 15 to 25
Kalanchoë blossfeldiana	September 25 to October 5
Lady Mac begonia	October 10 to 20
Poinsettia	October 10 to 20
Stevia	September 20 to 27

The earlier in the season they are exposed to short days, the sooner they will flower. If the treatment is started so early that the flower buds form before the days become naturally short, the treatment must be continued until the flower buds are well developed. If the short days of fall coincide with your artificially shortened days, treatment may be discontinued.

Short-day treatment of chrysanthemums is widely practiced. Their flowers will be ready to cut 8 to 13 weeks, depending on the variety, after the beginning of the darkening period. Varieties of chrysanthemums which naturally flower in late October can be made to flower in September or even August by starting short-day treatment at the appropriate time. The days must be kept shortened until the flower buds of the spray types (pompons) show color and until those of the standards are the size of a nickel. When the buds are of this size they will complete their development with either long or short days. For kalanchoë, when the darkening period is begun July 20 and continued until September 20, the plants flower October 20. If they are shaded from August 15 to October 1, they flower early in December. Christmas begonias, such as Lady Mac and Melior, will flower in late November if they are grown with short days from September 1 until they bloom. The Christmas cactus flowers at Christmas if given short days beginning August 15. *Euphorbia fulgens* flowers in mid-December when given short days from September 20.

If you wish to delay the flowering of short-day plants, you act on the fact that they normally do not set flower buds when the days are long. You can postpone their flowering by artificially lengthening the days before, during, and after their normal bud-forming period. Then when you wish them to set flower buds, you simply discontinue the long-day treatment, and let them be exposed to the normally short days of the season.

The artificial light used to augment the day hours need not be strong. Ordinary 40- or 60-watt incandescent bulbs in reflectors are placed 2 feet above the plants and 4 feet apart, or if you wish you can use 100-watt lamps spaced 6 feet apart and 4 or 5 feet above the plants. These are turned on at sunset, and turned off at 10 P.M., and serve to give the plants a day length of 14 hours or more. This is often referred to as "lighting." A time switch may be used to control the lights.

By controlling the day length, chrysanthemums can be brought into flower during any month. For February flowering of chrysanthemums, the plants are given long days until December 1, when supplemental lighting is discontinued. Thereafter, the plants are exposed to the naturally short days and hence they produce flower buds. Flowering of other short-day plants can be controlled in the same way.

If you do not wish to delay the flowering of short-day plants during fall or winter, be careful not to prolong the days unintentionally by keeping the greenhouse light on in the evening, or by exposing them to lights being used for long-day plants. Intense yard and street lights may also prevent flowering.

Long-day plants. Long-day plants produce flower buds when the days are more than 13 or 14 hours long. In Miami, Florida, the days are more than 14 hours long (including civil twilight) from April 26 to August 15. (Civil twilight is the time after sunset or before sunrise during which, on clear days, there is enough light for ordinary outdoor occupations. It ends, or begins, when the sun is about 6° below the horizon.) In San Francisco the period of long days extends from April 11 to September 1; in Ithaca, New York, from April 1 to September 15. Many of the plants which flower in late spring and summer are long-day plants. Feverfew, scabiosa, rudbeckia, and the China aster are typical ones. Long-day plants can be flowered in winter by supplementing the day length with artificial light. The method is the same as that just described, the lights being turned on at sunset and off at 10 P.M.

Many plants, certain day-neutral ones as well as long-day plants, will flower earlier if they are grown in the area where the days are prolonged and in some instances they will be more floriferous. Among those which respond in this way are China aster, Boston

Fig. 7–5. Centaurea, a long-day plant, flowers when days are 16 hours long, right, but not when they are 8 hours long, left. (U.S.D.A.)

yellow daisy, centaurea, clarkia, feverfew, gardenia, lily, marigold, nasturtium, pansy, salpiglossis, and violet. There are a few kinds which, although they can be flowered earlier with supplemental light, give low quality flowers borne on weak stems. For this reason do not light bouganvilleas, calendulas, carnations, cinerarias, snapdragons, and freezias.

Indeterminate or day-neutral plants. Plants such as carnations, African violets, snapdragons, roses, and tomatoes, which flower when the days are either short or long, are known as day-neutral plants. These plants flower almost continuously.

Length of Night and Flowering

Instead of altering the length of day we can interrupt the night by turning on lights near midnight to control flowering of long- and short-day plants. Early investigators put emphasis on day length as the major factor controlling flowering and, as we have seen, it is easy to control flowering by modifying the day length. More recent investigations demonstrate that the length of the night, the dark period, is the major factor that determines when plants flower. Under natural conditions day length and night length are interrelated; when days are short, nights are long and when days are long, nights are short.

The long uninterrupted nights associated with short days bring about flowering of short-day plants. If the long night is interrupted by turning on lights near midnight the short-day plants will not flower. Some plants are extremely sensitive to such lighting, for example kalanchoë, a short-day plant. If a light remains on for just one minute at midnight, it will not flower, even though the days are short. The illustration on page 103 shows this extreme sensitivity. The plant on the right was grown with short days and long nights which were interrupted at midnight by turning on a red light (white would give the same result) for just one minute. Not all plants are as sensitive as kalanchoë. To prevent flowering of chrysanthemums when days are short, the days can be lengthened or the nights can be interrupted by having lights on for four hours.

On the other hand, long-day plants don't flower when days are short primarily because the nights are too long. By interrupting the long night they can be brought into flower even though the days are short.

Temperature and Flowering

Night temperatures markedly influence the initiation of flowers. If night temperatures are not appropriate for the individual variety, it does not flower.

During winter, stocks flower profusely when the night temperature is 50 degrees, but do not do so at 60 degrees. Other plants which flower only when the night temperature is less than 60 degrees are greenhouse buddleia, calceolaria, cineraria, Martha Washington geranium, and wallflower.

The response of some plants to length of day can be modified by temperature. At one temperature a plant may flower when the days are short, but at a different temperature it may flower when the days are long. Poinsettias are generally considered to be short-day

Long uninterrupted   One minute of
dark period   red light at
                                      midnight

Fig. 7–6. Interrupting a long night prevents flowering of kalanchoë, a short-day plant. (Agricultural Research Service, Plant Industry Station, U.S.D.A.)

plants, flowering at Christmas. Poinsettia plants exposed to night temperature of 60 to 62 degrees are indeed short-day plants, but if they are grown at a night temperature of 55 degrees, they become long-day plants and at this cooler temperature will not flower during the short days of winter. If they are raised with nights of 70 degrees, they do not flower at all. The flowering of Christmas cactus is also affected by both day length and temperature. This plant flowers well with nights of 60 to 65 degrees and short days. With nights of 55 degrees, it is day-neutral, flowering when the days are either long or short. At nights of 70 to 75 degrees, it does not flower under either long- or short-day conditions.

Length of Day and Dormancy

In the autumn you may notice that the leaves of trees growing near street lights are still green on the side toward the light and of autumnal coloring on the side away from it. Where the days are artificially prolonged by the light, the leaves are active; where the light is too low to influence the branches, the branches are dormant.

One year we thought that we could get a head start by planting seeds of tuberous begonias in late fall instead of January or February, the recommended months. The seeds germinated promptly, but the seedlings did not grow appreciably until the following spring, when the days became longer than 12 hours. We know now that we could have kept those seedlings growing through the winter months by lengthening the days artificially until 10 P.M. When the days are 14 hours or more in length flowering sized tuberous begonia plants come into bloom. When the days are 12 hours or less, and the night temperature 60 degrees or above, growth ceases and mature plants stop flowering. During the short days of autumn the tuber below the ground grows. Gloxinias seem to behave in a similar manner. Not only do gloxinia seedlings benefit when grown with supplemental light during the short days of winter, but so also do plants grown from tubers. If such plants are grown with supplemental light, they will make better growth and produce more and earlier flowers than those grown during short days.

We can keep orchid seedlings growing actively during the winter months by prolonging the days, thereby growing plants to flowering size in a shorter time.

You will find still other uses for the lighted area. Leaf cuttings of Lorraine and Elatior begonias remain healthy and root more quickly if they are grown with long days. Both stem and leaf cuttings of many plants respond in a similar manner if they are planted during the short days of December, January, and February.

The length of day may even influence the germination of some seeds. For example, seeds of *Begonia evansiana* do not germinate when days are shorter than nine hours, but they germinate promptly when days are longer than twelve hours.

8

Plant Pests

Pests weaken plants, deform and disfigure flowers, and spread disease organisms. It requires constant care to keep them under control. It is better to spray regularly, say at biweekly or monthly intervals, than to wait for the insect population to build up before control measures are taken. Pests can increase at an alarming rate when prevention is not practiced.

Good culture and cleanliness will help in controlling pests. Crowding of plants leads to a vicious circle of events. Crowding makes it difficult to reach plants with insecticides, and populations of insects build up. It also makes it difficult to water and fertilize plants, and the starved plants are more susceptible to many insects. If the greenhouse is continually too hot and dry you can expect an outbreak of red spiders as well as certain other pests.

You will need a good sprayer and a duster, as well as insecticides for specific pests. A tank sprayer with a pump to build up a pressure great enough to break the spray into fine droplets is suitable for liquid sprays. If your greenhouse is very small you may find a hand sprayer adequate. When spraying or dusting, direct the insecticide to the tips of the shoots, the undersides of leaves, and the junction between stem and leaves, where the insects congregate.

In her book *Silent Spring* Rachel Carson alerted us to the dangers of pesticides. Not only have the facts she gave us been proven indisputable, but new evidence of the harm wreaked in our environment by pesticides comes to light every day, and not just to the wild creatures but to man himself. Many fatalities have occurred from the careless use of insecticides, both to the users and to innocent persons who have drunk, eaten, or otherwise taken in the chemicals. In the discussion which follows, we have selected where possible, nonpersistent kinds and those which are relatively safe. Even so, we advise you to wear a mask and rubber gloves when handling them, to wear old clothes that protect the body and to take a bath immediately afterward. The clothing used should be thoroughly aired, preferably washed, between times.

When spraying or dusting, use just enough to cover the plants thoroughly. Too little may be inadequate; too much wastes material. Before using any spray, read the manufacturer's directions carefully. Some can be used safely on flowers, but not on vegetables. The concentration is very important; too strong a solution may injure some plants and do more harm than the pests against which it is used. No one chemical is effective against all pests. Malathion (Cythion) is a good general insecticide, as is also Sevin (Carbaryl), but these are not particularly effective for mites. For the latter, Dimite, Kelthane, or chlorobenzilate must be used, but these will undoubtedly be replaced by less persistent chemicals in the future. Metaldehyde dusts, baits, and suspensions are used against slugs and snails. Each year new pesticides are put on the market. Before using anything new on all your plants, try it on a few or assure yourself that they have been tested professionally on the kinds you have. Smoke fumigants are available and must be used with great care. *Some chemicals, such as calcium cyanide and parathion and all the organophosphates (except Malathion), are dreadfully poisonous and should never be used.*

Systemic insecticides have been developed to give more thorough control, especially of such kinds as scale and mealy bugs which are difficult to eradicate. Where they have been thoroughly tested for certain plants and have been proved not to be injurious, they are quite regularly used by commercial growers, and there is no reason why amateurs should not also use them. Most are very toxic to man, so great care should be taken in handling them and in handling the plants afterwards. Some require certain environmental conditions in order not to harm the plants, e.g., if it is too warm they may burn certain kinds, so directions should be carefully followed. Some kinds of plants are definitely injured easily and should not be treated with systemics. Experimental work is turning out new kinds and eventually there may be some that are not so hazardous to use.

Many sprays are on the market that combine an insecticide, a miticide, and a fungicide. Some also contain a systemic insecticide,

Fig. 8–1. Upper, webbing of two-spotted mite on chrysanthemum. (Agricultural Research Service, USDA). Lower left, mealy bugs. Lower right, aphids.

Fig. 8–2. Upper left, cottony sacs of the wooly cactus scale. Upper right, leaf miner injury on chrysanthemum. Lower left, injury of carnations by the carnation leafroller. Lower right, galls of the chrysanthemum gall midge. (Upper right, Agricultural Research Service, USDA; others A. Earl Pritchard and California Agricultural Experiment Station)

but if you do not wish to use such, better find another kind. In fact, always know what the spray contains before you use it; one may have an ingredient that would be harmful to your particular plants, or which you do not want to have in your greenhouse because of its very poisonous nature. As new products appear during the years, find out all you can about them before using them.

While there is no necessity to over-treat your greenhouse, a regular spray program is a good idea. The owner of a new greenhouse may think at first that he is not going to be bothered by pests. But most of the pests we battle are those common in gardens, and they inevitably enter the greenhouse. Moreover, they can survive the winter in the warm atmosphere. It is advisable to spray preventively once a month during the summer and every six weeks to two months in cold weather. If a particular pest increases suddenly in population, treat it with a chemical specific for it. If it continues in spite of this, use a different chemical to overcome its resistance. In general, a combination of Malathion and chlorobenzilate, which can be mixed in the sprayer, gives good control. The old standbys, rotenone, pyrethrum, and nicotine sulfate, can also be used, perhaps occasionally or alternating with Malathion-chlorobenzilate to prevent buildup of resistance.

Insect Enemies of Greenhouse Plants

Ants. These are annoying in the greenhouse, and the soil-dwelling ones may change the soil texture for the worse. Moreover, they transport aphids from one plant to another. Malathion is an effective control.

Aphids. You may know these ubiquitous insects as plant lice. They are small, plump-bodied, pale white or greenish to blackish insects with or without wings. Practically all greenhouse plants are vulnerable to their attack. Aphids may be controlled with Malathion, nicotine sulfate, pyrethrum, or rotenone.

Beetles. Various kinds of beetles feed on greenhouse plants. Be alert for their damage on asters, hydrangeas, orchids, and roses. Beetles can be controlled with rotenone or Malathion.

Chrysanthemum midge. This is a small fly which lays eggs inside the leaves of chrysanthemums. The eggs hatch into larvae and, concurrently, galls appear on the undersurfaces of the leaves. The galls extend out from the leaf about an eighth of an inch. Insecticides cannot reach the larvae to kill them. However, the emerging flies are readily killed by Malathion. Weekly spraying with this insecticide or with nicotine sulfate gives good control.

Cutworms. You may find cutworms feeding on the foliage of chrysanthemums. Scattering a metaldehyde bait will usually control them. Spraying or dusting with Sevin is also very effective, as is hand-picking at night with the aid of a flashlight.

Leafhoppers. Leafhoppers are wedge-shaped, slim, winged insects about ⅛ to ¼ inch long. Asters, chrysanthemums, and lettuce are their favorite plants. Sevin or Malathion give good control.

Leaf miners. These are the larvae of minute flies which feed on the soft tissues inside leaves. They make characteristic tunnels in the infested parts. Leaf miners attack azaleas, chrysanthemums, carnations, cinerarias, and other plants. The larvae cannot be reached by sprays. Control consists of killing the adults with Malathion before they begin to lay eggs. You should remove and burn infested leaves.

Leaf rollers. Leaf rollers are green or bronze caterpillars that bring about a rolling of the leaves. Aster, azalea, calceolaria, carnation, calendula, chrysanthemum, cineraria, geranium, rose, snapdragon, and sweet pea may become infested. Spraying or dusting with pyrethrum, Sevin, or Malathion gives good control.

Mealy bugs. Mealy bugs are troublesome pests of African violets, amaryllis, azaleas, begonias, cacti, chrysanthemums, gardenias, geraniums, kalanchoë, lantana, poinsettias, and orchids. They are generally oval in shape, about a quarter of an inch long, smaller in the young crawling stages, and have hairlike projections on the body covered with a waxy white powder. Malathion and Sevin (carbaryl) give good control when a few drops of a household detergent are mixed with the solution to penetrate the waxy covering. Treatment should be repeated in three weeks to get the newly hatched crawlers. Bad infestations may require a systemic insecticide, but make sure that this will not harm the plants in question.

Scales. These are small insects that are covered with a flattened scale which is variously gray, orange, brown, or black in color. They move about after they are hatched, but they soon locate, insert their beaks into the plant tissue, and develop a covering scale. Scale insects are likely to attack cacti, ferns, orchids, palms, poinsettias, and succulents. Sevin and Malathion will control many scale insects, and nicotine with soap is fairly effective.

Springtails. These are small, jumping insects which live in the soil and come to the surface when the plants are watered. The common springtail (Collembola, a relative of the silverfish) may be controlled with Malathion.

Thrips. Practically all greenhouse plants are subject to injury by thrips, among them African violet, aster, azalea, calceolaria, carnation, chrysanthemum, cineraria, cyclamen, geranium, gladiolus, hydrangea, orchid, primula, rose, snapdragon, and sweet pea. Thrips are minute, narrow, yellowish to brown or blackish insects that feed on both flowers and leaves. Petals of attacked flowers are often brown, and infected flowers may fail to open properly. Thrips feed by rasping and scraping the surface, leaving tiny irregular scars. Their presence can often be detected by small black dots of excrement scattered over the injured areas. Malathion, nicotine sulfate, rotenone, or pyrethrum can be used for control.

White fly. These tiny flies (about $\frac{1}{25}$ inch long) have white powdery wings. They generally occur in large colonies and fly off in clouds when the plants are disturbed. Their young stages, extremely small nymphs, feed by sucking sap from the leaves, and can be very destructive. Calceolaria, calendula, cineraria, geranium, gerbera, lantana, pelargonium, tomato, and cucumber are especially susceptible to their attack. Malathion gives good control.

Mites. Mites are in the spider family. They have eight legs, as do true spiders, whereas insects have six legs. Some of them spin fine webs on the leaves, usually on the underside. They feed by sucking and produce a stippling and silvering of the leaf surface.

Red spiders. Also called *two-spotted spider mites,* these very small spiders spin webs and are red to yellow in color. They can be seen with the unaided eye, but often a hand lens is a help. They are a serious pest of asters, azaleas, bouvardia, calceolaria, calla, carnations, chrysanthemums, cineraria, gardenias, gerbera, gladioli, hydrangeas, lantana, orchids, roses, and sweet peas. They thrive in greenhouses that are hot and dry. Keeping the temperature down and the relative humidity high will aid in keeping down the population of red spiders. Forceful syringing helps rid plants of both eggs and adults. Spraying with Dimite, Kelthane, Malathion, or chlorobenzilate gives good control.

False spider mites. These are an even worse enemy for they do not spin webs, and are so small that they cannot be seen with the ordinary hand lens. A low-power binocular microscope or a ten-power hand lens is usually necessary to detect them. On some plants they cause large brown scars or pits, so serious as to cause leaf fall; on other kinds the damage is less severe but usually worse

Thrip

Two-spotted spider mite

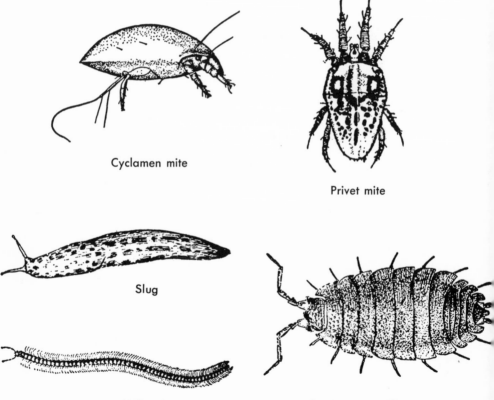

Cyclamen mite

Privet mite

Slug

Millipede

Sowbug, or pillbug

Fig. 8–3.   Troublesome pests.

than that of red spiders. Malathion gives only poor control. Better control is given by Kelthane, Dimite, or chlorobenzilate. One of these should be used when spraying as a precautionary measure.

Sowbugs. Sowbugs are related to crabs, lobsters, and shrimp. They have seven pairs of legs, a hard, gray shell, and frequently they will roll into a ball when disturbed. They feed on organic matter and on stems and roots of plants. They can be controlled by spraying the area with Malathion.

Millipedes. Like sowbugs, these are also related to the crustaceans. Ordinarily they feed on organic matter in the soil, but at times they eat the roots of plants. A spray of Malathion or Sevin will eliminate them.

Nematodes. Nematodes are minute roundworms that are abundant in some greenhouse soils. Some nematodes cause a serious disease known as root knot. The nematodes invade the feeding roots and cause galls to form on them. Infected plants are stunted and have difficulty in absorbing water and minerals. Among the plants that may be affected are African violets, gardenias, and roses. If nematodes are a problem in your greenhouse, you should sterilize the soil before use with steam, Pano-drench, Sarolex, or Vapam. *Use great caution in handling these chemicals and follow directions carefully.* Remove and destroy badly affected plants.

Leaf blotch or blight of begonias and chrysanthemums, is caused by nematodes which enter the leaves through the leaf pores. The first symptoms on begonias are small brown spots with water-soaked edges. Later the spots merge to form large brownish blotches. Infected leaves of chrysanthemums exhibit brownish-black, wedge-shaped areas. Foliar nematodes are difficult to control. Some suggestions for control are: use sterilized soil; keep foliage dry; destroy infected leaves; space plants so their leaves do not touch.

Slugs and snails. Slugs and snails are related to clams and oysters. The soft bodies of snails are protected by a shell, whereas the bodies of slugs are not protected. Slugs and snails usually hide during the day and feed at night. When abundant they may raise havoc with young plants. They can be controlled by scattering a bait containing metaldehyde or, better, by dusting the soil surface with a powder containing metaldehyde or by watering with a metaldehyde slurry. Many slugs can be picked off by hand at night with the aid of a flashlight. Scattering lime under the benches will also aid in controlling these pests.

9

Diseases of Greenhouse Plants

Plants may suffer from unsuitable environmental conditions and from diseases caused by viruses, bacteria, and fungi. Ailments which result purely from poor culture are not contagious, so the sick plants need not be isolated. However, diseases caused by organisms are contagious. The viruses, bacteria, and fungi reproduce in the plants and the infective agents may be spread to other plants. Be careful not to transfer an infectious disease to healthy plants when flowers are cut. Likewise, when making cuttings, pruning, and dividing plants, sterilize the knives, pruning shears, and other tools to make sure they do not carry a disease to healthy plants. Simplest and most effective is to flame them, using an alcohol lamp, a candle, or a small blow torch. Small items such as razor blades can be boiled for ten minutes. Used pots should be washed, soaked in Clorox (1 part in 10 of water), then thoroughly rinsed and aired. Plants harboring harmful agents should be disposed of, or at least isolated from healthy plants. Sanitation is most important; the more closely you approach surgical conditions, the more likely are your plants to be healthy.

Plants are more susceptible to infection when they are weak, poorly grown, and crowded. The ravages of disease may be reduced by paying attention to such cultural practices as careful preparation of the soil, proper watering, giving the plants ample light and space, keeping weeds down, and by purchasing top-quality seeds and plants.

Virus Diseases

Infectious agents so small that they cannot be seen with the ordinary microscope are known as *viruses*. These minute agents can be seen with the powerful electron microscope which gives magnification up to 100,000 times. Viruses are capable of reproducing themselves in the body of an appropriate host; there are many kinds. Some can infect only human beings, others cattle, others orchid plants, still different ones asters, and so forth.

Plant diseases known as *mosaics* are caused by several viruses. The leaves of infected plants are mottled with irregular light- and dark-green areas. Furthermore, the plants are dwarfed and often the flowers are streaked or splotched. The mosaic disease is seen in beans, carnations, cinerarias, coleus, geraniums, gladioli, irises, lilies, daffodils, orchids, petunias, stocks, sweet peas, and others.

Diseases known as *yellows* are also caused by viruses. Aster yellows is one of the best known of this class. The first symptom is a slight yellowing along the veins; later the leaves become yellow throughout. The growth is spindly, the plants are dwarfed, and frequently they do not flower. If flowers develop, they are yellowish green, regardless of the normal color of the variety. Carnations and chrysanthemums are other plants which may have the yellows disease.

All virus diseases—mosaics, yellows, and others—are systemic; that is, they develop throughout the whole plant. Hence, the removal of parts of the plant, such as picking off mottled leaves or the stems bearing them, will not control the disease, and no external control has yet been found. To keep other plants from contracting a virus disease, ruthless elimination and burning of diseased plants is necessary. Most viruses are spread by aphids, thrips, or leafhoppers, which feed on infected plants and then on healthy ones. Control of insects will go a long way toward keeping your plants free of virus diseases. Plants harboring a virus should never be propagated, and only disease-free stock should be planted. Frequently weeds serve as reservoirs of plant viruses which are transmitted to greenhouse plants. Eliminating weeds in the greenhouse is a safeguard against some virus diseases. Some growers, Yoder

Brothers for example, take great care to produce cuttings of chry-santhemums and carnations which are free of virus. Hence, many commercial growers prefer to purchase new cuttings each year instead of making their own.

Bacterial Diseases

Bacteria are one-celled plants, extremely small, but visible with the ordinary microscope. Some of them are so small that fifty billion could be contained in a volume the size of a drop of water. Some bacteria have a spherical shape; others are rod-shaped or of spiral form. They reproduce rapidly by splitting in two. Some bacteria divide in two every 20 minutes. Starting with one bacterium and assuming a division every 20 minutes, the population would be astronomically large at the end of one day. The division does not usually proceed in such a regular manner, fortunately, being limited somewhat by a decreasing food supply and by poisonous substances produced by the bacteria themselves.

Certain species of bacteria cause plant disease. Usually a specific bacterium attacks a specific host, so that one which infects one kind of plant will not infect any other. There are a few, however, that are nonspecific, capable of infecting many kinds of plants, from carrots to orchids.

Many greenhouse plants are susceptible to the *bacterial leafspot* disease. Typically, the first symptom is small, dark, circular spots on the leaves. The spots enlarge and frequently appear water-soaked. An ooze containing countless bacteria may appear on the leaves, and it is this ooze which may be carried to other plants by splashing water, insects, or contaminated hands. Begonia, carnation, dieffenbachia, geranium, gladiolus, ivy, various orchids, and others are a few of the susceptible plants. The species which causes leafspot on begonia will not cause leafspot on carnation or other hosts; for example, *Phytomonas begoniae* causes bacterial leafspot of begonia and *Phytomonas woodsii* infects carnations.

The bacterial leafspot may be controlled. First, isolate infected plants from healthy ones. Then remove and burn all infected leaves. If more than just a few plants are infected, spray with a good fungicide, such as Captan, Fermate, or Zerlate. Certain sound cultural practices aid in disease prevention, such as giving the plants plenty of space so that there will be free air circulation, and watering early in the day so that the foliage and stems will be dry by nightfall.

Carnations are susceptible to the *bacterial wilt* disease. The most striking symptom is the sudden wilting of the plant or some of the branches, brought about by damage to the water-conducting system. Furthermore, the root systems of diseased plants are rotted. In this case it is best to remove all infected plants to check the spread of the disease, rather than to try to save any by cutting off infected parts. Only disease-free plants should be benched.

Soft rots of African violet, calla, cyclamen, hyacinth, iris, and orchid are caused by bacteria. In soft rot of African violet and cyclamen the leaf stalks and flower stalks become soft and watery, with resulting wilting and death. Care in watering plants and the use of sterilized soil and pots are control measures. Some hyacinth bulbs may be infected with soft rot. Infected bulbs do not produce flowers or if they do, the flowers open irregularly and rot at the top of the bulb. Plant only healthy bulbs.

Roses may have a disease known as *crown gall,* a disease characterized by the development of galls on the stems or roots. Diseased plants should be destroyed and new plants should be set out in sterilized soil.

Frequently bacteria are transmitted from diseased to healthy plants when plants are propagated, often when the presence of disease is not suspected. Sterilization of tools between each cut is effective in preventing the spread of bacteria.

Fungus Diseases

True *fungi* cause many diseases of greenhouse plants. These fungi have a cobweb-like body made up of many fine threads that penetrate the plant tissue. They reproduce by microscopic spores, formed on the plant surfaces, which are scattered by wind, insects, splashing water, and even by human hands.

Parasitic fungi injure plants by interfering with the conduction of food and water, by withdrawing nutritive substances for their own use, and by producing poisons which kill part or all of the plant. If the poisons are localized near the fungus, dead spots form on the leaves, stems, or flowers. In some diseases the poisons are carried from the point of infection to other parts of the plant where they kill the tissues.

Parasitic fungi enter plants in various ways. Frequently spores land on the leaves, and if moisture is present and other environmental conditions are favorable, the spores send out tubes which enter the leaf through open stomata (natural leaf pores). Insect punctures and wounds may allow some fungus parasites to gain entrance. Roots of plants may become infected through root hairs. Young seedlings often become infected at the crown, especially if the plants are crowded and kept too moist.

In most fungus diseases the body of the fungus (the threadlike *mycelium*) develops inside the plant (in the flowers, leaves, stems, or roots) so that it cannot be reached and killed by a fungicide sprayed on the surface. Spraying is generally a means for preventing infection or checking its spread rather than for curing a diseased plant. However, the coating left on the leaves kills any spores which subsequently light on the leaves, so if a plant is only slightly infected it can be saved. Hence you should spray plants with a fungicide as soon as the first symptoms of a fungus disease become evident. All diseased parts should be cut off and burned.

There is a notable exception to the rule that the body of a fungus is inside the plant tissue. The body (mycelium) of the one which causes *powdery mildew* remains on the outside of the plant parts; therefore a fungicide can come in contact with its body. This fungus sends absorbing organs into the plant, and these do not survive when the mycelium is killed. Plants infected with powdery mildew can be cured by dusting them with sulfur or by spraying them with Pipron or Phaltan.

Preventive spraying with a fungicide is effective in controlling many plant diseases. Some that are frequently used are dusting sulfur, Captan, Daconil, Ferbam (Fermate), Karathane, Maneb, Parzate (Zineb), Phaltan, Tersan, and Zerlate. As with insecticides, test the fungicide on a few plants before spraying the entire collection. Some manufacturers sell a mixture of an insecticide, a miticide, and a fungicide for control of insects, mites, and disease. You may find these effective and convenient to use. For example, some general purpose sprays contain Sevin for insect control, Kelthane for mites, and Maneb for fungi.

Spraying and dusting are only parts of the control program. Many varieties of plants are naturally disease-resistant. These have been selected by nurserymen and it is to your advantage to use them. For example, some varieties of chrysanthemum are resistant to the disease known as verticillium wilt. If you have had trouble with this disease, your best bet is to select resistant varieties.

Many diseases can be avoided by planting only those seeds, cuttings, bulbs, and corms which are free of disease. If a tulip bulb is infected with *Botrytis blight,* the resulting plant is sure to be infected and it will produce spores which will spread the disease. Similarly, carnation plants grown from cuttings taken from a plant suffering from fusarium yellows will harbor the disease and spread it to healthy plants. Seeds obtained from fields in which plants are diseased are likely to have some spores on them. When such seeds are planted, spores are also planted, and the plants become infected. To minimize seedborne diseases, secure seed from reliable dealers.

If seeds are planted in unsterilized soil, the seedlings may damp off, and they are particularly susceptible if they are crowded. The disease known as *damping-off* is caused by *Pythium debaryanum* and related fungi. These fungi are widely distributed in soil and practically all kinds of seedlings are vulnerable to their attack. Infected seedlings topple over suddenly, and the stems are seen to be watersoaked at the ground line. Sterilization of the soil will rid it of harmful fungi. Soil may be sterilized with heat or with Vapam. Good cultural practices will also reduce the losses from damping-off. The soil should be well aerated and the plants given ample room. Overwatering should be avoided. Seeds started in vermiculite or sphagnum moss are less likely to damp off than those planted in unsterilized soil.

In the table which follows some common diseases of greenhouse plants are listed. As you go through the table you will notice how the several control methods previously discussed are used.

SOME COMMON DISEASES OF ORNAMENTAL PLANTS

Host	Name of disease and fungus	Symptoms	Control
African violet	Crown and rootrot *Phytophthora*	Glassiness and collapse of leafstalks.	Burn diseased plants.
	Rhizoctonia canker or stem rot *Rhizoctonia*	Petiole rots where it joins stem, but crown and roots healthy.	Remove diseased leaves and brush. Fermate over cut surfaces.
	Rootrot and vascular wilt *Verticillium* and *Fusarium*	Wilting of plant, collapse of petioles, premature withering of flowers.	Burn diseased plants.
Amaryllis	Red Fire Disease *Stagonospora crini, S. curttisii*	Red streaks on leaves and flower stalk. Flower stalk deformed.	Cut off and burn diseased parts. Don't syringe plants. Secure healthy bulbs.
Aster	Wilt *Fusarium oxysporum*	Wilting and withering of foliage. Stems blackened at the base.	Use wilt resistant varieties. Do not plant in soil which harbors the fungus.
	Rust *Coleosporium solidaginis*	Orange-red pustules on under side of leaves.	Spray with Fermate, Captan, Phaltan or Bordeaux mixture.
Azalea	Flower spot *Ovulinia azaleae*	Pale or whitish spots on colored flowers and rust-colored spots on white flowers. Spots enlarge, and infected flowers cling to shrubs. Disease spreads very rapidly.	Pick and destroy affected flowers. Spray with fungicide when flower buds first show color.

Plant	Disease / Organism	Symptoms	Control
Begonia	Crown and stem rot *Pythium* sp.	Crown and lower portion of stem watersoaked and soft.	Keep plants well spaced. Avoid overwatering.
Cacti	Bacterial spot or rot *Phytomonas cactivorum*	Rotted areas on shoots.	Water sparingly and keep water off shoots. Cut out infected parts and cover cut surface with fungicide.
Calendula	Leafspot *Cercospora calendulae*	Spots on leaves which later fuse.	Spray with fungicide.
Calla lily	Bacterial soft rot *Erwinia aroideae*	Tuber and base of stem rotted.	Destroy infected plants. Use sterilized soil and healthy tubers.
	Phytophthora rot of tuber *Phytophthora richardiae*	Leaves streaked. Flowers brown and malformed.	Destroy infected plants. Use sterilized soil and healthy tubers.
Camellia	Flower blight *Sclerotinia camelliae*	Irregular brownish spots on petals. Eventually flowers become dull brown and drop.	Remove and destroy infected flowers. Pick up any fallen flowers and burn them.
Carnation	Fusarium wilt *Fusarium oxysporum*	Withering of the shoots and pale straw-yellow foliage.	Because fungus remains in soil indefinitely, it is necessary to sterilize soil or use fresh soil. Take cuttings only from healthy plants.
	Rust *Uromyces caryophyllinus*	Reddish brown pustules on leaves and stems.	Keep foliage dry so spores cannot germinate. Spray with fungicide. Use disease-free cuttings.

SOME COMMON DISEASES OF ORNAMENTAL PLANTS (*Cont.*)

Host	Name of disease and fungus	Symptoms	Control
Chrysanthemum	Verticillium wilt *Verticillium dahliae*	Wilting of foliage. Plants stunted.	Plant disease-free stock. Select resistant varieties.
	Powdery mildew *Erysiphe cichoracearum*	Deformed leaves covered with a white powdery growth.	Dust with sulfur or spray with Pipron.
Cyclamen	Leafspot	Brown or black spots on foliage	Remove infected leaves and burn. Spray with Fermate or Zerlate.
	Soft rot	Leafstalks and flowering stems soft and watery.	Avoid overwatering. Use sterilized soil and pots.
Dahlia	Stem rot *Sclerotinia sclerotiorum*	Sudden wilting and dying of plants. Water-soaked areas at the base of the stem.	Remove and destroy diseased plants. Use well-drained soil. Wide spacing of plants.
	Storage rot Various species of *Botrytis, Fusarium,* and others.	Rotting of tubers during storage.	Because most tuber rots start in wounds made during digging, careful digging will reduce rot. Maintain a temperature of 40°F. in storage room.
Fuchsia	Gray mold	Rotting of buds.	Avoid wetting foliage and buds. Provide good ventilation. Cut off and burn infected parts.
Gardenia	Stem canker *Phomopsis gardeniae*	Stem near soil surface enlarged and cracked. Plants stunted.	Destroy infected plants. Avoid injury to plants. Use sterilized soil. Use disease-free cuttings.

Geranium	Blossom blight and leafspot *Botrytis cinerea*	Premature fading and drying of petals. Irregular brown, water-soaked spots on leaves which later become dry and wrinkled.	Prompt removal of infected flowers and leaves. Proper spacing and ventilation. Keep flowers and foliage dry.
Gladiolus	Yellows *Fusarium orthoceras*	Foliage becomes pale or yellow. Corm shows a brown rot and may rot in soil. Corms slightly infected survive, but disease increases during storage.	Use such resistant varieties as Alice Tiplady, Apricot glow, Dearborn, Hopi, Minuet, Picardy, and Souvenir. Eliminate diseased stock. Disinfect corms before planting with a 3-hour soak in one pint lysol to 25 gallons of water, or 6 to 8 hours immersion in 1:1000 mercuric chloride.
Hydrangea	Powdery mildew *Erysiphe polygoni*	White powdery growth develops on the leaves.	Dust with sulfur or spray with Pipron
Iris	Leafspot *Didymellina macrospora*	Minute brown spots on the leaves, surrounded by watersoaked areas. Spots may fuse and the leaves may die.	Remove and burn infected leaves. Spray with Captan or Fermate.
Lily	Botrytis blight *Botrytis elliptica* Foot rot *Phytophthora cactorum*	Circular orange or reddish-brown spots on the leaves. Sudden wilting and death.	Spray with Captan. Plant only healthy bulbs secured from reliable source.
Narcissus	Basal rot *Fusarium bulbigenum*	Rotting of the bulbs begins at the base of the scales and spreads through the inside of the bulb.	Discard diseased bulbs.

Host	Name of disease and fungus	Symptoms	Control
Orchids	Leafspot *Rhizoctonia*	Black areas on leaves.	Don't syringe. Spray with Fermate or Zerlate.
	Soft rot *Erwinia carotovora*	Watersoaked areas on leaves followed by collapse of tissue with wrinkling of leaf surface.	Cut off infected leaves and destroy. "Paint" cut surface with Fermate. Destroy badly infected plants.
	Bacterial leafspot *Phytomonas cattleyae*	Watersoaked spots on leaves.	Remove infected leaves and destroy. Spray with fungicide.
	Anthracnose *Gleosporium* and *Colletotrichum*	Reddish brown circular or oval sunken spots on leaves which later become brown or gray.	Remove infected parts and destroy. Spray with Bordeaux mixture, Fermate, or Tersan.
	Petal blight *Botrytis*	Small spots on petals often with pink rings.	Cut off and destroy diseased flowers. Spray with Zineb or Ferbam.
Pansy and violet	Anthracnose *Colletotrichum violae-tricoloris*	Dead spots on leaves and flowers.	Remove infected leaves and flowers and burn.
Poinsettia	Stem rot *Rhizoctonia* sp.	Decay and blackening of lower portion of stem.	Root cuttings in sterilized sand. Pot in sterilized soil.
Rose	Black spot *Diplocarpon rosae*	Circular black spots on the leaves. Spots have a fringed margin. Leaves may become yellow and fall off prematurely.	Remove diseased leaves and burn. Spray with Captan or Phaltan. Repeat at weekly intervals.

Plant	Disease	Symptoms	Control
Snapdragon	Brown canker *Diaporthe umbrina*	Purple to white cankers on the stems, which ultimately girdle the stem. Purple or purple with white spots on the leaves.	Plant disease-free plants. Prune out and destroy infected parts. Make cuts well below infected area and sterilize the pruning shears between cuts. Dust with sulfur.
	Rust *Puccinia antirrhini*	Reddish-brown, powdery pustules on the leaves, stems, and seed pods.	Purchase varieties resistant to rust. Spray young plants with Fermate or sulfur.
Stocks	Rootrot *Corticum vagum*	Plants yellow, dwarfed, and sometimes wilted. Roots decayed.	Bench healthy plants. Use sterilized soil.
Sweet pea	Black rootrot *Thielavia basicola*	Plants dwarfed, yellow, and sickly. Root system partially or completely destroyed.	Plant seeds in disease-free soil. Do not use same plot year after year.
	Rhizoctonia rootrot *Rhizoctonia solani*	As above.	As above.
	Anthracnose *Glomerella cingulata*	General wilting of affected parts at flowering time. White areas on leaves. Flower stalks wither before flowers develop.	Use disease-free seed. Pull and burn infected plants.
Tulip	Blight or fire *Botrytis tulipae*	Yellowish spots on leaves surrounded by darker, watersoaked area. Spots often enlarge, fuse, and turn whitish gray. Lesions also develop on flowers, flower stalks, and bulbs.	Plant disease-free bulbs. After plants are up, remove all infected plant parts. Spray with Fermate, 2 lbs. per 100 gallons of water, when plants are 4 inches high. Repeat at 7- to 10-day intervals.

10

Cut Flowers

By raising plants in benches you can have an abundance of flowers at all seasons of the year and with a minimum of work. Raising plants in this way requires no more time than growing them in the garden, and many favorite outdoor kinds grow much better in a greenhouse, among them calendulas, candytufts, carnations, chrysanthemums, daisies, feverfew, marigolds, pansies, salpiglossis, scabiosas, snapdragons, stocks, and sweet peas.

With the exception of chrysanthemums and gerbera all of the plants discussed in this chapter thrive in a cool greenhouse, one maintained at 50° at night with a 10° to 15° rise during the day. Except during the bright, hot, summer months they should be grown with full sun.

They grow vigorously in a soil consisting of two parts loam; one of peat moss; and one of coarse sand, or vermiculite, or perlite. Add six ounces per bushel of 5–10–5 fertilizer, or three ounces of 10–20–10 fertilizer, or twelve ounces of Mag Amp. If Mag Amp is used subsequent feeding may not be necessary because the nutrients are released over a long period. If a 5–10–5 or 10–20–10 fertilizer is used no additional fertilizer will be needed for the first month or two. Thereafter the plants should be fed biweekly with a solution of a water soluble fertilizer prepared according to the manufacturer's directions.

If well-rotted manure is available you may wish to use a mixture of two parts of loam to one of well-rotted manure. With this mixture no fertilizer need be added.

Fill the bench with the desired mixture to a depth of five inches, water thoroughly, and when the excess water has drained out, plant the crop.

When one variety has finished flowering, you should have plants of some other kind to take its place. For example, after the chrysanthemums are through, you can remove them from the bench and fill it with snapdragons or stocks, the seeds of which were sown in flats in June or July.

The plants are discussed in alphabetical order by their common names followed by the name of the family to which each belongs.

Aster (Compositae)

The China Aster, *Callistephus chinensis*, is the common garden aster. Asters may be grown to perfection under glass, and they will make the greenhouse colorful from July through September if you grow early, midseason, and late varieties. For flowers during the summer, sow seeds in April and move the plants into the bench in May, with a spacing of 8 by 8 inches. The stems should be disbudded in order to obtain large flowers.

If you want asters in flower during the spring months you must furnish the plants with long days by giving them supplemental light from sundown until 10 P.M. The Royal varieties are reliable for growing with supplemental lighting. Seed may be sown December 1 for flowering from April to June. After they have germinated (about December 10), give the seedlings additional light. The seedlings will be ready to plant in the bench about February 1. Continue lighting the plants until they are through flowering.

Aster wilt is a serious disease. However, if you select wilt-resistant varieties you will not be troubled by it. A destructive virus disease, known as *aster yellows*, is spread by a leafhopper. The elimination of this insect with Malathion will aid in control. Aphids, red spiders, thrips, and leafrollers are other pests.

Calendula (Compositae)

Varieties of calendula (*Calendula officinalis*) which bear large flowers on long stems have been developed especially for greenhouse culture. Among the choice varieties are Gold, Lemon Queen,

Orange King, and Masterpiece, plants which should be spaced 12 × 12 inches. Plants grown from seed sown in late July will begin to flower in October or November and produce flowers through the winter. For better-quality flowers, you can remove the first flower buds as they form, after which the plants will branch. Each branch will then flower in January. The branches should be disbudded to secure large flowers. After these flowers are cut you can get a second crop in April. The flowers of the second crop may be somewhat inferior to those of the first. For choice flowers from February to March it will pay you to sow seeds in October, and for flowers from April through June, in November.

Carnations (Caryophyllaceae)

For a generous supply of fragrant, beautiful flowers of good lasting quality from September through June you can depend on carnations, *Dianthus caryophyllus*, a member of the pink family. Their requirements are simple: plenty of light and fresh air, an even supply of water, and a night temperature of 50 degrees with a 10-degree rise during the day.

You can get a start by purchasing rooted cuttings in winter or early spring. There are white, pink, red, yellow, and novelty varieties from which to select. When the cuttings arrive, pot them in 2½- or 3-inch pots. Don't let the young plants become potbound and hard-stemmed; keep them moving along, shifting them into larger pots if necessary. When they are 6 to 8 inches tall and thoroughly established in their pots, pinch the plants to promote branching. In May they may be planted in the bench with a spacing of 8 by 8 inches. The plants in the greenhouse need light shade only during the bright summer months. At other seasons they should have full sun. Give them ample water and syringe them frequently.

If you prefer, you can raise the plants outdoors from late spring, when the danger of frost is over, until August. Prepare an outdoor bed in late spring and plant them 8 inches apart in rows 16 inches apart.

Those plants grown outdoors should be moved into the greenhouse in early August. If they are kept on the dry side for 2 weeks before they are dug, they can be moved with less injury. Lift the plants from the outdoor bed, keeping as much soil around the roots as possible. Plant them in the bench at the same depth they were

Fig. 10–1. Companionable plants for the cool greenhouse. Upper left, Aster. Upper right, Calendula. Lower left, Candytuft. Lower right, Snapdragon. (Bodger Seeds Ltd.)

Fig. 10–2. Upper left, a carnation flower. Upper right, the stamens and pistil are revealed when the petals have been removed. Lower left, carnations are readily increased by stem cuttings. Lower right, carnation cuttings in a propagating bench.

in the field. Give them a good watering, then wait about 10 days before watering again. Until the plants are established, provide shade and syringe them frequently. When they are established give them full sun, which is essential for strong stems and quality flowers.

It will be necessary to install supports for the plants. A frame of pipes, which can be purchased from a greenhouse supply company, is installed at each end of the bench, or you can rig up a frame of your own design. Attach wires to the frames and run them lengthwise of the bench between the rows. Then tie cotton strings to the wires and extend them across the bench with one string between each two rows of plants. You will need two or three tiers of wires and strings, one above the other.

Instead of the wire and string method many growers prefer to use welded wire fabric, having the wires spaced in 8-inch squares. The welded wire fabric is placed on the bench and then one plant is planted in the center of each square. As the plants grow, the wire net is raised progressively higher above the bench by anchoring it to vertical posts which are fastened to the frame of the bench.

The plants will not require fertilizer for the first two months after benching. Then apply 4 pounds of 4–12–4 fertilizer for each 100-square-foot area of bench. Repeat in October, February, March, and April. The soil should be moist when the fertilizer is sprinkled between the plants and it should be watered in thoroughly. Instead of using dry fertilizer, you may prefer to feed the plants with a liquid fertilizer at biweekly intervals. If Mag Amp was added to the soil no further fertilizer will be needed.

Plants benched in early August and not pinched after June 1 will begin to blossom in September. Plants pinched in early July will generally not flower until November or December. For quality flowers let only one flower bud develop on each stem. Remove the side flower buds on that stem as soon as they are large enough to handle. With good cultural conditions you will get a sequence of blooms as lateral branches develop and flower, as many as 25 from each plant during the season.

You can purchase new cuttings each year, as many commercial growers do, or you can take cuttings from your flowering plants. Cuttings are best made from December to February. The vigorous side shoots that develop on the lower part of the stem make good cuttings. You can pull the cuttings from the parent plant or cut them off. Peel off the lower pair of leaves and insert the lower ¾ inch of the stem in sand. With a bottom heat of 60 degrees, the cuttings will root in three or four weeks. Move the rooted cuttings into pots and keep them actively growing. Pinch the plants in the manner described previously. In May the plants may be benched or planted outdoors when danger of frost is past. Because the old plants will still be flowering in May, you may not wish to remove them to make way for the young ones. That is why you may prefer to raise the young plants outdoors until August, when the old plants may be replaced with the young ones. It is desirable to replace the old soil in the bench with fresh soil each year. By so doing the incidence of disease is kept down. However, some growers use the same soil for many years; each year they sterilize the soil with steam to rid it of harmful organisms.

If you wish to grow the year-old plants a second year and even a third year instead of starting with new ones annually, keep them actively growing throughout the year. Do not cut them back and do not keep them on the dry side during the summer. In other words, carnations are perennial and will flower during all months, year after year.

Carnations are easily raised from seed. Many of the resulting plants may be inferior, but there is always the possibility of obtaining a variety of exceptional merit. Seeds are sown in the spring. Pot the seedlings and grow them on as you would cuttings. You may wish to hybridize some plants and collect seed for growing. Remove the stamens before they shed their pollen from the flower selected as the female parent. When the stigma appears fuzzy, it is ready to receive the pollen from the male parent. The pollen can be transferred from the anthers of the male parent to the stigma of the female with a brush. After the petals wilt, remove them and slit the calyx down the sides so that water will not stand inside the calyx and cause the developing pod to rot. As soon as the seeds are ripe, which requires six to eight weeks, plant them.

Pests. Carnations are attacked by aphids, leaf rollers, thrips, and red spiders; all of these can be controlled with a Malathion spray. They may become infected with such diseases as rust, bacterial leaf spot, alternaria leafspot, septoria leafspot, and *fairy-ring*, diseases which can be controlled with Fermate or Zerlate. Stem rot and bacterial wilt are other diseases. Stem rot can be controlled by reducing syringing, avoiding injury to the plants, and by using sterilized soil. To avoid bacterial wilt, propagate only from disease-free plants; discard infected plants at once.

Chrysanthemums (Compositae)

For beauty and fragrance in the greenhouse during autumn, chrysanthemums are hard to beat. They will reward you greatly for your efforts. People everywhere enjoy these magnificent plants. The Chinese have admired chrysanthemums for more than 2000 years, and the Japanese since at least 1186 A.D. The chrysanthemum is the national flower of Japan. Over many years countless beautiful varieties have been developed and their culture has been perfected. It is believed that the cultivated forms of chrysanthemum have been derived from *Chrysanthemum indicum*, which grows natively in China and Japan. The chrysanthemum is in the sunflower family.

If you are just getting a start, purchase rooted cuttings. Plants which are wilted upon arrival should be soaked in water for about an hour before potting or planting. Dip any cuttings which show fungal damage into a solution of 2 tablespoons of Fermate to a gallon of water. The rooted cuttings may be planted directly in the bench or they may be potted in 2½-inch pots and later benched. Plant the cuttings or plants with a spacing of 8 by 8 inches or 8 inches by 10. Frequent syringing and temporary shade are beneficial until they become established.

After benching, provide the plants with some means of support. The varieties bearing small flowers, sometimes called pompons, may be supported by wires running lengthwise and strings crosswise, in the manner described for carnations. The large flowered kinds, called standards, are grown with just one large flower to a stem, and they are too tall to be supported in this way. If you are raising just a few standards you can tie the plants to wooden stakes pushed into the soil. If you are growing quite a number it is more convenient to tie them to metal stakes or vertical strings which are held upright by wires running 3 to 5 feet above the bench. Fasten an upright pipe or 2 x 4 at each corner of the bench and fasten a crosspiece at a level of 5 feet above the soil. Run wires from the crosspiece at one end to the crosspiece at the other end, each directly above a row of plants. Metal stakes are pushed into the soil next to each plant and the upper end of each stake is tied to the overhead wire. Another method substitutes strings for the metal stakes. Run a set of wires just above soil level adjacent to the plants, in addition to those higher up. Beside each plant, tie a piece of string from the lower wire to the overhead wire. As the plants

Fig. 10–3. Chrysanthemums add beauty and fragrance to the greenhouse during autumn. (Lord and Burnham)

grow they can be fastened loosely to the vertical strings with string or Twist-Ems.

Chrysanthemums require a great deal of water. Once they are established it is difficult to overwater them. Frequent syringings are beneficial. In cloudy regions shade is not necessary, but in hot, bright areas a light shading may be needed during the summer.

Pinching chrysanthemums on definite dates makes for better quality flowers and a more certain crop. You may wish to pinch the spray types more than once, although fine plants will develop with just one pinch. Standards, those with one large flower per stem, are pinched once. The date of making the last pinch, which may be the only one, for both spray and standard types varies with the variety. Catalogs published by chrysanthemum specialists list the date for the last pinch for each variety.

Culture of standards. By the proper selection of varieties you can have several types of standards in flower from October through December. The standards should be pinched on definite dates as shown in the table on page 136.

Professional growers plant rooted cuttings two weeks prior to the "pinching date." For example, if they are to be pinched on July 15, the rooted cuttings are planted on July 1. You will notice that some varieties which are pinched on July 15 flower sooner than others; Amber Bright flowers on October 15, Ambassador on October 25, and Indianapolis White on November 5.

The short days that come in late August induce flower formation. Some varieties flower nine weeks after the beginning of the short days, others after ten weeks, still different ones after eleven weeks, and so on. Yoder Brothers Inc., Barberton, Ohio issues a catalog of hundreds of varieties, classified as 9, 10, 11, 12, 13, or 14 week varieties. During the time of flower bud initiation and development the temperature should be 60 degrees at night with a 10-degree rise during the day.

After the standards are pinched, side shoots will develop. Remove all but one, two, or three of the side shoots. Commercial growers generally permit two of the shoots to grow. If you leave one shoot you will get one flower per plant; if two are left, two flowers will be obtained.

If side shoots begin to grow on the flowering stems, remove them, as well as any basal shoots that form. In time the top of the stem

DATES TO PINCH STANDARD VARIETIES AND TIME OF FLOWERING

Variety	Color	Pinch	Flower
Ambassador	Cream	July 15	Oct. 25
Amber Bright	Amber Bronze	July 15	Oct. 15
Anaconda	Coppery Red	July 20	Nov. 8
Betsy Ross	Ivory	July 15	Nov. 5
Bonaffon Deluxe	Golden	July 25	Nov. 20
Bronze Mistletoe	Buff Bronze	Aug. 5	Dec. 5
Bunbu	Lavender	July 20	Nov. 1
December White	White	Aug. 5	Dec. 5
Glitters	Red Orange	July 20	Oct. 28
Golden Mistletoe	Golden	Aug. 5	Dec. 5
Good News	Lemon	July 20	Nov. 1
Helen Frick	Rose	July 22	Nov. 20
Indianapolis Bronze	Buff Bronze	July 20	Nov. 5
Indianapolis Pink	Pink	July 20	Nov. 5
Indianapolis White	White	July 15	Nov. 5
J. W. Prince	Lavender	July 20	Nov. 5
Major Bowes	Dark Lavender	July 15	Oct. 15
Meteore	Lemon	Aug. 5	Dec. 5
Mrs. H. E. Kidder	Yellow	July 10	Oct. 20
Peggy Hoover	Pink	July 20	Nov. 10
Silver Sheen	White	July 10	Oct. 20
Smith's Late White	White	Aug. 10	Dec. 11
Yellow Ambassador	Light Lemon	July 15	Oct. 25

will form a cluster of flower buds, consisting of a central flower bud surrounded by others generally smaller. As soon as the smaller buds are large enough to handle, they should be rolled off, using the thumb and index finger. Be careful not to break off the topmost large bud or there will be no flower at all. By removing the side shoots as they develop and by removing all but one flower bud from each stem the energy of the branch is diverted to one flower, which becomes very large (see Fig. 7–2, page 94).

Generally, when varieties are pinched on the recommended dates a cluster of flower buds will form at the top of each stem. The dates work very well for most regions, but in certain areas it may be necessary to make the last pinch earlier or later. In Canada the pinching date should be about seven days earlier, and in the southern areas of the United States a week later than the dates

Dates To Pinch Spray Types and Time of Flowering

Variety	Color	Size and type of flower	Pinch	Flower
Betty	Pink, Rose Center	Med. Decorative	July 10	Oct. 14
Cassandra	Orange Bronze	Med. Pompon	July 20	Nov. 5
Cordova	Cream	Med. Decorative	July 28	Nov. 30
Firebird	Red Bronze	Med. Decorative	July 15	Oct. 25
Freida	Light Lavender	Large Anemone	July 22	Nov. 15
Holiday	Crimson	Med. Single	Aug. 15	Dec. 10
Moonlight	Yellow	Med. Decorative	June 25	Oct. 1
Nuggets	Golden	Single Pompon	July 20	Nov. 5
Pink Dot	Pink	Med. Pompon	July 15	Oct. 25
Red Velvet	Crimson	Single Pompon	July 5	Oct. 10
Riviera	Luminous Pink	Med. Decorative	Aug. 10	Dec. 15
Rusticon	Rust Scarlet	Med. Pompon	July 25	Nov. 20
September Morn	White	Med. Single	June 25	Oct. 1
Shasta	White	Med. Anemone	July 22	Nov. 10
Silver Ball	White	Large Pompon	July 10	Oct. 15
Talmeda	White	Med. Pompon	Aug. 15	Jan. 5
Valencia	Orchid	Large Single	July 30	Nov. 28
White Doty	White	Large Pompon	July 20	Nov. 1
Yellow Cordova	Lemon	Med. Decorative	Aug. 5	Nov. 30
Yellow Doty	Buff	Large Pompon	July 20	Nov. 1
Yellow Nevada	Yellow	Med. Anemone	July 28	Nov. 20
Yuleflame	Yellow	Large Decorative	Aug. 15	Dec. 25

recommended. If the pinch is not made at the correct time a crown bud may form instead of a cluster of buds. You can easily recognize a crown bud. Only one flower bud, the crown bud, is formed at the top of the stem, instead of a number of flower buds. Below this solitary flower bud there will be a number of side shoots bearing leaves. The crown bud will develop into a flower, but with certain varieties it develops into a less choice flower. For most varieties, remove the crown bud if it forms and then remove all but one of the sides shoots. The remaining side shoot will probably produce a cluster of flower buds at the top. The center one of the cluster should be retained, the others removed. It sometimes happens that the side shoot produces a crown bud. If so, remove the crown bud and let one of the branches develop as before.

Culture of spray types. We are going to call the varieties which are generally grown with a number of stems, each bearing several to many flowers, *spray types*. There are a great many varieties which are excellent for growing in this way. Some bear single flowers, others anemone types, others decorative types, and different ones are true pompons. Sometimes all of these are called pompons, but strictly speaking the true pompons are characterized by small blooms, small leaves, and a dwarf habit.

After pinching the spray types, let several to many branches develop. Many commercial growers allow three or four stems to grow on each plant. If you wish many flowers, do not disbud the branches. If you want more open sprays with fewer, but larger, flowers, disbud them. As with standards, pinching of spray-type chrysanthemums on definite dates results in flowers of better quality. The date of the last pinch for many spray type chrysanthemums is given in the table on page 137.

Conditions necessary for setting of flower buds. Chrysanthemums need short days and a night temperature close to 60 degrees to form flower buds. Many varieties will not flower satisfactorily at night temperatures below 55 degrees or above 65 degrees. Under natural conditions flower buds form when the days become short in late summer. In most regions the night temperatures are favorable for flowering at this season. If they are less than 60 degrees in your region, you should use artificial heat until the flower buds are visible, after which the night temperature may be allowed to drop to 50 degrees.

Controlling flowering. When days are naturally short, flowering can be delayed by artificially lengthening the day. Install 100-watt lamps, spaced 4 feet apart and 2 feet above the plants. Turn them on at sundown and keep them on until 10 P.M. Interrupting the long nights that are associated with shorter days has the same effect as prolonging the days, a practice favored by commercial growers. They turn on the lights at 10 P.M. and off at 2 A.M., using a time switch. This lengthening of the day or interrupting the night is referred to as lighting.

The day length can be shortened at will by covering the plants with light-proof black cloth from 6 P.M. to 7 A.M. the next day. The cloth is stretched over a frame built on the bench and it covers the top, sides, and ends of the frame. As we have previously mentioned, this practice of covering is sometimes called shading.

Young chrysanthemum plants are grown with long days (or interrupted nights), which promotes the development of leaves and stems. After the plants have made sufficient vegetative growth they are grown with short days, which favor flower-bud formation. If cuttings are planted from August 15 to April 30 they must be lighted until they are large enough to be given short-day treatment. Three or four weeks after being planted the young plants are pinched. The time required from then for ample vegetative growth varies from about nine weeks in the fall and spring to about ten weeks during the winter months. After they have made sufficient growth they are provided with short days. The interval between the beginning of exposure to short days to flowering varies with the variety. Some flower in nine weeks, others in ten, eleven, or twelve weeks. Propagators and sellers of chrysanthemum cuttings classify varieties on the basis of the time required for flowering and they also publish schedules that are used for flowering plants throughout the year. The foremost propagator is Yoder Brothers, Inc., Barberton, Ohio.

The plants may be raised in benches or in pots. Both spray and standard kinds can be grown for year-round flowering. Let us see how the variety *Shasta* may be flowered at any month of the year. This schedule can be used:

Plant Cuttings	Light	Pinch	Black Cloth	Flower
Jan. 5	Jan. 5–Mar. 9	Feb. 2	None	May 18
Feb. 16	Feb. 16–Apr. 9	Mar. 12	Apr. 9	June 18
Mar. 30	Mar. 30–May 11	Apr. 20	May 11	July 19
Apr. 27	None	May 18	June 8	Aug. 17
May 25	None	June 15	July 6	Sept. 10
June 22	None	July 13	Aug. 3	Oct. 12
Oct. 12	Oct. 12–Dec. 28	Nov. 2	None	Mar. 9
Nov. 23	Nov. 23–Feb. 16	Dec. 18	None	Apr. 27

A large number of other varieties can be grown with this schedule. Of the spray types the following can be raised in like manner: Encore, Madonna, Constellation, Barcarole, Yellow Shasta, Rubicon, Chevron, Paragon, Memorial, and Taffeta. Some standards which can be grown with the same schedule are Betsy Ross, Indianapolis White, Crystal Queen, Giant Betsy Ross, Monument, Indianapolis Yellow, Yellow Queen, Indianapolis Bronze, Indianapolis Pink, and Orchid Queen.

Plants started in January, February, March, October, and November need supplemental light to promote vegetative growth and

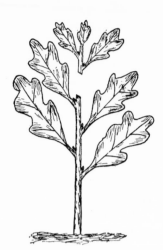
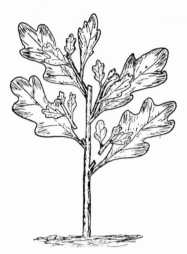

Fig. 10–4. Growing standard chrysanthemums. Upper left, pinch on recommended dates. Upper right, after branches have developed, remove all but one to three of them; here two branches have been left. Lower, disbud the stems, allowing only one flower to develop on a stem.

to retard flowering until they have reached sufficient size. From the table it will be seen that plants started January 5 will need to be lighted each day until March 9. The plants are pinched February 2. By March 9 they are large enough to produce good blooms. From then on they are not lighted; because the days are naturally short it is not necessary to cover them with black cloth. Plants started from April 27 through June 22 do not need extra light because the days are naturally long enough to promote vegetative growth and to prevent flower buds from forming. But for early flowering it is necessary to shorten the days, beginning June 8 for those started on April 27. For these plants the black cloth should be drawn over them at 6 P.M. each day and removed at 7 A.M. the next. This covering may be discontinued when the flowers of the spray types show color and when the flower buds of the standards are the size of nickels. Remember that flower buds form when the days are naturally short or when they are artificially shortened, and when the night temperature is about 60 degrees. During the black-cloth period or period of naturally short days, keep the night temperature at 60 degrees.

Getting a start the second and subsequent years. Many commercial growers prefer to purchase cuttings each year. When they buy from a reliable dealer they are assured of disease-free cuttings. Perhaps you will also want to buy new cuttings each year.

However, you can carry your plants over and make cuttings of your favorite varieties. After they have finished flowering, select healthy plants of the varieties that you like. Cut the plants back to a height of 4–6 inches, remove them from the bench, and plant them in pots or deep flats. These plants are in a semi-dormant stage and should be kept in a cool place and on the dry side. They can be kept under a bench in a cool greenhouse, or if the region is not extremely cold, in a protected hotbed or cold frame. The cold frame should be well banked with leaves and protected with mats in extreme weather. In a very cold climate the cold frame will not give sufficient protection. Most greenhouse varieties of chrysanthemums are easily winter-killed. During the dormant period, water the plants occasionally, pinch them once or twice to prevent spindly growth, and keep pests under control.

Start the old plants into active growth in April by placing the flats or pots on a greenhouse bench and giving them ample water. About a month later you can start to make cuttings. If cuttings are taken in May the plants may be too tall at flowering time. If cuttings of early varieties are made the first week of June and of later varieties about the last week in June the mature plants will be of a more desirable height. For varieties listed on pp. 136–37, a suitable date for making the cuttings would be five weeks prior to the pinching date. Allow three weeks for the cuttings to root and two weeks for the young plants to make sufficient growth prior to the pinching. The cuttings root well in sand. If the cuttings stay too long in the propagating bench, they will become stunted and will not develop into choice plants. As soon as roots have formed, pot them in 2½-inch pots. If you prefer, you can root the cuttings in 2½-inch pots filled with a medium made up of equal parts of soil, sand, and peat moss. Keep the young plants growing. Don't let them dry out or become potbound.

Another way to keep plants from one season to the next is to make cuttings immediately after the plants have flowered. Pot the rooted cuttings, keep them well watered, and light them. Pinch the plants at intervals to stimulate branching.

Pests. Spider mites, aphids, thrips, Lygus bugs, chrysanthemum gall midge, leaf miners, and leaf rollers are principal pests. Malathion gives good control of all but chrysanthemum gall midge. However, Malathion may injure certain varieties. Better try it on a few plants before spraying all of them. Some growers use a combination spray of Malathion and Captan to control both insects and disease. One combination spray is "Isotox," available at most garden stores, which contains Sevin, Meta-Sytox R (a systemic), and Kelthane. Verticillium wilt, rust, leaf spot, and mildew are diseases to guard against.

Clarkia (Onagraceae)

Clarkia elegans is excellent for cut flowers, in shades of white, rose, and salmon. However, there is a cultural peculiarity that must be observed. If it is planted in rich deep soil and watered frequently, clarkia produces an abundance of leaves, but few flowers. On the other hand, good flowering can be obtained by keeping the plants on the dry side or by raising them in flats, about 3 inches deep, filled with sandy soil. Seed should be sown in January for flowers during April and May. When benching, space the plants 8 by 10 inches.

Didiscus *(Umbelliferae)*

Didiscus coeruleus, commonly called Blue Lace Flower, produces beautiful blue flowers on good stems. Because the plants are set back by transplanting, it is best to sow seeds in pots or directly in the bench. Leave one seedling in each pot, and bench when the roots fill the pot. If you sow the seeds directly in the bench, thin the plants so that they will be 6 inches apart in rows 12 inches apart. Seed sown in June will develop into plants flowering at Christmas; those sown in August will flower in March.

Gerbera *(Compositae)*

Gerbera jamesonii, the Transvaal Daisy, a native of South Africa, bears beautiful 4-inch daisy-like blooms of yellow, orange, red, pink, or white. The flowers are becoming increasingly popular with florists. They are long lasting, remaining attractive on the plant for three to four weeks, and as old flowers fade new ones keep coming. They stay fresh a week or more when cut. The plants are perennial. The clumps are divided in June and then planted outdoors. Dig them in the fall before frost, and plant them in a greenhouse bench with a spacing of 12 by 12 inches. They grow and flower best at a night temperature of 60 degrees. Gerbera can also be grown from seed. Plants grown from seed sown in March will start to bloom in January and continue until summer.

Gypsophila *(Caryophyllaceae)*

You know *Gypsophila elegans* by the common name of Baby's Breath. The graceful lacelike sprays are useful in bouquets. In addition to white varieties, there are those which bear rose or crimson flowers. Seeds may be sown directly in the bench in rows 8 inches apart. You can have flowers in March by sowing seeds in January. If you sow seeds at monthly intervals you will have a succession of blooms.

Pansy *(Violaceae)*

Few flowers have more character and appeal than pansies (*Viola tricolor hortensis*). Their texture, brilliance, arrangement of colors, shape, and fragrance have made them one of our favorites. Some of the varieties are indeed elegant.

The seeds are best sown about the middle of July in a cold frame. If you do not have a cold frame, make a frame out of four boards 10 to 12 inches wide and place it over finely prepared soil. The soil must be finely raked, and then watered. A day or two after watering, sow the seeds in grooves $\frac{1}{16}$ inch deep. The rows should be 3 inches apart. Cover the seeds with $\frac{1}{16}$ inch of sand. Then cover the frame with boards, spaced so that there will be good ventilation. Pansy seeds require a temperature of less than 75 degrees for germination. Don't let the seed bed become dry. As soon as the seeds germinate, remove the boards and replace them with light muslin tacked to the top of the frame.

Four or five weeks after sowing, the seedlings will be ready for transplanting. They may be planted in a cold frame or in a raised bed in the garden. Space them 4 by 4 inches. In October they may be benched in the greenhouse, spacing them about 10 inches apart. If you raised the seedlings in a cold frame and have more than you need for the greenhouse, you can winter the surplus in the cold frame. Before severe weather sets in, mulch the plants with straw or salt hay. Of course, you can move plants from this frame into the greenhouse at any time.

Pansies thrive when it is cool. Do not let them become dry at any time. If you grow the plants with long days, furnished by turning on 60-watt lamps at sunset and off at 10 P.M., they will flower more profusely and the stems will be longer. Continued removal of old flowers is essential for good flowering.

Snapdragons (Scrophulariaceae)

Snapdragons, *Antirrhinum majus*, are among the finest flowering plants for the 50-degree greenhouse. There are a great many varieties which have been developed for growing in the greenhouse; these must be selected instead of garden ones. Some varieties flower in less time than others. You can select varieties of the following colors: white, light pink, rose pink, red, ivory, bronze, and lavender. Obtain a catalog from a seed company that caters to florists and make selections from it. The seed is quite expensive and, unless you have a large greenhouse, you may prefer to buy a package of a greenhouse mixture of varieties.

Seeds should be sown thinly, in light soil, during June or July for a winter crop. Scatter the seeds over firmed soil and cover the seed pot or pan with a pane of glass. Remove the glass as soon as the seeds begin to germinate. When the seedlings are large enough to handle, move them into 2½-inch pots. Keep the young plants in a warm spot, preferably where the night temperature is 60 degrees until they are 4–6 inches tall. They may then be grown with a night temperature of 50 degrees. The plants may be benched during August with a spacing of 8 by 8 inches.

In August or September the plants may be pinched, leaving three sets of leaves. Generally a branch will develop above each leaf giving a plant with six branches.

Plants pinched in August will generally flower by Christmas. The plants will produce additional flowers later in the season, but the second and third crops may have shorter stems than the first spikes. For better-quality flowers in May and June you may wish to sow seeds in January. When the plants are large enough, pinch them to three sets of leaves.

Snapdragons require supports of wires and strings, as recommended for carnations. The removal of the side shoots on the flowering branches usually does not result in better flowers although it does make a more attractive spike. However, do not remove all the side shoots, otherwise the plants will be useless after they have produced their first flowers. During late fall and winter, snapdragons do not respond to applications of fertilizer. During the spring, biweekly applications of a fertilizer solution are beneficial.

Raising snapdragons with a single stem. Most amateurs and many professional growers prefer to raise snapdragons in the manner suggested, that is, with several flowering branches to a plant. However, a recent trend among some commercial growers has been to raise them to a single stem. With this method the plants are not pinched. They are spaced 4 by 4 inches or 5 by 5 inches in the bench. After the flowers are cut, the plants may be disposed of or the plants may be thinned. If the latter method is followed, remove every other row and alternate plants in the remaining rows. The plants remaining will then be spaced 8 by 8 inches or 10 by 10 inches and will produce flowers at a later date.

Skillful growers obtain year-round flowering by sowing seeds at intervals. When the seedlings are large enough to handle, generally two to four weeks after sowing, they plant them directly in the bench. A brief schedule of when to sow, when to bench, and when the plants flower appears on page 146.

Sow	Plant in bench	Flowers ready for cutting
Jan. 7	Feb. 7	May 15–July 5
Mar. 3	Mar. 27	June 5–June 19
Apr. 14	May 5	June 23–July 7
May 12	June 2	July 14–July 28
June 9	June 26	Aug. 7–Aug. 11
July 7	July 21	Sept. 1–Sept. 15
July 21	Aug. 4	Oct. 27–Nov. 17
Aug. 18	Sept. 4	Dec. 11–Jan. 1
Sept. 1	Sept. 22	Jan. 1–Feb. 9
Sept. 29	Oct. 23	Mar. 12–Apr. 2
Nov. 10	Dec. 8	Apr. 4–May 4

This schedule is only approximate. It fluctuates with varieties, temperature, light, and latitude. Vaughan's seed catalog gives more precise schedules for a great many varieties.

Pests. Aphids, cyclamen mites, leaf rollers, red spiders, and sow bugs are pests that attack snapdragons. Rust is the most serious disease of snapdragons.

Stocks (Cruciferae)

Stock, *Mathiola incana* of the mustard family, produces sturdy flower spikes 2 or 3 feet tall, bearing beautiful, fragrant flowers. Some plants bear single flowers, others double ones, which are more attractive. You cannot buy seeds all of which will develop into plants bearing double flowers. However, if you keep only the strong seedlings and discard the weak ones, nearly all of the plants will bear double flowers. When the seedlings have four leaves you can rather easily tell the difference between them; those that will bear single flowers are noticeably weaker than those that will produce double ones.

There are varieties which produce only one stem and those which develop many branches. The former are called *nonbranching* or *column* stock. Both kinds come in a variety of colors—white, rose, lilac, and yellow.

Seeds of both types are generally sown in August for flowering in January. The branching types will continue to flower. For this reason they are often preferred by amateurs, even though the flower spikes are not so large as those of the column types.

Fig. 10–5. Swiss giant pansies will reward you with elegant flowers on long stems. (Bodger Seeds Ltd.)

Plants started in August may be brought into flower in December by growing the plants with additional light or by keeping the young plants at a temperature of 40 degrees for two weeks before benching them. Lighting should begin about two weeks after the plants are benched. Early flowering can also be obtained by putting the young (2–3 weeks old) plants in a cold frame for about two weeks before they are benched. The ideal temperature for the cold frame is 40 degrees.

The leaves on cut flower stems may wilt severely. To prevent wilting, immerse the stems deeply in water for 24 to 36 hours.

After the flowers are cut from the nonbranching types the plants are discarded. For a sequence of flowers, successive sowings may be made every other month, beginning in August and continuing until February. Plants grown from seed sown in November will flower at Easter; those from seed sown in February, in late May.

Sow the seed thinly and cover lightly with sand or soil. When the seedlings are large enough, move them into flats, from which they may be planted in the bench sometime in October from an August sowing. The nonbranching stocks are planted close together, about 3 inches apart in rows 6 inches apart. A spacing of 6 by 8 inches is about right for the branching varieties. Remove the top of the stem of the branching types when the stem is 6 inches tall. This pinching will stimulate branching. To keep the stems straight, some means of support should be provided. The wire and string method is suitable.

A night temperature of 48 to 50 degrees in the greenhouse results in good growth and flowering. Stocks will produce an abundance of foliage when the night temperature is 60 degrees, but they will not flower at this temperature.

Aphids, thrips, and mites are pests that attack stocks. The wilt disease is characterized by a yellowing of the foliage, sudden wilting, and then death. Removal of diseased plants and the use of sterilized soil will help control this disease.

Salpiglossis (Solanaceae)

The showy, velvety flowers of this easily grown plant (*Salpiglossis sinuata*) are fine for cutting. The deep colors of the petals—red, purple, blue, yellow, or brown—are attractively set off by the gold veins. Seeds are started in January for flowering in May. The plants are set 10 inches apart in the bench.

Sweet Pea (Leguminosae)

Perhaps you can find a place in your greenhouse for a few sweet peas (*Lathyrus odoratus*). Make sure that you select varieties which have been specially developed for greenhouse culture. These winter-flowering varieties flower much earlier than the garden varieties and they have a different habit of growth. The garden varieties form side shoots when they are young and during this period the plants appear to be checked in their growth. The winter-flowering varieties grow rapidly to a height of 2 feet or more and then flower, after which side shoots, bearing additional flowers, form. You may wish to grow some in boxes at the end of the greenhouse or perhaps a few around the posts that support the greenhouse.

Of course, you can raise them in a bench or in a ground bed. For flowers from December to March, sow seeds during September, either directly where the plants are to mature or in 3-inch pots or plant bands. From seeds sown in October you will get flowers from February through May.

Sweet peas may be planted in double rows. Plant seeds or plants in a row, then 7 inches from this row plant another one. Leave about 2 feet and plant another double row. After the plants are established, thin them so that the remaining plants are 3 inches apart in the row. Strive to furnish them with good light and ventilation, a night temperature of 50 degrees, and moist soil. On cloudy days the day temperature should be kept at 55 degrees and on bright days at 60. When the plants are a foot tall, if the days are bright, they should be fertilized monthly with a complete fertilizer. Avoid feeding them during the dull weeks of winter. Do not allow the vines to be crowded by other plants, as this cuts out the light they need. Crowding is particularly bad in dull weather.

When the plants are a few inches high they will require support. Vertical strings tied between an overhead wire and one just above soil level are ideal for the plants to climb on. You will have to train the tendrils to the strings by hand at first.

The dropping-off of flower buds may be troublesome during the winter months. A lack or excess of water, improper temperature, and too much fertilizer during the cloudy winter months may be responsible. Various root rots can be troublesome. To control them, use clean or sterilized soil. Remove infected plants and water with a fungicide. Among the pests of sweet peas are snails, red spiders, thrips, aphids, and cutworms.

Violet (Violaceae)

The delightfully fragrant violet flowers make this plant (*Viola odorata*) a desirable one for the greenhouse. Both single and double varieties are available. To get a start, purchase plants in September and plant them in a bench about 10 inches apart. Provide shade for the newly set plants and syringe them each day until they become established. After the middle of October, syringing should cease and the shade may be removed gradually. The runners which develop should be removed as they form. The runners will not produce flowers the first season. The runners can be rooted in sand and potted, if you desire to increase the stock. Throughout the growing season, water judiciously, provide the plants with good ventilation, a night temperature of 45 to 50 degrees, and a day temperature 10 degrees higher.

When the plants are through flowering, remove them from the bench and divide them. If you wish, you can move the plants into a shaded part of the garden for carrying through the summer. In September put them back in the greenhouse.

Aphids and red spiders attack violets, as do such diseases as leafspot and rootrot. Keep the plants healthy, use disease-free soil, and remove dead, dying and spotted leaves to minimize disease.

Additional Plants

In this chapter we have singled out a number of plants which you can grow in benches in a 50-degree greenhouse. Other which you might like to try, the time to sow seed, and the spacing are:

Plant	Sow	Space	Flower
Candytuft (Iberis amara)	January	6 x 6 inches	May
Centaurea	January	8 x 8 inches	May
Cynoglossum amabile	September	12 x 12 inches	March–April
Erysimum perofskianum	January	6 x 6 inches	May–June
Feverfew (Chrysanthemum parthenium)	October	12 x 12 inches	May
Forget-me-not (Myosotis sylvatica)	March	10 x 10 inches	December on
Larkspur (Delphinium ajacis)	September	8 x 8 inches	April–May
Lupine (Lupinus luteus)	September	8 x 8 inches	January
Marigold (Tagetes erecta)	February	4 x 4 inches	May
Mignonette (Reseda odorata)	July	8 x 8 inches	December
Nemesia strumosa	August	8 x 8 inches	October–February
Statice (Limonium suworowii)	October	8 x 8 inches	February–May

11

Pot Plants for the Cool Greenhouse

Many pot plants of great beauty can be raised in a greenhouse maintained at 50 degrees during the night, among them calceolaria, camellia, chrysanthemum, cineraria, cyclamen, fuchsia, geranium, primrose, rose, and schizanthus. You may wish to grow a variety of these, or you might enjoy specializing in one kind. Building up a collection of geraniums would be fascinating, as would the culture of camellias, fuchsias, and primroses.

Unless otherwise indicated in the subsequent discussion, the plants will thrive in a soil consisting of two parts loam, one part peat moss, and sufficient coarse sand, vermiculite, or perlite to make it porous. Fertilizer should be added when the ingredients are mixed.

Abutilon (Malvaceae)

Abutilon hybridum, the flowering maple, is a shrubby evergreen that grows to a height of about three feet. The hairy maple-shaped leaves add interest to the greenhouse throughout the year. Pendant, bell-like flowers of red, yellow, or white (depending on the variety) give a magnificent display over a long period throughout the summer and into winter. They are grown with light shade during the brightest months and with full sun during the winter. They are

151

easily propagated from stem cuttings. Branching should be induced by pinching in early spring.

Blue Marguerite (Compositae)

Felicia amelloides, a native of South Africa commonly called Blue Marguerite, is a free-flowering perennial plant that bears exquisite sky-blue, daisylike flowers that are fine for cutting. Plants are started from seed sown in January or from cuttings made in the spring. The plants flower the following winter. They should be pinched two or three times to produce a bushy habit. They require light shade only during the brighter months of the year.

Bouvardia (Rubiaceae)

Bouvardia longiflora humboldtii from Mexico is a beautiful flowering shrub that flowers from fall to winter. The shrub bears small, oval, evergreen leaves and large terminal trusses of delightfully fragrant white flowers. Another interesting species is *Bouvardia ternifolia* from Texas and Mexico, which bears terminal clusters of tubular, fiery-red flowers throughout the year. Bouvardias are readily increased by stem cuttings taken in the spring. They can also be propagated from root cuttings. Cut a thick root into 1-inch segments, lay them on sand, and barely cover. Young plants will develop which can be moved into pots. Bouvardias are grown without shade during the cloudy winter months and with light shade the rest of the year.

Calceolaria (Scrophulariaceae)

The favorite species is *Calceolaria herbeohybrida,* the Pocketbook Plant, so called because the lip resembles a handbag. The hybrids have been derived principally from *C. crenatifolia,* a species native to the cool Andes of South America. There are several fine strains, Grandiflora, Multiflora Nana, and others. The plants bear showy flowers, often attractively spotted or blotched, in shades of yellow, orange, red, and rose. The color schemes are gay and of great contrast.

Calceolarias are started from seed sown in July or August. The

Fig. 11–1. Calceolaria bears showy purse-shaped flowers.

minute seeds are scattered over a slightly firmed soil surface and should not be covered. When the seedlings are large enough to handle, put them into 2¼-inch pots, preferably Jiffy-Pots. Later, shift them into 5- or 6-inch pots, in which containers they will flower. To prevent the leaves from rotting, keep the plants well spaced so that the leaves of one plant do not overlap those of another. During the bright months, shade them, and maintain the night temperature as near 50 degrees as possible. At all times keep them actively growing. When the roots fill the pots, either large or small, water with dilute commercial fertilizer at weekly intervals.

Calceolarias generally flower in April or May. However, they may be induced to flower earlier by giving the plants lengthened days. If they are lighted from the middle of November they will flower in February. Plants lighted from December 20 will flower in March.

There is a shrubby species of calceolaria, *C. integrifolia*, which is not so frequently grown in greenhouses. The seeds of this species are generally sown in March and raised in the same general way as *C. herbeohybrida. C. integrifolia* can also be propagated from cuttings taken in August.

Thrips, aphids, greenfly, whitefly, and red spiders may attack calceolaria as well as such diseases as leafblight and graymold. The latter may be controlled by removing infected leaves and giving the plants adequate spacing.

Camellias (Theaceae)

These beautiful shrubs, members of the tea family (Theaceae), are natives of China and Japan, and deserve a place in the cool greenhouse. They have handsome, evergreen, glossy leaves and beautiful flowers of white, pink, or red color, and of formal double, semidouble, or peony form. By selecting different varieties, you can have camellias in flower from September to March. For the little care that they require you will be rewarded with flowers of exquisite form, generous size, and pleasing color. The flowers make choice corsages and are attractive when floated on water, lasting about a week.

Three species of camellia, *Camellia japonica, C. sasanqua,* and *C. reticulata,* are available for growing in the greenhouse. The most popular varieties belong to the species *C. japonica;* the flowers are white, pink, red, and variegated. *Camellia sasanqua* has a more straggly growth habit and flowers earlier than *C. japonica.* Certain varieties have pink flowers, others white ones. *Camellia reticulata* has a less compact growth form than *C. japonica.* Certain varieties of *C. reticulata* have wavy, rose-pink flowers, 5 to 7 inches in diameter. There are, of course, numerous named varieties of camellias, and many new ones are introduced each year.

Camellias should be shaded from bright sun during all months of the year. Under glass the buds, blooms, and occasionally the leaves will burn in bright sunshine. From autumn until after flowering a night temperature between 40 and 45 degrees is ideal, with a day temperature of around 50 degrees. Camellias should be syringed when actively growing and when the flower buds are developing. Syringing the flower buds favors their development and syringing flowers during the night gives them better substance.

When the plants have finished flowering, a night temperature of 55 degrees is desirable because at this temperature vegetative growth is stimulated. Potting should be attended to after the plants have finished blooming and before new growth begins, generally in March or April. Small plants require potting each spring. Larger ones do not require annual potting, but only a top dressing of new soil. Large plants may need repotting every third year. Potting time is also the time to prune camellias, although they require very little pruning. You may wish to shorten very long branches and remove unwanted and weak ones. When the plants are developing new leaves they require a good supply of water and benefit from frequent syringing, which also increases the humidity. During the entire year a high humidity is beneficial. If not recently repotted, the plants should be fertilized periodically with cottonseed meal or a 15–30–15 fertilizer, using 1 ounce to 2 gallons of water. Specially prepared camellia fertilizers are available. Plants should be fertilized just before they begin their new growth and then at biweekly intervals until flowering time. If the new foliage is yellow, water the plants with a solution of 1 ounce of iron sulfate in 2 gallons of water or with an iron chelate solution.

From June to September the plants grow better if they are kept outdoors than if left in the greenhouse, although they may be maintained in the greenhouse all year. If they are kept in the greenhouse during summer, provide shade and good ventilation. Outdoors, they may be placed in a lath house, in a cloth house, or under large trees. The pots should be plunged in the soil. At no time during the summer should the soil become completely dry, because drought causes flower buds to fall off. However, bud drop may also be caused by low humidity, by high temperatures during winter, and by wide fluctuations of temperature. The roots should be kept moist, but avoid excess water as well as drought.

If two flower buds develop on a branch and if you want especially choice flowers, remove the weaker of the two buds when it is about the size of a pea. Then if you want larger and earlier flowers add one drop of a solution of gibberellic acid in the cup formed as the bud is removed. The gibberellic acid solution is prepared by adding 1/3 gram of 85 per cent gibberellic acid to one ounce of distilled water and then adding 12 drops of non-sudsy household ammonia.

Camellias may be started from seeds, by air layerage, from cuttings, and by grafting. Usually they are started from cuttings taken from the mature wood of the current season's growth. Cuttings are taken any time between August 15 and February 15. From one branch a number of cuttings can be made. The cuttings may be 3 to 6 inches long and have three or four nodes, or they may be shorter with just one node. If you prefer the latter, cut a branch into segments so that each piece has one leaf with a live bud at the top and 1½ inches of stem below the leaf. Treat the basal portions of the cuttings with Rootone or Hormodin and then insert the cuttings, about an inch and a half apart, in sand with all the leaves facing in the same direction. Bottom heat of 70 degrees hastens rooting, which normally takes two or three months. After the cuttings have rooted move them into 2½-inch pots. When the roots fill the pots, transfer the plants to 4-inch size pots. Shift into larger pots when necessary. When plants are large enough to move into 8-inch containers or larger, wooden tubs are better than clay pots.

It requires four to seven years for camellias to flower if grown from seed. Young plants produce only a few flowers; those large enough to be in 14-inch tubs will produce about 150 flowers per plant. Flowers from seedlings may or may not be of excellent quality. Certain seedlings may produce inferior blooms. However, there is always the possibility that one or more seedlings will be outstanding. The chances of getting excellent plants from seed are increased if especially choice parents are used for seed production.

Some growers hasten seed germination by carefully nicking the seed coat. Seeds are sown about ½ inch deep in the soil previously mentioned. When the seedlings are 6 inches high they are moved into pots.

Red spiders, mealy bugs, aphids, and scale insects are pests to watch for. Flower blight is the most prevalent of the fungal diseases and is evidenced by a discoloration of the flowers. It may be controlled by gathering and destroying all diseased flowers. It also pays to remove the upper three inches of soil and replace it with fresh soil.

Carnivorous Plants

Plants that capture and digest insects hold a special fascination. Carnivorous plants live in bogs or other wet places where the super-abundance of water causes lack of certain minerals necessary for plant growth. They have evolved remarkable ways of obtaining these minerals by snaring insects (sometimes also small worms or other animal life) and secreting enzymes to digest them. In cultivation these plants do not need the insects, since we can make up for the lack by giving an occasional very dilute solution of fertilizer. (They, therefore, do not need to be fed hamburger!) If insects do

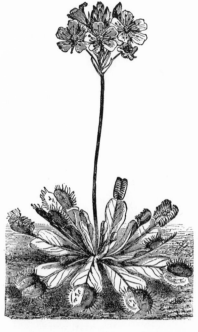

Fig. 11–2. Carnivorous plants. Below, a sundew, *Drosera binata*, from Australia and New Zealand, which has cylindrical branching leaves. Right, Venus flytap, from North Carolina.

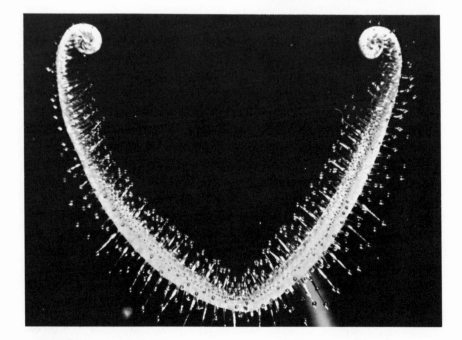

happen into their traps, however, they will act upon them as they do in nature.

Carnivorous plants native to temperate climates can be grown in the cool greenhouse. Those native to the tropics, such as *Nepenthes* which is epiphytic, need more warmth and will be discussed later.

The sundews (Droseraceae) have leaves that are covered with sensitive hairs that secrete glistening drops of mucilaginous fluid. Insects that are enticed by the shining droplets are instantly entangled when they light upon them, and as they struggle to free themselves adjacent hairs bend over to aid in holding them. Cells on the leaves secrete digestive enzymes and the plants absorb the substances released by their action. *Drosera rotundifolia* carpets the ground in damp North Carolina woods. It has a rosette of spoon-shaped leaves, of which the "bowl" is covered with red secreting hairs. *D. filiformis*, which grows in wet sandy places along the coast from Delaware to Massachusetts, has thread-like leaves equipped with red glandular hairs. A number of attractive droseras from Australia are sometimes grown in this country. *D. peltata* and *D. auriculata* have pin-cushion-like leaves all along a 6-inch, slender, upright stem. The glandular hairs are all green or tipped with red. *D. spathulata* has a ground-hugging rosette of spatula-shaped leaves fringed with red hairs, and *D. binata* looks like some creature from the sea with its branched, tentacle-like leaves covered with gold hairs. All have attractive flowers that look like pink or yellow buttercups. The plants can be grown in two parts silica sand, one part finely screened peat, one part fine perlite, and a very small amount, perhaps 0.5 part, of garden loam. Water them with rain water or distilled water. Twice during the growing season give them a very dilute fertilizer solution—half the concentration you would give other plants. After the leaves die down in the fall, put them in a shaded place in the coolest part of the greenhouse, keeping the pots damp all winter, or else put pot and all in a polyethylene bag in the refrigerator at 45 degrees. Do not let them freeze. When spring comes, put them back in the greenhouse.

Venus flytrap, *Dionaea muscipula*, is another member of the family Droseraceae. Its leaves are two-lobed, hinged together like a clam shell, and fringed around the edges with bristles. There are sensitive hairs on the inside leaf surfaces, and when an insect touches at least two of these, the leaves snap together, imprisoning the visitor. The insect is then digested, and when the "meal" is finished the trap spreads wide again, revealing only the indigestible parts. Venus flytrap thrives when potted in pure fresh-dried sphagnum, kept constantly wet in a pot with free drainage. Best to use rain or distilled water on it, too.

Pitcher plants have leaves transformed into upright traps that act as pitfalls. Insects are lured by nectar secreted by glands situated toward the upper part and particularly concentrated just within the rim. As an insect seeks the nectar it travels over the rim and plunges to the bottom into a pool of fluid. Escape is prevented by downward-pointing hairs or bristles, or by a slippery surface on which it cannot gain a foothold, and it soon drowns. It is then digested by enzymes secreted by the plant. The family Sarraceniaceae has three genera, of which *Darlingtonia* and *Sarracenia* grow in North America. *Darlingtonia californica,* the cobra plant, has green pitchers with red and yellow blotches. The tops are rounded and hooded like the head of a cobra, with down-hanging flaps that look like a mustache. The nodding, purplish flowers appear in May. *Sarracenia* has many species, trumpet or urn shaped and luridly colored, which inhabit bogs east of the Mississippi River, some extending north to Labrador. *S. purpurea, S. rubra, S. drummondii,* and *S. sledgei* and their hybrids are kinds frequently grown. Their flowers are beautiful and intricate. All can be grown in a mixture of two parts silica sand, one part peat moss, and one part loam, preferably watered with rain water, and not allowed to become dry. When flowering is over the pitchers die down and the plants become dormant, during which time they should be kept cool and damp as for the droseras. In the spring active growth begins and new pitchers form.

Chrysanthemum (Compositae)

Many varieties of chrysanthemum make excellent pot plants, and all kinds can be raised in pots if you so desire. In catalogs of chrysanthemums, such as that issued by the Vaughan Seed Company, certain ones are designated as pot plants. There are many named varieties in this category, and they come in the following colors: white, yellow, bronze, orange, red, pink, and lavender. Moreover, there are varieties with large flowers, others with medium blooms, and different ones with small flowers. Varieties with the following flower shapes are available: single, anemone, decorative, pompon, incurved, and semi-incurved. Contrast in size and shape adds variety to a collection.

By proper selection, chrysanthemums can be had in flower from September to January. Some varieties flower in September, others in October, November, or December. Catalogs indicate flowering periods.

Except during the period when flower buds are forming, chrysanthemums thrive in a 50-degree house. A night temperature of not less than 55 degrees, preferably 60 degrees, is necessary for the initiation of flower buds. In many regions the night temperature will be naturally about 55 degrees during late August and early September, when the early and midseason varieties form flower buds. For late-season varieties you may have to turn on the heat to raise the night temperature to 60 degrees during the natural bud-forming period. After the flower buds are well developed, the temperature may be lowered to 50 degrees.

In many localities no shade is necessary during the summer months. In hot regions with bright sun, a light shade will be necessary. A soil mixture consisting of two parts loam and one of peat moss suits chrysanthemums. If the soil is heavy, add some sand, vermiculite, or Perlite to the mixture.

Chrysanthemums are started from cuttings, generally made in April, May, or June, and rooted in sand. Three uniform rooted cuttings may be potted in a 6-inch azalea pot. If you prefer, you can pot the cuttings singly in 2½-inch pots, later shifting them singly into 4-inch pots and then into 6-inch ones. Water thoroughly after potting and syringe the plants several times each day to reduce wilting. When the plants are well established and about 6 inches tall, pinch them to promote branching. Use a soft pinch, removing only the very soft tip of the stem. At least six leaves should be left on the plant after the first pinch. When the branches are about 4 inches long, pinch them to induce additional shoots to form. If you wish a very bushy plant, these in turn may be pinched after they have grown to a length of 3 or 4 inches. Plants should not be pinched too late in the season. Varieties which flower in early October should not be pinched later than August 15; those which flower late in October, not later than August 20. Varieties which flower during the first half of November should not be pinched after August 25; those flowering the last two weeks in November, not later than September 3; and those which flower in December, not later than

September 13. The last pinching dates vary somewhat with the variety. The exact dates for the last pinching may be obtained from catalogs, such as the chrysanthemum catalog put out by Vaughan.

During the growing period, the plants benefit from being syringed several times each bright day. Never let the plants become starved. Move them into larger pots or feed them. Well-established plants can be fed every two or three weeks with a dry fertilizer or a liquid one. A half-teaspoon of 4–12–4 fertilizer for a 6-inch pot is the correct amount. Add the dry fertilizer to the pots when the soil is moist and then water the plants.

The plants may be allowed to flower naturally, or you may disbud, or remove the center flower bud from each spray. If you desire a plant bearing a few large flowers, disbud each shoot by removing all flower buds except the terminal one from each branch. A plant with many small flowers can be developed by removing the center flower bud and permitting the side buds to develop.

You will have to be alert for the presence of these insects: aphids, red spiders, thrips, leaf rollers, midges, cutworms, mealybugs, and leaf miners. Verticillium wilt, mildew, leaf or black spot, and yellows are diseases of chrysanthemums.

After flowering is through, retain sufficient healthy plants of the varieties you like to furnish a supply of cuttings next year. These stock plants should be cut back and then moved into flats or a bench, or be repotted. Place them in a cool part of the greenhouse, water as necessary, and keep free from insects and disease.

Cineraria (Compositae)

There are a number of good strains of cineraria, among them Cremers Prize, Multiflora Nana, Potsdam, Siter's Rainbow, and Grandiflora. The Multiflora Nana strain is preferred by florists. It has a very compact growth habit and flowers profusely. The flowers are blue, red, or pink in color. In some catalogs cineraria is listed as *Cineraria cruenta*, but its correct botanical name is *Senecio cruentus*, a native of the Canary Islands.

Cinerarias grow rapidly and thrive in a 50-degree house. They may be had in flower from January through April, by successive sowings in June, July, and September. The seeds are small and should be sown on fine soil. After sowing just barely cover the seed with sand or soil. When the seedlings are large enough to handle,

Fig. 11–3. Stages in the culture of cinerarias. The seedlings in the flat are ready to be moved into 3-inch pots. When good root growth is evident, center, the plant is shifted into a 5-inch pot, in which it flowers. Lower, a flowering cineraria. (Bodger Seeds Ltd.)

transfer them to 2¼-inch Jiffy-Pots, then later move into 5-inch pots. A mixture of two parts loam to one of peat moss with the addition of fertilizer is suitable. Cinerarias require frequent waterings. They should be fertilized every two or three weeks after they are established and until the flower buds just begin to show color, after which feeding should cease. Keep the plants well spaced. Be on the alert for attacks by aphids, red spiders, leaf rollers, white flies, and thrips. Malathion may injure or spot cineraria leaves. Nicotine sulfate or rotenone may be used. When the plants are through flowering discard them.

Cyclamen (Primulaceae)

Of the 20 species of cyclamen, only one, *Cyclamen persicum*, a native of Asia Minor, is generally grown in greenhouses. This species is noted for its distinctively shaped, nodding, attractively colored flowers and for its handsome marbled foliage. Few plants can surpass the cyclamen for display during the winter and spring months. There are many varieties from which you can select; some bear salmon flowers, others pink, red, white, or orange-vermillion.

The favored way to grow plants is from seed, best sown in August or September, although they may be sown as late as December. Sow the seeds individually ¼ inch deep and 1 inch apart in a mixture of equal parts soil, sand, and peat or leaf mold. After sowing, water thoroughly and cover the pot or flat with a pane of glass and a sheet of paper. At a temperature of 55 to 60 degrees, they will germinate in four to eight weeks. After the seeds have germinated, continue to provide the seedlings with light shade. Allow the seedlings to develop two or three leaves and then transplant them to a flat containing a mixture of one part soil, one part peat moss and enough sand, vermiculite, or perlite to make the soil porous. Space the plants 2 or 3 inches apart and insert the seedlings so that the corm is at soil level. If you prefer, you can move the plants from the seed flat to 2½-inch pots. In the spring the plants may be moved from the flats or 2½-inch pots into their flowering container, generally a 5- or 6-inch pot, or they can be potted in a 4-inch one. If the latter practice is followed, shift them into 5- or 6-inch pots in July or August. When potting, provide plenty of crock and keep the corm half in the soil and half out. After the plants are established in the pots apply liquid fertilizer every two or three weeks.

Throughout the growing period the plants should be well watered. Don't let them wilt before watering.

During summer the plants should be kept as cool as possible by placing them under trees outdoors or in a well-ventilated and shaded cold frame. The shade, either lath or a double thickness of cheese-cloth, should be supported well above the frame so that there is free circulation of air. Although it is preferable to keep the plants out-doors during the summer, you can maintain them in the greenhouse if you provide heavy shade and adequate spacing. Either outdoors or in the greenhouse they benefit from frequent syringings during summer.

In early September, bring the plants into the greenhouse. If they have been kept in the greenhouse during the summer, gradually reduce the shade, beginning in September. From September on, keep the night temperature at 50 degrees and allow the day tem-perature to go 10 degrees higher. Staging the plants on inverted pots from September on promotes good aeration and seems to en-courage the setting of flower buds. Flower buds which appear prior to October should be removed in order to encourage vigorous growth of the foliage. The time from seed sowing to profuse flower-ing is between fifteen and eighteen months.

It is possible to carry plants over for flowering the next and sub-sequent years, although commercial growers prefer not to do so. To carry the plants over, keep the plants on the dry side when flowering is through by watering them only at biweekly intervals. The drought will induce rest which should be maintained until August. Then remove the dead leaves, knock the plant out of the pot, reduce the ball of soil, and repot in a pot just slightly larger than the ball. Syringe the corms daily. In a few weeks growth will be active.

Cyclamen may also be increased by dividing the corm. After the plant has flowered remove the corm and cut it into sections, each with at least one leaf. Place the pieces in sand, where they will root. Then pot each piece. Plants started in this way will flower the following winter.

Leafspot and crown rot are two diseases of cyclamen. Leafspot is characterized by brown or black areas developing at the margins of the leaves and is controlled by pulling off infected foliage. If you see a white fungus growth at the base of the leaves, the plant has crown rot. This disease can be avoided by not burying the

Fig. 11–4. Left, cyclamen seedlings removed from the seed flat are ready to be moved into a flat. Right, seedlings just moved into a flat. The corm should be at soil level, not buried. These seedlings will flower in about twelve months.

corm when potting and by not letting water stand in the crowns during the night.

Nematodes, red spiders, aphids, thrips, and mites are pests that attack cyclamen. Nematodes cause knots to form on the roots and you can avoid them by using sterilized soil and containers. Mites, particularly the notorious cyclamen mite, *Tarsonemus pallidus*, so tiny it can be seen only with a powerful hand lens, deform leaves and flowers and must be kept under control with a miticide such as Kelthane. Thrips give the undersides of the foliage a scaly appearance and cause streaking of the flowers. Colored flowers have white streaks; white flowers, brown ones.

Fuchsia (Onagraceae)

Fuchsia (*Fuchsia hybrida* of the evening primrose family) is among the most ornamental of flowering plants. *Fuchsia hybrida* has been derived from several species that are native to Mexico, and Central and South America where they grow in the cool, moist climate of high elevations. Fuchsias begin flowering in the spring and continue through the summer. The flowers are pendulous, of a charming bell-like form, and attractively colored.

There are nearly 2,000 varieties; some bear single flowers, others double ones. Many varieties grow erect; but certain ones are trailing, and these can be grown in hanging baskets or other containers. A few varieties of trailing form and their descriptions are: Anna, magenta and red, double; Cascade, carmine and white, single; Falling Stars, red and scarlet, single; Marinka, all red, single; Muriel, lilac and scarlet, semi-double; San Mateo, violet and pink, double; Swingtime, red and white, double. Among the favorite erect varieties are California, orange and pink, single, tall; Cardinal, scarlet and red, single, tall; Don Peralta, burgundy, double, tall; Guinevere, lavender and rose, semi-double, medium height; Mazda, orange and pale orange, single, tall; Minuet, purple and red, single, medium height; Mrs. Desmond, rose-mauve and red, double, medium height; Patty Evans, pink and rose, double, tall; Treasure, violet-pink and rose, double, medium height; Violet Gem, violet and carmine, semi-double, medium height; Whitemost, white and pink, single, medium height. These, as well as other erect varieties, may be grown as bushy plants or treelike specimens, so-called standards.

You will have no difficulty in raising these splendid plants. They grow well in a 50-degree house. While actively growing they require plenty of moisture, a high humidity, and benefit from biweekly feedings with liquid fertilizer. From March 1 until fall they require light shade. You can keep them in a shaded, well-ventilated greenhouse during the summer; or plunge them outdoors under the shade of trees, or under lath roofing made by spacing laths ½ to ¾ inches apart. Fuchsias have a rest period after flowering, in November and December. During these months keep the plants on the dry side; give them just enough water to keep the wood plump. In January, bring the plants into active growth by watering more frequently and syringing.

Bushy specimens are obtained by pruning. Just as the buds become active, cut out the dead and weak wood, and cut the vigorous branches back. Trailing varieties are also pruned in the spring. The heads of standard fuchsias are shaped in the spring by cutting the main lateral branches, leaving each about 10 inches long.

In the spring, knock a plant from its pot and remove as much soil as possible from the ball without tearing it apart. Repot in fresh soil. A suitable mixture consists of one part loam, one part leaf mold or peat moss, one part manure, and a little sand. Provide good drainage. Don't overwater after potting. Syringe frequently, preferably with water at the same temperature as that of the greenhouse. When the plants are in active growth water frequently; avoid letting the ball get dry. Feed the plants at intervals.

Fuchsias are readily propagated from cuttings made in February or March, or in September. The cuttings are rooted in sand or in a mixture of half sand and half vermiculite. When rooted, pot singly,

Fig. 11–5. Fuchsia bears beautiful flowers from spring through summer.
(Bodger Seeds Ltd.)

generally in 2½-inch pots. Give further shifts as necessary. If you want bushy specimens, pinch the plants. Plants grown from cuttings started in the spring should be given a rest period during November and December; those started in September may be kept growing during the winter months.

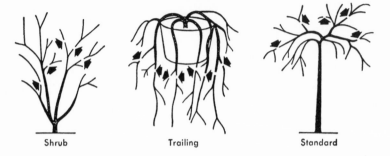

Shrub   Trailing   Standard

Fig. 11–6. Pruning fuchsias. (H. M. Butterfield and the California Agricultural Experiment Station)

The making of a standard, a tree-like fuchsia, starts with the cutting. Select a straight, stout, rooted cutting. Pot it, keep it growing, and stake it. If any side shoots appear, remove them. When the stem is of the desired height, pinch off the tip of the stem. Side growths will then develop near the top. After they have made sufficient growth, they should be pinched, the object being the production of a well-balanced head, on a stem about 4 feet tall.

Growing fuchsias from seed can be an exciting adventure. You can purchase superb mixtures resulting from crosses of a number of varieties. Such seed will probably produce new hybrid varieties as well as plants resembling the parents. Seeds may be sown in January; they germinate best at a temperature of 60 degrees. Seeds are sown in pots containing a mixture of equal parts of loam, peat moss, and fine leaf mold. Keep the seeds moist all the time; to let them dry out is fatal. Seed germination is sporadic; some seeds may germinate in ten days, others not for three or four months. When the seedlings have developed their second set of leaves they are potted in 2½-inch pots, best plunged in a flat of moist peat moss. The seedlings should be given shade. In about a month they can be moved into 4-inch pots and later, as needed, into 6-inch ones. After the seedlings have made sufficient growth—if you want bushy specimens—pinch off the top to promote the development of

Fig. 11–7. Potbound plants benefit from periodic applications of fertilizer. A scant quarter-teaspoon of fertilizer (for a 4-inch pot) is added to the soil surface, keeping it away from the stem and foliage. The fertilizer is worked into the upper quarter-inch of soil, then the plant is watered.

branches. Some of the seedlings may flower during the late summer and autumn months of the first year.

Fuchsias are remarkably free from disease. There are a number of insects which attack fuchsias, among them mealy bug, white fly, scale insects, aphids, thrips, and the cyclamen mite.

Genista (Leguminosae)

A species of *Cytisus*, *C. canariensis* (native in the Canary Islands), and the hybrid *C. racemosus*, are commonly called genista. Both are shrubs and produce yellow, pea-shaped flowers in the spring.

After they flower, cut the shoots back to within about 2 inches of their base and repot. At this time you can make cuttings, which root best with a bottom heat of 65 degrees. Cuttings may also be rooted in October. Pot the rooted cuttings in 3-inch pots and shift to larger pots as necessary. Regular pinching is necessary to produce compact plants. Genista benefits from being kept outdoors during the summer. Syringe the plants frequently and give them ample water.

Geraniums (Geraniaceae)

Many greenhouse owners give geraniums front rank and take pleasure in building up a collection of these interesting and attractive plants. They have many lovely varieties, classified in five groups, from which to select. The five groups of geraniums (all in the genus *Pelargonium* of the geranium family, Geraniaceae) are the zonal geraniums, the scented-leaved geraniums, the ivy-leaved geraniums, the show or fancy pelargoniums, and the succulent geraniums. All of the cultivated geraniums have come from South Africa.

The zonal geraniums (Pelargonium zonale). This group, the familiar geraniums, enjoys widespread popularity for greenhouse culture and for summer bedding. If you have had trouble raising geraniums in your home you will be delighted with how easy it is to raise them to perfection in a greenhouse. Certain varieties are distinguished for their abundance of beautiful flowers, others for their attractively marked and colored foliage, so charming that corsages can be made from them.

Fig. 11–8.   There are numerous varieties of geraniums. Some, upper, have beautiful foliage. Lower, the miniature geraniums are especially appealing. (Merry Gardens)

Among the choice varieties that are grown primarily for their flowers are: Springfield violet, with lavender flowers; Blaze, Cardinal, Irene, Sincerity, and Victory, all bearing red flowers; Salmon Irene, Enchantress Fiat, Wendy Ann, producing salmon-colored flowers; Dawn, Genie, Pink Camellia, Penny, with pink flowers; Modesty, Snowmass, and Summer Cloud, all bearing white flowers. All of these are of normal stature.

Other varieties are dwarf, some attaining a height of only a few inches, yet flowering profusely. These dwarf zonal geraniums are fascinating and in a small space you can maintain a very interesting collection. Among the choice dwarf geraniums are Little Darling, with green leaves and pink flowers; Pigmy, bearing scarlet flowers; Alpha, a variety with red flowers and golden leaves zoned with brown; and Black Vesuvius, with olive green leaves and huge flowers of a bright orange-scarlet. Other good dwarf varieties are Pixie, Madame Fournier, Bumble Bee, Sleepy, Perky, Saturn, Moonbeams, Peace, Snow White, Prince Valiant, Salmon Comet, and Sirus.

Certain varieties of zonal geraniums have beautifully colored foliage in shades of green, red, and yellow. Among the varieties with tricolored foliage and eye-catching leaf markings are Lady Cullen and Mrs. Pollock, with nicely lobed green leaves, edged yellow, and splashed brown and crimson. Skies of Italy has brilliantly colored maple-like leaves, and Mrs. Cox has leaves green in the center, then a zone of brown tinted with red, surrounded by a border of creamy white. Miss Burdett Coutts is another variety with beautiful foliage. The leaves are purple-zoned, green-centered, and cream-bordered.

Zonal geraniums are best grown in a 50-degree greenhouse, but can be grown in a 60-degree house. Except during the hottest summer months, when the glass should be shaded, they prefer an abundance of light. Although geraniums can withstand prolonged drought they grow better if watered regularly. However, avoid waterlogging the soil, which is harmful. Water thoroughly when the surface of the soil is beginning to get dry.

Geraniums are propagated from cuttings made in the fall, winter, and spring. The cutting should be about 4 inches long. Remove the lower leaf or two to facilitate inserting it in sand or vermiculite, both of which are excellent rooting mediums. After insertion, water the cuttings thoroughly and from then on keep them somewhat on the dryside.   Some growers prefer to root the cuttings directly in 2½-inch pots filled with a mixture of equal parts of loam, leaf mold, and sand.   The cuttings in pots or in a bench of sand or vermiculite should be shaded from the sun.   They will root either in a 50-degree or 60-degree house.

After the cuttings have rooted they should go in 2½-inch pots. A mixture of three parts soil, one part peat moss, one part sand, with the addition of one teaspoon per quart of commercial fertilizer, is ideal.   After the plants are established they should be pinched to induce branching.   If you have allowed the plants to become very leggy with many leaves, remove the top three or four inches of the stem, a so-called *hard pinch*.   The part removed may be rooted.   If the plants are short, roll or pinch off the tip of the stem; in other words, use a *soft pinch*.   When the roots become crowded the plants will need shifting into 4-inch pots, or into 5-inch ones if large specimens are wanted.   If you want flowers during the winter months, do not overpot.   Slightly pot-bound plants are more likely to flower than those which are in large pots.   When the pots are well filled with roots, apply commercial fertilizer (about one-quarter teaspoon for a 5-inch pot) at about monthly intervals or apply liquid fertilizer.

Raising geraniums from seed is an interesting venture.   Choice seed is now available or you can hybridize your plants and collect the seed.   Seeds are planted in a sterilized mixture of equal parts of loam, peat moss, and sand; cover the seeds with a quarter inch of soil.   When the seedlings are large enough, transplant to flats or individual pots.   Move into larger pots as necessary.   If seeds are planted March 1, you can expect the plants to bloom in late summer and continue through the winter.   You will wait with much anticipation for the first flowers and will be delighted at the variety of plants, some of which may be superior to named varieties.   All kinds of geraniums may be grown from seed; the zonal geraniums, the scented-leaved geraniums, the ivy-leaved geraniums, and the show pelargoniums.

Geraniums may become infested with red spiders, mealy bugs, leaf rollers, mites, and aphids.   If the leafspot disease appears, remove the infected leaves and eliminate overhead syringing.   Proper spacing of the plants and good ventilation are also helpful in controlling leafspot, as is the application of Fermate or Zerlate.   *Crinkles*, a virus disease, causes translucent spots on the leaves.   The only control is to dispose of the infected plants. Another disease is *blackleg*, which may be recognized by the blackening of the stem. This disease is most commonly seen in the propagating bench, although potted plants may be affected. Use fresh sand in the propagating bench or sterilize the old sand and dispose of infected plants. To avoid dieback or branch rot disease don't tear the flower stalk from the stem, because this leaves an open wound through which harmful fungi can gain entrance. Instead just pinch off the flower cluster, leaving 3 to 4 inches of the stalk. After it dies, the stalk naturally falls from the stem and a protective layer will form.

The scented-leaved geraniums. This group consists of a number of species with inconspicuous flowers and leaves which vary in shape according to the variety. The scented-leaved geraniums are grown chiefly for the fragrance which emanates when the leaves are rubbed lightly. Among the varieties are those with the fragrance of the rose, nutmeg, lemon, lime, strawberry, and mint. The culture of these interesting plants is the same as that of the zonal geraniums, with a night temperature preferably close to 50 degrees.

Ivy-leaved geraniums (Pelargonium peltatum). These geraniums are characterized by their trailing habit of growth, which makes them desirable for use in hanging baskets and window boxes. The leaves are glossy and green. There are many varieties: Intensity, with red flowers; Mexican Beauty, deep red; Charles Turner, rose-pink; Barbary Coast, lavender; Apricot Queen, salmon-pink; Snowdrift, white; and many others.

Show pelargoniums (Pelargonium domesticum). These are also known as the Lady Washington Geraniums, Martha Washington Geraniums, Fancy Pelargoniums, and Pansy-flowered Geraniums. The show pelargoniums are not in continuous bloom. They generally flower in the spring, from Easter on. Like other geraniums, they are propagated from cuttings made in fall, winter, and spring. The favorite time is soon after the flowering season. After rooting, the cuttings are potted in 2½-inch pots and moved along into larger pots as is necessary. During the growing period pinching is desired to promote branching. Plants soft-pinched for the last time in December will flower in March and April, those pinched in early February, in May and June. Pinching after February will prevent flowering.

The plants require rather heavy shade as well as syringing during the bright summer months. In the fall more light should be given and syringing stopped. Monthly applications of fertilizer are desirable. The plants do well with a night temperature of 50 degrees. After flowering, the plants should be kept on the dry side until August or September. Then prune them into shape, leaving one or two nodes on each branch. Remove most of the old soil, trim the roots and repot. The plants should be shifted into larger pots in December.

Some favorite varieties are Azalea, Edith North, Springtime, Easter Greeting, Gardener's Joy, Marie Vogel, Salmon Springtime, and Pink Vogel.

Succulent geraniums. A few geraniums are strikingly different from those previously described. The Knotty Storksbill (*Pelargonium gibbosum*) has fleshy stems knotted at the joints. Another, the Cactus Geranium (*P. echinatum*), has stems armed with spines and lobed leaves covered with white hairs.

Fig. 11-9. Show pelargonium, also called Martha Washington geranium, produces many delightful flowers in the spring.

Grevillea (Proteaceae)

Grevillea robusta, commonly called Silk Oak, is raised for its attractive fernlike foliage. In its native home in Queensland and New South Wales it grows into a mighty tree 150 feet high. The plants are raised from seed sown in the spring. The seeds are large and flat. They seem to germinate better if placed point downward or sideways, instead of flat. Pot the seedlings in 2½-inch pots and move to large ones as necessary. The plants require shade. Grevillea is best raised with a single stem; do not pinch the plants.

Passion Flower (Passifloraceae)

Because of the shape and arrangement of the floral parts, *Passiflora caerulea*, a vigorous vine from Brazil, is known as the passion flower. According to legend, the whorl of ten green-white petals represents the ten Apostles who witnessed Christ's crucifixion. Within the petals the corona of blue, white, and purple filaments suggests the Crown of Thorns. The five stamens represent the wounds and the three stigmas the nails. The vines flower in summer; the blossoms open at sun rise and close at sun set. The fruit is purple, plum-shaped and about 2 to 3 inches long. It is filled with seeds surrounded by juicy pulp with a delicious aroma. The fruits are edible and high in vitamins A and C. The vines may be grown along a wall or they may be trained on a trellis, totem pole, or wire mesh.

Among the other exotic species of passiflora are *Passiflora coccinea*, from tropical South America, with scarlet flowers of medium size; *P. coriacea* from Mexico to Peru, a vigorous climber that bears 1-inch flowers with pale green petals; and *P. trifasciata*, from South America, with small fragrant yellowish flowers. The last two are more interesting for their beautifully shaped and colored leaves than for their small flowers. Passifloras are easily propagated from stem cuttings and from seeds. Seeds may be sown in the fall or winter and should be lightly covered with a $\frac{1}{16}$ inch layer of vermiculite or sphagnum moss. The large-flowered types may take two or three years to bloom whereas the small-flowered kinds flower the first year.

Fig. 11–10. Passion flower, an exciting flowering vine to which many people attach religious significance. (W. Atlee Burpee Co.)

Primroses *(Primulaceae)*

Primroses produce a grand display of flowers during the winter and early spring. Among the favorites for greenhouse culture are *Primula malacoides, P. sinensis, P. obconica,* and the hybrid *P. Kewensis.* Except for *P. Kewensis* these grow natively in China. *Primula malacoides* (the Baby Primrose) bears myriads of flowers on slender stems, month after month. Numbers of superb varieties are now available with flowers of white, rose-pink, salmon-rose, lavender, pink, or red.

In the Star or Stellata group of the Chinese Primrose (*Primula sinensis*) are graceful and very floriferous plants that bloom over a long period. The flowers are long-lasting when cut, remaining fresh for many days. The color range includes white, pink, lavender, blue and ruby. The Giant varieties of *Primula sinensis* are also worthy, and they come in colors of red, orange-red, pink, salmon, and blue.

Primula obconica, sometimes called Poison Primrose, bears huge heads of flowers on strong stems well above the foliage. The plants are compact and neat. Pink, rose, red, and crimson varieties are available. This species has one serious drawback: the foliage, when handled, causes a severe irritating rash on some individuals. Some persons are immune but others are susceptible. If you are sensitive and desire to raise this plant, you will have to wear rubber gloves when handling it. Keep it where it will not be readily handled by visitors.

Primula Kewensis is strong-growing, floriferous and bears beautiful yellow flowers. It is a hybrid resulting from a cross of the Buttercup Primrose with the Arabian Primrose.

All of the primroses mentioned require the same cultural conditions. They are started from seed. Sow seeds of *Primula obconica, P. Kewensis,* and *P. sinensis* in April. Seeds of *Primula malacoides* are sown in June for Christmas flowering and in September for flowering at Easter and for Mother's Day. As soon as the seedlings are large enough to handle they should be moved into flats, spacing them an inch apart. A suitable soil mixture consists of two parts soil, one part sand, and one part peat moss. When the plants begin to crowd each other, move them into 2½-inch pots. Before the plants become potbound shift them into 4- or 5-inch pots. When potting, keep the crown at soil level. Too-deep planting may encourage a stem rot and too-shallow planting results in the plant's toppling over. During the bright months of summer the greenhouse should be shaded. In autumn the shade should be gradually reduced. If you prefer, you can keep the seedlings in a shaded, well-ventilated cold frame during the summer. Throughout the growing and flowering period, the ideal night temperature is 50 degrees.

Roses (Rosaceae)

The roses you see in flower shops have been raised in ground beds or raised benches. To grow long-stemmed roses to perfection requires considerable skill and, of equal importance, greenhouses of large size. However, certain varieties of rose grow well in a small greenhouse. Roses grown in pots make excellent greenhouse specimens. They can be raised at a night temperature of 50 degrees or at 60 degrees. Of course the plants will flower sooner in a 60-degree

Fig. 11–11. The baby primrose, *Primula malacoides*, bears myriads of lovely flowers over a long period.

house than in a 50-degree one. You can raise a large variety, selecting from the Hybrid Teas, Floribundas, and Climbers.

In November, dig rose plants from your garden or purchase top-quality plants. Then pot them, without delay, in 6-, 7-, or 8-inch pots, according to the sizes of the plants. They grow well in a mixture of two parts loam and one part peat moss with the addition of commercial fertilizer. As usual, provide good drainage. After potting, the climbers should be shaped on a wire form. Store the potted plants in a cold frame and protect them from winter injury by covering the canes with straw or leaves. In early January, bring the plants into the greenhouse and syringe them several times a day. Syringing promotes swelling and development of buds.

Pruning of roses, except for the climbers, can be done before they are put in the cold frame or just after you bring them into the greenhouse. The climbers are pruned after flowering; cut out the old wood nearly entirely. This encourages a few strong shoots to develop near the base. These new shoots will be 6 to 10 feet long by fall.

Commercial growers find a ready market for pot roses at Easter. The customers enjoy them as house plants and then plant them in the garden. A schedule to have roses in flower at Easter would be as follows: transfer the plants from the cold frame to the greenhouse on January 15, keep at a temperature of 45 to 48 degrees until February 15, then raise the temperature to 54 to 56 degrees, and in early March increase it to 60 degrees.

Roses prefer a high humidity, 60 to 70 per cent, and good ventilation. Water carefully, preferably with water at the same temperature as the greenhouse. Avoid both overwatering and dryness at roots. When actively growing, the plants respond to fertilizer.

In the spring you can plant the roses in your garden, or you can carry them over in pots to be raised in the greenhouse the next season. If you prefer the latter, and many growers do, plunge the pots in the garden in late spring. In the fall, repot the plants that need it, and top-dress the others with a mixture of half soil and half well-rotted manure. Early October is suitable for overhauling the plants. After they are overhauled, place them in a cold frame and cover with straw. Near the end of November you can bring some of the plants into the greenhouse. Others can remain in the cold frame until January.

Roses are increased by cuttings, generally taken in the spring. The best cuttings have three eyes on them, and they are best rooted with a bottom heat of 70 degrees. Cuttings root in one or two months. Pot the rooted cuttings in 2½-inch pots and shift into larger pots as necessary. Roses are also propagated by grafting and budding.

Roses can also be grown from seed. However, the offspring will not be uniform; some may be excellent, others worthless. Before rose seeds will germinate, they must be exposed to a low temperature. Store the clean seeds in moist peat moss at a temperature of 41 degrees for four to six months, and then plant them.

If the plants become infected with mildew, dust them with sulfur. Aphids and red spider are troublesome pests.

Fig. 11–12. Schizanthus is a fine pot plant, excellent for cut flowers. (Bodger Seeds Ltd.)

Schizanthus *(Solanaceae)*

This plant, an annual of the potato family from Chile, is known as the Butterfly Flower or Poor Man's Orchid. It grows 1 to 2 feet tall, has fern-like, light green leaves, and bears showy flowers in terminal clusters. The petals, in shades of lilac, purple, pink, carmine, reddish brown, or white, usually have streaks or spots of another color at the base.

For handsome plants that will flower in April or May, sow seeds about ⅛ inch deep in August or September. For flowering in late spring and summer, sow in January. The seeds germinate in a few days and the seedlings grow rapidly. The seedlings may be moved into flats, then into 3-inch pots, moving into larger pots as necessary. Or they may be moved from the seed pan directly into 2½-inch pots and later into larger ones. The plants should be pinched once or twice to get a bushy habit. A night temperature of 50 degrees is ideal.

If you wish schizanthus for cut flowers you can move them from the seed pan into flats, spacing the plants three inches apart. Do not pinch the plants; permit them to grow to a single stem. The plants will flower in the flat. Of course you can raise schizanthus in benches; space them about 8 inches apart.

Schizanthus may be flowered early, from February on, by lengthening the days with artificial light from sundown to 10 P.M.

Streptosolen (Solanaceae)

Streptosolen Jamesonii is a handsome evergreen shrub from Colombia. From January on, the plant produces clusters of attractive trumpet-shaped orange-red flowers. After flowering, cut the shrub back to promote bushiness, and then repot, using a compost of two parts loam and one of leaf mold. Established plants require plenty of water, occasional feedings, and a temperature of 50 degrees. The plants are easily propagated from cuttings made in the spring. Young plants should be pinched several times.

Swainsona (Leguminosae)

This shrub is a native of Australia. The favorite species is *Swainsona galegifolia,* which bears sprays of pea-shaped, red or white flowers, depending on the variety. The white variety is the one generally grown. Swainsona begins to flower in summer and continues well into winter. The plants do well in pots containing an even mixture of loam and peat moss. Swainsona may be started from seed sown in the spring or from cuttings taken in January. Pinch several times to get stocky plants. Plants may be kept growing for several years by cutting back and repotting when necessary. They flower better when they are potbound. During some years, only a top dressing of soil and manure will be necessary.

12

Pot Plants for the
60-Degree Greenhouse

A greenhouse with 60-degree nights provides a suitable environment for many plants, some of which are grown for their beautiful flowers, others because of their decorative foliage. Aphelandra, azalea, bouganvillea, browallia, gardenia, hoya, impatiens, kalanchoë, poinsettia, and strelitzia bear attractive flowers. Among the beautiful foliage plants are coleus, croton, dracaena, fittonia, maranta (the prayer plant), peperomia, pilea (the aluminum plant), and the ti plant. Some may be grown for their fascinating behavior, for example Nepenthes, a carnivorous plant, and the sensitive plant. Most of the plants will thrive in a soil consisting of one part loam and one part peat moss, with sand, vermiculite, or perlite to make it porous. Fertilizer in the form of manure or commercial fertilizer should be added to the mixture.

Separate chapters will be devoted to other plants that thrive in a 60-degree house—the aroids, begonias, bromeliads, ferns, gesneriads, and orchids.

Acalypha (Euphorbiaceae)

The family Euphorbiaceae to which Acalypha belongs includes many greenhouse favorites such as poinsettia, codiaeum (garden croton), euphorbia, and acalypha. In addition there are a number of species which are succulent and cactuslike in appearance; these we will consider in a later chapter. Most members of this family have a milky juice, which in some species is poisonous. Valuable products come from certain members; among the commercially important ones are the *Hevea* rubber tree, the castor plant, and the *cassava*.

One of the most attractive acalyphas is *A. hispida* from India, known as the Red-hot Cattail or Chenille Plant. It has green leaves and bears striking pendant tassels of red flowers. Other species of *Acalypha* are grown chiefly for their attractive foliage—among them *A. godseffiana*, with green leaves, spotted white; *A. macafeeana*, a plant with red leaves blotched with deeper red; *A. musiaca*, whose foliage is bronzy-green variegated with shades of red.

For excellent winter-flowering specimens of *Acalypha hispida*, the most interesting species, cuttings should be made in the summer. The flower spikes become 8 to 10 inches long as the plant increases in size. Be on the alert for mealy bugs, scales, and red spiders. In its native habitat acalypha grows to be a large shrub. In the greenhouse it may be kept within bounds by pinching or preferably by starting new plants each year. It prefers full sun during the fall and winter months.

Aphelandra (Acanthaceae)

Aphelandra squarrosa, sometimes called the Zebra Plant, comes from the rainforests of Brazil. It bears beautiful, shiny, emerald-green leaves with white veins and in autumn and winter has terminal clusters of waxy, long-lasting, yellow flowers tipped with green. Aphelandra should be grown with shade throughout the year and because it is evergreen the soil must be kept moist at all seasons. Plants are increased by stem cuttings. If the plants are not pinched they will flower the first year.

Azaleas (Ericaceae)

Greenhouse azaleas are handsome evergreen plants that flower profusely in the winter and spring. There are many varieties, some bearing single flowers, others double ones. The flower color ranges from white through many shades of pink to red. Azaleas are in the genus *Rhododendron,* a member of the heath family, which also includes heather, arbutus, mountain laurel, cranberry, and huckleberry.

To get a start, purchase during the autumn plants which have the flower buds well formed. When you receive them, unpack them and soak the root balls in water until they are wet through. Let each ball drain and then pot the plant in a 5- or 6-inch azalea pot. Azaleas should not be overpotted. If you know that the soil in your region is acid, mix one part of soil with one of peat moss and use this mixture. If the soil is not acid use plain peat moss or humus from a pine forest. Azaleas thrive only in acid soil; in alkaline soil they are weak, flower poorly, and have yellow leaves. Rainwater is ideal for azaleas. If you use tap water that is alkaline, a wise precaution is to water the plants at two- or three-week intervals with a solution of one ounce of iron sulfate in two gallons of water.

To have azaleas in flower by Christmas obtain plants which have been raised on the West Coast. Such plants will have well developed flower buds by early fall, whereas those grown in the midwest will not have mature buds until later in the season. Certain varieties of West Coast azaleas will flower by Christmas if they are placed in a 60-degree house the first week of November.

Among the varieties which are suitable for early season forcing and their flower colors are Paul Schame, salmon-pink; Jersey Belle, coral salmon; Dorothy Gish, deep salmon; Alaska, white; Constance, cerise pink; Pink Ruffles, deep rose pink. Varieties suitable for later flowering are Jean Haerens, rosy carmine; Coral Bells, coral pink; Snow, white; Pink Pearl, salmon rose; Salmon Perfection, salmon; and Niobe, white.

Flower buds of these azaleas do not grow when the temperature is less than 45 degrees. Hence, flowering can be delayed by keeping the plants at slightly below this temperature. You can then move them, a few at a time, from the cool place into the 60-degree greenhouse, thus obtaining a sequence of flowering. The cool spot used to retard flowering may be either a cool greenhouse, or a cold frame. In January and February, the plants flower six weeks after they are brought into the 60-degree house. During the brighter spring months, when the days are longer, only three weeks are required for flowering. These times for flowering are average ones; some varieties come into blossom in a shorter time than do others.

When the plants are in the 60-degree house and the flower buds are developing, remove new shoots that develop below the flower clusters. Keep them watered carefully. They must not be allowed to become dry, nor should they become waterlogged. Daily syringing promotes the development of fine flowers.

The plants can be grown for the next and subsequent years. Overhaul them after flowering, just as the new growths begin. After knocking a plant from its pot, remove some of the old peat and then put it in the same size pot or one slightly larger. Generally plants can be grown in the same size for two years. It is essential to pot firmly and to provide good drainage.

When the plants are established and actively growing, they benefit from fertilization with ammonium sulfate and iron sulfate prepared by adding 1 ounce of ammonium sulfate and 1 ounce of iron sulfate to 2 gallons of water. Water them with this solution every two or three weeks. The plants will also benefit from two applications of 4–12–4 fertilizer during the summer.

When the danger of frost is over in the spring, move the plants to a cold frame. They may either be removed from their pots and planted or they may be left in their pots, which should be plunged into peat moss. Shade the frame with lath until August 1, after which remove the shade and allow the plants to have full sunlight to check vegetative growth and promote the formation of flower buds. Keep the plants well watered throughout the summer and syringe them frequently.

If you have planted the azaleas, dig them up and pot them in early September. At this time the plunged ones should also be lifted. Then move them into the greenhouse and grow them for three weeks at a temperature of 55 degrees. During this period the flower buds will complete their development, after which the plants may be kept at a temperature of 45 degrees until it is time to force them. The first batch can be brought into the 60-degree house in early November and others at later dates.

Azaleas are propagated by grafting and from cuttings. The cuttings are made in May and rooted in a mixture of two parts sand and one of peat moss with bottom heat of 65 degrees. The cuttings should be shaded, and syringed frequently. They will begin to root in four or five weeks. The rooted cuttings are best moved into flats of peat. When the plants crowd each other, transplant them into other flats of peat, this time spacing them 4 inches by 4 inches. Young plants do better in flats than in pots because moisture is more

Fig. 12–1. Bougainvillea, left, has small flowers but brilliant beautiful bracts—purple in the *Sanderiana* variety of *B. glabra* and crimson in the variety Crimson Lake of *B. spectabilis*. Right, a year-old azalea plant flowering in a 3-inch plot.

uniform. From the second flat the plants are moved into pots. Young plants should be kept growing all of the time, by keeping them where the night temperature is 60 degrees. As the plants develop, pinch them at intervals to produce a bushy, compact plant and give them a complete acid fertilizer periodically.

Among the insect pests attacking azaleas are the red spider, thrip, mealy bug, leaf miner, and leaf roller.

Bougainvillea *(Nyctaginaceae)*

Bougainvillea is a showy plant that bears panicles of beautifully colored, leafy bracts in the center of which are the small flowers, generally white in color. Bougainvillea thrives best in a 60 degree greenhouse. However, we know a number of gardeners who have success with them in a 50-degree house. They are easily increased from stem cuttings made in the spring. The plants will be ready for 6-inch pots by fall and will flower during the coming winter or spring. Pot the plants in a mixture of half loam and half leaf mold or peat moss. Prune annually when flowering is over by cutting back each new growth so that 3 or 4 inches remain on each branch. Cut off all thin and weak growths.

B. glabra, from Brazil, and its many varieties make excellent pot plants when thus kept small, although they grow to a height of ten feet out-of-doors in warm climates and can do the same in a green-house. If you have the space for a trellis the trailing branches can be trained upon it or they can be fastened overhead by strings to give a glorious mass of color reminiscent of a tropical garden. Among the popular varieties are Barbara Karst, bright red bracts; Texas Dawn, pink bracts; Orange King, orange bracts; Jamaica White, white bracts.

Browallia *(Solanaceae)*

Of the six species of this South American genus of the potato family, one species, *Browallia speciosa major,* is commonly grown in greenhouses. This species flowers during winter and early spring, giving blooms of a rich deep blue that have a white throat and are about 2 inches across. It is also suitable for outdoor bedding. Sow seeds in July for winter flowering plants. Barely cover them with soil. Transplant six seedlings to a 6-inch pot, in which the plants will flower, or pot the seedlings singly in 2½- or 3-inch pots and later shift them into larger ones. The plants should be pinched about three times to encourage a bushy habit. Seeds may be sown in February for plants to set out in the garden. These can be moved back into the greenhouse in the fall.

Christmas Pepper *(Solanaceae)*

The Christmas Pepper, *Capsicum species,* is a perky plant for the Christmas season and makes a much appreciated gift. The compact plants with glossy green foliage produce a profusion of upright, lacquered, cone-shaped fruits that change from green to purple to red as they mature. Sow seeds from April to June, and finish one plant in a 4-inch pot or three in a 5-inch pot. They are most attractive when grown with full sun.

Clerodendron *(Verbenaceae)*

Clerodendron thomsonae (glorybower), from tropical West Africa, is an easily grown vine with large, prominently veined green leaves. The vine continuously produces brilliant, long lasting, red flowers enclosed in a white bag-like calyx. The vines can be trained in a variety of patterns on a trellis, stake, or wire form.

The glorybower is easily increased by stem cuttings. Once the plants are in 8-inch pots they may remain in them for many years, if periodically fertilized. Except during the brightest months they should be grown without shade. Water frequently during spring, summer, and fall and moderately during the winter.

Coleus *(Labiatae)*

There are many varieties of *Coleus blumei,* a native of Java, which are grown for their colorful and variegated foliage. The colors of the leaves are seemingly endless in combinations of chartreuse, light and dark green, brown, bronze, yellow, pink, and red. The leaf shapes also come in many patterns and may be fringed or ruffled. Favorite varieties are quickly and easily propagated from stem cuttings; if cuttings are taken in summer you will have large plants by spring. Coleus is readily increased by seeds. You can purchase seeds of specific varieties or you can purchase hybrid seed from which many types will develop. From seed planted in February you can expect large plants by early summer some of which you may wish to grow in your garden. Encourage bushy growth by pinching the plants from time to time. Coleus thrives with ample water and biweekly feedings of a liquid fertilizer. Although the plants prefer full sun they will also thrive in shade. Coleus develops spikes of small blue-purple flowers, but, because its chief attraction is the foliage, growers often remove the developing flower cluster.

Croton *(Euphorbiaceae)*

The decorative crotons, grown for their beautiful foliage, are in the genus *Codiaeum,* a group of six species native to Malaya and the Pacific Islands. There are over a hundred horticultural varieties of the species *C. variegatum pictum,* varying in leaf shape and foliage color, which ranges from almost white to light and deep yellow, orange, pink, and red, often in charming combinations. The flowers of crotons are small and inconspicuous.

The crotons do best with a high night temperature, about 70 degrees, but do moderately well at 60 degrees. During the brighter months of the year, light shade is necessary because bright light will burn the leaves. They do well with a high humidity. The plants are easily propagated by cuttings taken from October to June and by air layerage. Cuttings may be rooted in sand with bottom heat of about 80 degrees. The potting mixture should consist of equal parts of sand, loam, and leaf mold with the addition of some cow manure (one-sixth) and bone meal. During the period of active growth they should be well-watered. When they are resting, keep the plants on the dry side. Red spiders and mealy bugs are the most common pests.

Dracaena (Liliaceae)

Dracaenas are grown for their ornamental foliage. The leaves are sword-shaped in some species, broader in others. A number have variegated leaves. During the brighter months of the year they should be furnished light shade. Dracaenas should not be over-potted.

A few species of dracaena may be started from seed and all may be propagated by air layerage or from cuttings. The top of the plant may be cut off and rooted. Cut the rest of the old stem into pieces about 2 inches long and embed them horizontally just below the surface of a medium of half sand and half peat. Or, if you prefer, embed the entire cane in this mixture without cutting it into segments. Shoots develop rapidly from the whole cane or the pieces if the temperature is kept at 80 degrees and the humidity is high. You should use a heated propagating case if you wish quick development. One or more shoots will develop from each cutting. Remove the shoots from the cane whether they have rooted or not and pot them in a mixture of three-fourths loam and one-fourth leaf mold or peat.

Some favorite species of dracaena are *Dracaena indivisa* (more correctly, *Cordyline indivisa*), *D. fragrans*, *D. godseffiana*, *D. goldieana*, and *D. sanderiana*. *Dracaena indivisa* has dark green leaves about 2 to 3 feet long. There are a number of named varieties of this species which have more distinctive foliage, among them Doucettii, with variegated leaves, Veitchii Superba, with a bright red midrib, and Atropurpurea, whose foliage is a deep reddish brown. *Dracaena fragrans* grows almost too rapidly for the small greenhouse; it has arching corn-like leaves about 2 feet long and 3 inches wide. *Dracaena godseffiana* has a branching habit and bears deep green leaves, about 4 inches long, which are irregularly spotted with yellow or white. It is indeed a decorative plant. *Dracaena goldie-*

Every greenhouse gardener is his own decorator.

The greenhouse in winter is a hospitable haven
of warmth and color.

The tuberous begonia is a showy and satisfying
hobby flower. (Photograph by Bea Slinger for
Flower Grower, The Home Garden Magazine)

The greenhouse is a blaze of color with the popular autumn crop of chrysanthemums. (Photograph, Lord & Burnham, *Popular Gardening*)

ana is another fine foliage plant with glossy green leaves conspicuously spotted and banded with white. The leaves are about 8 inches long and 4 inches wide. *Dracaena sanderiana* bears leaves about 8 inches long and 1 inch wide, and they are glossy green, broadly margined with white.

Euphorbia *(Euphorbiaceae)*

Three species of *Euphorbia* make good greenhouse plants, *Euphorbia fulgens*, the scarlet plume; *E. splendens*, crown of thorns; and *E. pulcherrima*, the poinsettia. The genus is a very large one with more than 1000 species. The flowers of all members lack petals and sepals and they would not be showy if it were not for the highly colored bracts. The bracts, modified leaves, of the poinsettia are conspicuous, the flowers hardly noticeable. Similarly, the bracts are the beautiful part of the flower cluster of the scarlet plume and crown of thorns. All of the euphorbias have a milky sap, and in certain species the juice is poisonous.

Scarlet Plume (Euphorbia fulgens). This is a tropical shrub, native of Mexico, with slender drooping branches. The leaves are long-petioled, bright green, and lance-shaped. The bracts of the flowers are orange-scarlet and most attractive. The flowers are borne on long clusters that are suitable for cutting. After cutting the spray, sear the cut end to stop the flow of the sap. The flowers last about three weeks after cutting.

The scarlet plume grows well with good light and a night temperature of 60 to 65 degrees, and is potted in a mixture of four parts loam and one of well-rotted manure. Periodic feedings are desirable. The plants are readily propagated from cuttings taken after April. The cuttings should have about three nodes and be inserted in a mixture of half sand and half peat with a bottom heat of 65 to 70 degrees. The plants should be pinched in order to secure bushy specimens.

The normal flowering season is December and January, but the plants may be flowered earlier by shading them with black cloth from 5 P.M. to 7 A.M. If shading is started July 15, the plants will flower in September; if started August 15, in late October. In all cases the shading period should continue until the flower buds are well developed.

After flowering, plants which were not covered with black cloth should be repotted and brought into active growth. When sufficient new growth has been made, cuttings can be taken. Plants which were shaded may be kept growing. They will produce a second, short-stemmed crop of flowers in March or April.

Crown of Thorns (Euphorbia splendens). This plant blooms throughout the year, but most profusely in the winter. It is a shrub armed with spines. The leaves are few in number and clustered at the tips of the branches. The scarlet bracts, which look like petals but are not, furnish the color. Plants may be propagated by cuttings and grown under the same conditions as the scarlet plume. It is a native of Madagascar.

Poinsettia (Euphorbia pulcherrima). The true flowers of poinsettia are small, greenish-yellow, and not especially attractive. The beauty lies in the brilliant bracts below the cluster of flowers. The species is native to Mexico and it was named for Joel R. Poinsett, a Charleston, South Carolina, physician. Poinsettias are not only excellent pot plants for the Christmas season but they are also good cut flowers. The flowers last well after cutting, at least ten days. A number of excellent varieties are now available with red, pink, or white color bracts; Paul Mikkelsen is a short plant with stiff stems and red bracts, Mikkelpink bears pink bracts and has good keeping qualities, and a beautiful white is Mikkelwhite.

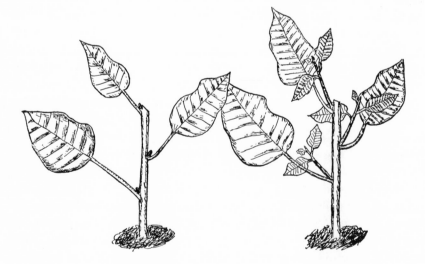

Fig. 12–2. Left, a pinched poinsettia plant. Right, the plant at a later date when three branches have developed.

Poinsettias, like the scarlet plume and crown-of-thorns, are sun-loving plants and do not form their colored bracts well if shaded during autumn. During the summer months, good ventilation is desirable. Throughout the growing period avoid letting the temperature drop below 60 degrees. Also, keep the plants out of drafts and don't let the soil become either dry or waterlogged. Low temperatures, drafts, waterlogging, and drought cause the leaves to fall, which detracts from the beauty of the plants. A mixture of three parts soil, one part well-rotted manure or peat moss, and one part sand with the addition of a 4-inch potful of superphosphate per bushel is an excellent potting medium.

After the plants have flowered, stop watering them and keep them where the temperature is 50 to 55 degrees. In April, cut them back so that each branch is about 8 inches long, then repot. Place the plants on the bench where the temperature is 60 to 65 degrees and encourage active growth by syringing them frequently and by watering the plants. After growth is active, water with a solution of 1 ounce of ammonium sulfate to 2 gallons of water. When the new growths are 8 to 12 inches long, the terminal 4 to 6 inches may be cut off and rooted. Cuttings are best made in the morning, and they should be kept in water for an hour to prevent excessive bleeding. The cut need not be made at a node. Just one cut is needed, the one made when the cutting is removed from the plant. You can take cuttings from the plants throughout the summer. After the last cuttings are made, as late as September, the stock plants are grown on at 60 degrees until they flower. Plants grown from late cuttings will flower at the same time as those started earlier and will be shorter and more marketable. At all times leave at least two leaves on each cut stem of the stock plant to make food for the new growths. The thicker the cutting, the larger the flower; avoid taking cuttings from spindly growths. One or two basal leaves may be removed from each cutting to facilitate insertion into the rooting medium.

Cuttings are best inserted into a mixture of one part of peat to two parts of sand, contained in 2½- or 3-inch pots. Firm the mixture in the pot, poke a hole with a dibble, insert the cutting, firm the medium, and then water. Cuttings may also be rooted in sand, contained in a bench. The sand should be firmed, and then the cuttings dibbled in, spacing them 3 inches apart in rows 5 inches apart. After inserting the cuttings, firm the sand about them, and water. Cuttings in pots or in a bench should be syringed three or four times each day for the first ten days. The cuttings require shade, which should be some distance above them. Don't place paper or cheesecloth directly on the cuttings. Cuttings root in about three weeks.

Commercial growers often do not carry over stock plants, but prefer to purchase them each year. When the stock plants arrive, usually in early April, they are potted, and as the growths come on, cuttings are made. One stock plant will yield thirty-five to sixty cuttings.

After the cuttings in a bench are rooted, they should be potted in 2½-inch or 3-inch pots in the soil previously mentioned. Water thoroughly after potting and keep the plants shaded until they are established. Frequently syringing is beneficial at this time.

Each plant will bear one "flower" if not pinched, and more than one if pinched. The top of a young plant may be removed and rooted, but make sure at least two leaves remain on the parent plant. The removal of the top of the plant with several leaves is known as a hard pinch, and plants should not be hard pinched after August 15. Instead, just roll off the tip of the stem (a soft pinch). Like the hard pinch, the soft pinch promotes branching. Soft pinching may be practiced until about September. Don't pinch plants that are not well established.

Most of the plants sold at Christmas will be those started from cuttings made in late August and early September. Such plants should not be pinched; instead they should be grown with a single stem which will be of a desired height at Christmas.

The plants should be repotted as necessary. They may be grown singly in pots, or a number of plants out of 2½-inch or 3-inch pots may be planted in a pot. Placing two or more plants in an azalea pot is called panning; this is generally done in September, but may be done as late as early November. A 6-inch azalea pot is about the right size, but larger ones can be used. Three or four pinched or unpinched plants may be placed in a 6-inch pot; a 7-inch pot will hold about 4. Select uniform plants for each pot and avoid breaking the ball of soil. Rooted cuttings made late in the summer may be panned directly. Pinched plants with two or three stems may be grown singly in 4- or 5-inch standard pots and smaller plants from late cuttings will flower in 3-inch pots.

Immediately after panning or repotting, water the plants. Throughout the growing period neither overwater nor underwater.

Either practice will cause leaf drop. The plants should be grown at a night temperature of 60 to 62 degrees without drafts. It may be necessary to fertilize the plants once between the time of panning and November 15, when the color of the bracts should be showing. After the color appears, fertilize the plant every two or three weeks, using a complete fertilizer dissolved in water.

Poinsettias require night temperatures of 60 to 62 degrees and short days with long uninterrupted nights for flowering. If you prolong the days during the autumn by turning on lights the plants will not flower for the Christmas season. Even a bright street light close to the greenhouse may prevent flowering. Interrupting the night by turning on lights at 10 or 11 P.M. may also prevent flowering; hence when checking temperatures at night use low wattage globes for only a very short time.

Throughout the season, watch for mealy bugs, scale, and root aphids and control them. Poinsettias may become infected with a virus disease which causes a mottling of the leaves. Plants showing symptoms of this mosaic disease should be burned. Occasionally poinsettias get a bacterial disease which results in watersoaked longitudinal streaks on the stem. In time the streaks crack open and a yellow ooze containing countless bacteria becomes evident. Plants with this disease should be burned.

Fittonia (Acanthaceae)

Fittonia is a compact plant of dwarf habit with beautifully netted leaves. *Fittonia argyroneura* is characterized by bright green leaves with conspicuous silver-white veins. *F. verschaffeltii* has deep green leaves with red veins. Fittonias are easily propagated from stem cuttings rooted in a medium of half sand and half peat. The plants grow well in soil which is rich in peat or leaf mold.

In Peru, their native home, they grow only in shaded niches and hence in a greenhouse they should be located where the light intensity is about one-tenth of full sun.

Gardenia (Rubiaceae)

This beautiful evergreen shrub, a native of China, with glossy foliage is prized for its delightfully fragrant, waxen, white flowers. *Gardenia veitchii* and such variations of *G. grandiflora* as Belmont,

Fig. 12–3. Some attractive foliage plants for the 60-degree greenhouse. Upper left, Coleus. Upper right, Watermelon begonia. Center left, Fittonia. Center right, Aluminum plant. Lower left, Prayer plant (W. Atlee Burpee Co.) Lower right, Sensitive plant. The leaflets on the right are just beginning to respond to touch.

Hadley, and McLellan's 23 are favorites for growing in the 60-degree house. Gardenia was named for a South Carolina physician, Alexander Garden.

Gardenias are propagated by cuttings taken from November through March. Make cuttings, 3 to 5 inches long, from healthy plants and root them in sand or in a mixture of sand and peat. Treatment with Rootone or Hormodin hastens rooting. A bottom heat of 70 degrees and a close atmosphere are desirable.

The rooted cuttings are potted in 2½-inch pots in a mixture of equal parts of loam and peat moss. If the loam is alkaline, add a tablespoon of iron sulfate to each bushel of the mixture. When the roots fill the pots, shift the plants into 4-inch ones, using the same mixture. By August the plants should be ready for shifting into 6-inch pots. A high humidity, a night temperature of 60 degrees, and a uniform water supply promote good growth.

In summer, occasional applications of 4–12–4 fertilizer promote good growth. During the bright months light shade is needed and the plants should be syringed frequently. Remove the shade gradually, beginning in September. During winter, monthly applications of ammonium sulfate (prepared by dissolving 1 ounce of ammonium sulfate in 2 gallons of water) and periodic applications of iron sulfate or iron chelate are beneficial.

Gardenia plants can be grown for several years. However, the largest flowers of the best quality are produced by one-year plants. In May one-year-old plants should be cut back to 24 to 30 inches, and repotted.

Gardenias can be cantankerous plants, often dropping their flower buds. Temperatures too high or too low, and an inadequate or excess supply of water may bring about flower drop. Mealy bugs and red spiders can be serious pests. Frequent syringings are helpful in controlling them, as is periodic spraying with an insecticide and miticide.

Hoya (Asclepiadaceae)

Hoya, a genus of over 50 species of Asian or Australian origin, includes plants which are mostly climbers of a succulent nature. Two species, *Hoya carnosa* and *H. bella*, are the most frequently grown. *Hoya carnosa* bears succulent dark green leaves and tight, round clusters of fragrant, perfectly formed star-shaped flowers that appear to be made of pink and white wax; hence the name wax plant. The flowers develop from cone-like spurs present on the previous year's stems. The vine may be trained to the wall of the greenhouse or to stakes or a trellis. *Hoya bella,* the miniature wax plant, bears small, pointed, thick green leaves on arching stems and pink and white flowers. There are many other species, some with peculiar and interesting foliage, and collecting them can be a fascinating specialty. Hoyas are easily propagated from stem cuttings. When established, feed biweekly. They thrive with full sun except during the bright months of the year when they should be given some shade.

Hydrangea (Saxifragaceae)

Hydrangea macrophylla, a native of China and Japan, can be forced for early- or late-spring flowering. Certain varieties bear blue flowers; others have white, pink, or red blooms. Merveille and Strafford are good dark pink varieties; Rosabelle, Kunert, Gertrude Glahn, and Helen Merritt are pink. Regula and Engels White are good whites. The flower color of pink varieties can be changed to blue by adding aluminum sulfate to the soil.

Hydrangea plants may be purchased in the fall. Pot them, using a soil consisting of two parts loam, one of leaf mold, and one of peat, plus a 4-inch pot of superphosphate per bushel of soil. After the plants are potted keep them in a cold frame until early November, when they should be placed in storage until late December. A dark place where the temperature is 40 to 45 degrees is ideal for storage. Perhaps you have a basement room at such a temperature or a frame which can be covered with boards, heavy cloth, or straw mats to exclude light. The temperature in the frame should never drop below 20 degrees; if it does the plants will be killed. The plants will do reasonably well if stored under the bench in a cool greenhouse, but the other storage methods are preferred. During the storage period clean up the leaves as they fall and never let the pots become dry. You can bring them into the greenhouse from late December on. Bringing them in at intervals gives a sequence of flowers. Plants brought in the last week of December should flower at Easter, those brought in during mid-January on Mother's Day. When the plants are in bloom, provide shade from strong sun.

Until growth begins, the greenhouse temperature should be 50 to 55 degrees. Then grow the plants at 60 degrees. Frequent syringing produces longer stems and better-quality flowers. When the pots are filled with roots an occasional application of fertilizer is beneficial. If the soil has good reserves of phosphorus and potassium, you need only fertilize with iron and nitrogen, both of which will produce a rich green color of the foliage. One ounce of ammonium sulfate dissolved in 2 gallons of water and applied at intervals will give the plants ample nitrogen. For iron, use a solution made by adding 1 ounce of iron sulfate to 2 gallons of water, or an iron chelate solution following manufacturer's directions.

To obtain blue hydrangeas, add aluminum sulfate to the soil after the plants are growing actively and have good root action. Add a teaspoon of aluminum sulfate to each 6-inch pot and then water it into the soil. Repeat in about two weeks. Three to seven applications are necessary to give blue flowers. All pink and rose-colored varieties will bear blue flowers if given aluminum sulfate. Of course, white-flowered ones cannot be changed, because they produce no pigment, and therefore do not contain the chemical basis for color.

When the plants are through flowering, cut the flowering shoots back to two joints and repot. When danger of frost is over the plants can be moved outdoors. The pots may be plunged in sand or soil in a cold frame equipped with lath shading. Partial shade promotes vigorous growth. The plants should be well supplied with water and fertilized every two weeks, using ammonium sulfate and 4–12–4 fertilizer, alternately. Biweekly applications of iron sulfate or iron chelate may be needed to prevent yellowing. The plants can be pinched early in the summer, but not after July 10. Remove the lath shading on August 1 and thereafter grow the plants with full sun, which promotes the setting of the flower buds which will open the following spring. In September the plants may be repotted if necessary and transferred to a cold frame where the temperature does not drop below 20 degrees. In November place them in a cool, dark storage place. Bring them into the greenhouse at intervals, beginning in late December.

Hydrangeas are easily propagated from stem cuttings or by leaf-bud cuttings, rooted in sand or in a mixture of two parts sand to one of peat. Cuttings are made in February or March, using the blind wood (that which will not produce flowers) of older plants.

Rooted cuttings are potted in 3-inch pots, then into 5- or 6-inch ones in May. The plants are grown with a temperature of 60 degrees. They should be pinched in May. The young plants are placed in a frame during summer and the same cultural conditions are followed as for older plants; that is, remove shade in August, place in cold frame in September and in storage in November. Plants started in February will flower in spring of the following year. Rooted cuttings are sold by some supply companies for spring delivery and are inexpensive.

Red spiders, thrips, and aphids are pests that attack hydrangeas.

Impatiens (Balsaminaceae)

Few plants are more bountiful in flowering than impatiens, also called Sultana. The varieties now available have been derived from *Impatiens holstii*, native to tropical East Africa, and *Impatiens sultanii* from Zanzibar. Tall varieties (20 inches high), dwarf va-

Fig. 12–4. A cutting of impatiens which is ready to be planted in moist sand.

rieties (about 12 inches tall), and elfin varieties (8 to 10 inches high) are available. The plants are always in flower. The bright red, pink, white, or orange iridescent flowers contrast beautifully with the glossy deep green leaves. Impatiens grows well with light shade and can be started from seeds or from cuttings. For blooming plants in November to December sow seeds August 1. Space the seeds and do not cover them. Transplant the seedlings into 2¼-inch Jiffy-Pots from which they can be moved into 4-inch pots. They thrive quite well in a mixture of half loam and half peat moss.

Kalanchoë (Crassulaceae)

This is a large genus of succulent plants. We will consider some species of kalanchoë in a later chapter on cacti and succulents. Of the many species of kalanchoë, one, *K. blossfeldiana,* from Madagascar, is an attractive flowering plant. It bears many small crimson flowers that last a long time.

The plants may be propagated from leaf or stem cuttings taken in January, but the choicest plants are raised from seed. Sow seeds in the spring for flowering the following winter and spring. Move the seedlings into 2½-inch pots. When the young plants are ready for shifting move three of them into a 6-inch azalea pot, or pot them singly in 4-inch pots. A soil consisting of two parts of sandy loam and one of peat moss or leaf mold is suitable. Kalanchoës grow rapidly at a temperature of 60 degrees, but slowly at 50 degrees. They benefit from occasional feedings.

The normal flowering time is spring. However, you can have them in flower from October on by artificially shortening the days. Plants placed in a chamber made of black cloth from 5 P.M to 7 A.M. each day from July 20 until September 20 will flower in October; those shaded in like manner from August 15 to October 1 will flower in December. *Kalanchoë blossfeldiana* is extremely sensitive to any amount of light during the long night. An interruption of just one minute will prevent flowering.

Kalanchoës are perennial, but two-year-old plants are not as attractive as those one year old. Mealy bugs and red spiders are the most serious pests.

Maranta (Marantaceae)

Maranta, a member of the arrowroot family, is a tropical American genus of about 23 species whose leaves are so strikingly marked they appear to be painted. Two frequently grown ones are *Maranta arundinacea variegata*, that grows natively from Mexico to South America, and *M. leuconeura*, from the jungles of Brazil. The former, a source of arrowroot starch, grows about a foot tall and has beautiful oblong green leaves variegated with yellow. The leaves of *M. leuconeura* are grayish-green, velvety, with large decorative purple spots between prominent veins; they are broadly elliptical and about 6 inches long. When evening comes the leaves fold upward as if in prayer; hence the common name "Prayer Plant." Other species sometimes grown are *M. splendida* and *M. bicolor*. Another genus, *Calathea* has members very much like the marantas and equally beautiful.

Marantas require shade during the entire year and plenty of water during their growing period. During winter the plants should be kept somewhat on the dry side. A soil made up of peat and loam in equal parts with some leaf mold and sand suits them. The pots should be well drained. Marantas are increased by dividing the crowns in the spring just before growth begins. They are also increased by tubers. If you remove a plant from a pot and shake out the soil you will see tubers bearing buds. The tuber may be cut into sections each with a bud. Plant the sections and soon new plants will develop.

Mimosa (Leguminosae)

Mimosa pudica, from Brazil, is an intriguing conversation piece. The slightest touch or tap on the plant causes the leaflets to close together in pairs and the leaf to droop, from which it gets its name "sensitive plant." The plant is attractive as well, with fern-like leaves and fluffy balls of purplish flowers in summer. If seeds are sown in January the plants will be well developed by summer. Although the sensitive plant is perennial, many growers prefer to raise new plants annually.

Nepenthes *(Nepenthaceae)*

These tropical Pitcher Plants are climbers. The midribs of the leathery leaves are prolonged to form climbing tendrils which bear pitchers at their tips. The rims of the pitchers are thickened and are sheltered by a lid. Insects are lured into the pitchers by nectar secreted by glands on the outer and inner surfaces. As the insects reach the neck of the pitcher they lose their footing on the slippery surface and fall into the pool of fluid in the bottom. Here they drown and are then digested by enzymes produced by the plant. The resulting substances are utilized to make up for minerals lacking in the plant's environment. These carnivorous plants are intriguing and the pitchers are beautifully formed and colored. A number of species and many hybrids are available.

Nepenthes gracilis, from Malaya and Borneo, is a slender climber with flask-shaped pitchers that are pale green with purple spots. *Nepenthes papuana* is an epiphyte that thrives in the rain forests of New Guinea; the slender yellowish green pitchers are decorated with a blood-red mouth and lid. Among the other interesting species are *N. ampullaria, N. maxima, N. mirabilis, N. rafflesiana, N. sanguinea,* and *N. ventricosa.*

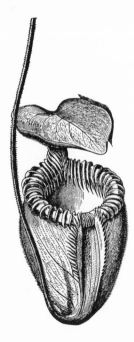

Fig. 12–5. Nepenthes, a carnivorous plant. (Kerner)

They may be potted in medium-grade chopped fir bark, or in a mixture of 2 parts bark and 1 of peat moss, or in osmunda fiber. Some growers have had success with sphagnum moss. The plants should be fertilized periodically with a dilute liquid fertilizer. The plants require shade and thrive with a high humidity. The pitcher plants described in the previous chapter may also appeal to you, those unrelated to Nepenthes and which grow in our own country instead of the jungles of the tropics.

Peperomia (Piperaceae)

Peperomia, a member of the pepper family, is an enormous genus of tropical plants grown for their beautiful foliage. Of the 500 species, two are very popular, *Peperomia sandersii* variety *argyreia* and *P. obtusifolia*. Peperomias thrive in a warm greenhouse with a minimum night temperature of 60 degrees, and with shade during the bright months. During their active growing season, which usually begins in February, they require a good supply of water, but during their inactive period be careful neither to overwater nor to let them get completely dry. The plants can be quickly increased by leaf cuttings rooted in sand with a bottom temperature of about 75 degrees.

Peperomia sandersii var. *argyreia*, from Brazil, commonly called Watermelon Begonia, is one of the most beautiful. This is a stemless plant with heart-shaped, fleshy leaves, and red petioles about 4 to 8 inches long. The leaves have attractive silver bands alternating with green stripes. *P. obtusifolia*, from Venezuela, bears thick green leaves on erect or semitrailing stems. A variegated variety of this has cream-colored markings on the foliage.

Pilea (Urticaceae)

An attractive member of this genus is *Pilea cadierei*, the "aluminum" plant, whose home is Vietnam. It is dainty and graceful, and adds a striking note to a group of foliage plants. The oval variegated leaves have the appearance of being quilted and brushed with strokes of aluminum paint. They must be kept carefully watered and not be allowed to become dry. A half-shaded location suits them nicely. The aluminum plant is easily increased from stem cuttings.

Fig. 12–6. Bird-of-paradise, *Strelitzia,* produces beautiful, distinctive flowers.

Sansevieria (Liliaceae)

These are bold plants of the lily family which have stiff marbled leaves. The plants are grown chiefly for their distinctive forms and attractive leaves. They produce conspicuous, slender-tubed flowers of white or greenish-white color, sometimes tinted with purple or pink. The flowers are fragrant, short-lived, and generally open in the evening. The genus is a tropical one containing more than fifty described varieties. Many species grow in tropical Africa, and others in India, Burma, and Ceylon. Some species are cultivated for their valuable fibers.

Sansevierias, commonly called Bowstring Hemp, Snake Plant, Leopard Lily, or Mother-in-Law's Tongue, grow well in an even mixture of loam, sand, and peat moss or leaf mold. They can survive prolonged periods of drought but make better growth when watered regularly. During the brighter months of the year they should be shaded. Sansevierias are propagated by seed, rootstock divisions, or leaf cuttings. To increase a plant by leaf cuttings, cut a leaf into pieces 3 inches long and insert about half the length into sand. In a month or two, one or more young rooted plants will form at the base of, each piece. The plant, plus the old leaf segment, may be potted, or the new plant may be severed from the parent piece and potted.

Among the choice species of *Sansevieria* are *S. trifasciata* (usually sold as *S. zeylanica*), *S. ehrenbergii*, *S. aethiopica*, *S. arborescens*, and *S. hahnii*. *Sansevieria trifasciata* is a stemless plant bearing two to six erect, leathery leaves 3 to 4 feet long. The leaves have alternate bandings of silver and dark olive green. *S. ehrenbergii* produces a short stem which is completely hidden by the clasping leaves. The five to nine bluish-green leaves, with conspicuous white edges, spread out in a fanwise manner. *S. aethiopica* is a stemless plant with pointed bluish-green leaves about 18 inches long and 1 inch wide. *Sansevieria arborescens* has a stem that gets to be 4 feet high which is covered with spreading, twisting, grass-green leaves. The leaves vary from 5 to 18 inches in length, and they are thick with a wavy white margin. *Sansevieria hahnii* has comparatively short leaves arranged in a rosette.

Shrimp Plant (Acanthaceae)

Because the long-lasting reddish-brown flower bracts highly resemble a shrimp, *Beloperone guttata* is known as the shrimp plant. The small protruding white flowers, spotted purple, contribute to the similarity. The plant is an evergreen shrub from Mexico that grows to a height of 2 to 3 feet and blooms almost continuously. The shrimp plant is propagated from cuttings made in the spring. The rooted cuttings are moved into 3-inch pots, and when established they should be pinched to promote branching. Later they are moved into 5-inch pots in which containers they will flower. They thrive with good light and a humid atmosphere.

Strelitzia (Musaceae)

Strelitzia, the bird-of-paradise, is in the banana family. It is a native of South Africa and is a good companion plant for orchids, begonias, African violets, and gloxinias. All of these plants grow well in a shaded 60-degree house.

Strelitzia is well worth growing. The foliage is attractive and the orange and blue flowers, reminiscent of tropical birds, are most exotic and striking. The flowering season is winter and spring.

The plants become very large, about 5 feet tall, so unless you have a big greenhouse limit yourself to one or a few. You can purchase young plants from nurserymen or start them from seeds, planted singly in small pots plunged in peat. Those started from seed will flower in four or five years. As the plants grow repot them as necessary. By the time flowering size is reached the plants should be in 8- or 10-inch pots, and eventually require large tubs to accommodate their carrot-thick roots.

Provide good drainage and use a mixture of half loam, one-fourth well decayed manure, and one-fourth peat. Periodic waterings with fertilizer are beneficial. The plants should be kept well watered. If grown in too small pots and with insufficient water they become stunted and flower sparsely or not at all.

Ti Plant (Liliaceae)

Cordyline terminalis, the ti plant, a native of India, Malaysia, and Polynesia, is cultivated outdoors in tropical countries and in greenhouses for its ornamental spear-shaped leaves which have shades of red running through the olive green background. The satiny leaves are about 1 foot long and 2 to 4 inches wide, wonderful for arrangements and decorative uses. The height of a ti plant may vary from 2 feet to 8 feet. If you desire a dwarf plant keep it in a small pot, whereas if you want a tree-like one for a tropical touch transplant it to a larger container every spring until it attains the desired height. They are easily propagated from "logs" which are sections of the stem that have been stripped of leaves. The "log" is placed horizontally on moist sphagnum moss and then covered halfway with damp moss. Soon shoots appear. After they have grown several inches remove them with a bit of the bark and then place the basal end in the moss to promote rooting. When well rooted move them into 3-inch pots. Ti plants can also be propagated by air layering.

13

Exotic Foliage and
Flowering Plants
of the Arum Family

Many of our fine greenhouse plants are in the Arum family (technically known as Araceae, and familiarly called aroids), which includes such exotic plants as alocasia, anthurium, calla lily, caladium, dieffenbachia, nephthytis, philodendron, and pothos. Many aroids come from the rainforests and cloudforests of Central and South America, a land of trees, climbers, and epiphytes. In these enchanting forests the boughs and trunks of the trees are crowded with epiphytes often in harmonious arrangement and balance. The various tree dwellers (epiphytes) compete with each other for positions where moisture and light are favorable. Too often the collector of aroids and other epiphytes is dismayed when he sees choice plants on the highest branches where they are out of reach. Collecting is additionally difficult and treacherous because of the steep slopes of the canyons where the vegetation remains in its natural state; in many tropical areas the forests have been cleared from the more gentle slopes. Ferns, begonias, bromeliads, gesneriads, and orchids of great variety share the perches with the aroids. However, many aroids are ground dwellers, living a terrestrial life in the fluffy humus of the forest floor, and some live in swamps.

In greenhouses these plants are companionable and grow under similar conditions of high humidity, shade, and a night temperature of 60 to 65 degrees with a 10-degree rise during the day. These temperatures may seem low for tropical plants, but many of the aroids and other epiphytes come from moderate to high elevations where temperatures are temperate or cool. For example, at 3,000 feet in the tropics the average temperature is 75 degrees and at 9,000 feet only 54 degrees. The terrestrial aroids prefer a soil high in humus; a suitable medium consists of one part loam, one part peat moss or leaf mold, and one part of coarse sand, vermiculite, or perlite. Alocasia, anthurium, and other epiphytic aroids thrive when potted in fir bark. Well-established plants should be periodically watered with a dilute fertilizer solution.

For the past century, and today as well, plant explorers have searched the jungles of tropical America for new aroids to enhance the beauty of the greenhouse. And the plant breeders, too, are working to produce ever more beautiful forms. Although a majority of the aroids are confined to the tropics a few are native to the United States, among them sweet flag, jack-in-the-pulpit, and skunk cabbage.

Certain aroids have beautiful foliage while the flowers, although interesting, are without beauty; these we use as foliage plants. Others—anthuriums, for example—have distinctive "flowers" of decorative value. The true flowers of all aroids are minute and inconspicuous. They are crowded on a finger-like spike, technically known as a *spadix*, with the male flowers generally on the upper part, the female on the lower. Below the spadix, there is a leaflike bract, known as a *spathe*. In certain species the spathe is colored and very attractive. The spathe and spadix of certain ones, such as anthuriums and calla lilies, are very decorative. We loosely refer to this attractive arrangement as a flower. Technically, of course, it is not a true flower, since the spathe is a leaf. When seed is desired, pollination is performed by rubbing the male (pollen-producing) flowers of one spadix over the female flowers of another when their pistils are receptive.

Aglaonema

The Chinese evergreen, *Aglaonema simplex* from Java, is the most widely grown species of this genus. It grows to a height of 2 or 3 feet and bears oblong glossy green leaves, about 10 inches long. A more compact species is *A. costatum,* which is about 8 inches tall and has foliage which is heart-shaped, green, and prominently marked with white patches. *A. robelenii* (also known as *Schismatoglottis*) has handsome gray-green leaves, but it is especially noted for its clusters of shiny red berries. *A. marantifolium* is another species with beautiful fruits. The plants are readily propagated by divisions and by cuttings rooted in sand.

Alocasia

The alocasias are gems among the foliage plants, with their beautiful forms and attractively colored leaves. Three species in which you may be interested are *Alocasia cuprea* from Borneo, *A. lowii* from Malaya, and *A. sanderiana,* a native of the Philippines. In addition to these there are many hybrids. Among the best is *A. sedeni,* a hybrid of *lowii* and *cuprea. A. cuprea* has oval, nearly bronze leaves, rich purple below, and deeply indented veins. *A. lowii* is characterized by heart-shaped leaves, which are olive green above, purple below. The silvery bands along the veins add beauty to the leaves. The hybrid, *A. sedeni,* is vigorous with heart-shaped leaves and beautiful vein markings. *A. sanderiana* has deeply indented, arrow-shaped leaves with prominent veins that make a bold pattern against the dark green foliage with its metallic sheen.

The alocasias thrive in a mixture of half peat moss, one-fourth leaf mold, and one-fourth loam or sand. With this compost, occasional feedings with a liquid fertilizer should be given to established plants, especially during the active growing season, which begins in March and extends to early winter. They can also be grown in a mixture of sphagnum moss and small pieces of charcoal or in fir bark, with regular applications of liquid fertilizer. Alocasias like ample moisture, a humid atmosphere, a shaded location, and do best with a night temperature of 65 to 70 degrees. Hence, select a warm spot in the 60-degree house for them.

The plants may be propagated from suckers or cuttings of the rhizome which should be inserted in small pots containing an equal mixture of peat moss and sand. Plunging the pots into a propagating box with bottom heat of 75 degrees is beneficial. Alocasias may also be grown from seed.

Anthurium

In this genus, native of tropical America, there are about six hundred species, many of which are epiphytes. It is a genus that could well appeal to a collector or hybridizer. Some members are noted for their handsome, velvety foliage and others for their attractive flowers. The most conspicuous part is the large, brightly colored patent leather-like modified leaf (spathe) below or around the fingerlike spadix that bears many inconspicuous flowers. The

Fig. 13–1. Right, many attractive foliage plants are in the Aroid family. Here are several varieties of philodendron and anthurium. The benches in the rear contain interesting philodendron seedlings, many of which are quite distinctive. Left, Maranth-leaved Aglaonema (1), *Aglaonema marantifolium,* has decorative bright red fruit. The true flowers (2) are clustered on a white spadix 2 inches long, below which is a greenish-white spathe. (3) shows a female flower magnified almost three times. (Aglaonema, Addisonia and the New York Botanical Garden)

Fig. 13–2. Anthuriums are noted for their attractive flowers and foliage.

spadix with its surrounding spathe is beautiful, and lasts extraordinarily well, up to five weeks after it is cut and three months or so on the plant. A well-grown specimen is continually flowering. The flowers are prized for use in exotic arrangements and for corsages. Anthurium's provide an interesting accent among other collector's plants such as orchids, begonias, and gesneriads.

Anthurium andreanum (Colombia) and *A. scherzerianum* (Costa Rica) are the species generally grown for their flowers. *Anthurium andreanum* has a yellowish-white spadix, and a heart-shaped orange-red spathe, 4 to 6 inches long. The leaves are heart-shaped, green, and about 12 inches long and 6 inches wide.

Anthurium scherzerianum, called the Flamingo Flower, is the most popular species. The spadix is coiled and yellow. The spathe is red, yellow, rose, or white depending on the particular horticultural variety.

Anthurium crystallinum (Colombia, Peru) and *A. veitchii* (Colombia) are grown for their beautiful foliage. Both species have large velvety leaves but rather unattractive flowers. The leaves of *A. crystallinum* are somewhat heart-shaped, 14 inches long, 10 inches wide, green with white stripes above, pale rose-pink below. The spathe of the flower is narrow and green.

Anthurium veitchii is perhaps the best-known foliage plant of the group. The drooping leaves are oblong and very large, about 3 feet long and 10 inches wide, of metallic green color, with showy veins.

The spathe of the flower is about 3 inches long and greenish-white in color.

Other species with beautiful leaves are A. *forgetii* (Colombia), a dwarf plant with velvety olive green leaves and silver veins; A. *bakeri* (Costa Rica), a dwarf plant with leathery, deep green, strap-shaped leaves and a green spathe; and A. *warocqueanum* (Colombia) with long (to 3 feet) velvety green leaves marked with ivory veins and bearing small flowers with a green to yellowish spathe.

All the anthuriums grow well with a night temperature of 60 to 65 degrees and benefit from frequent syringings. They require shade, but during December, January, and February, only a very light shade is needed. A suitable potting mixture consists of equal parts of peat moss, leaf mold, and coarse sand, to which can be added a small quantity of well-rotted manure and charcoal. They can also be grown in osmunda fiber without other ingredients but with a monthly feeding of fertilizer. The newest medium is chopped fir bark, which has been used with great success and is easy to handle. Add crock or gravel to the pot for drainage, hold the plant in position with the roots spread out, and then add bark. Tap the pot to firm the bark. They should be given a dilute fertilizer solution every two weeks.

Plants require repotting every two or three years. This is best done in January. Established plants should be furnished a uniform supply of water. Keep the medium moist but not wet; if it is continually soggy the roots will die.

The roots of anthurium have a tendency to extend above pot level. Therefore, in the interval between potting it is desirable to build up the compost around the stem to catch the roots. A fresh top dressing each year is also beneficial.

If a plant becomes too leggy, you can cut off the top, root it in sand, and give it a fresh start in a new pot. The old stock will send up new shoots which may be removed and potted in small pots or they may be permitted to develop on the plant.

Anthuriums can be increased by dividing the crown and by removing suckers. The suckers are inserted in small pots containing a mixture of peat, chopped sphagnum, and sand, in equal parts. In this medium they root rapidly if the pots are plunged in a propagating bed maintained at a temperature of 75 to 80 degrees, with bottom heat. Anthuriums may also be started from seeds sown on a mixture of peat and sphagnum. After sowing, cover the seeds lightly with chopped sphagnum. Seeds germinate best at a temperature of 80 degrees, at which temperature they germinate in about eight days. About six or seven weeks after sowing, the seedlings will be ready for transplanting into a flat. When they are six to eight months old, they can go into 3-inch pots, from which they can be shifted into larger ones. Well-grown plants will flower when they are three years old.

In their native shaded habitats of tropical America, anthuriums are pollinated by insects which are lacking in our greenhouses. If you wish the plants to set seed you will have to pollinate the flowers by hand. Many minute flowers bearing stamens and many bearing pistils occur along the spadix. You can recognize the stamen-bearing flowers by the powdery pollen which they liberate, and the pistil-bearing flowers by their sticky secretion and spicy fragrance. To perform pollination it is necessary to use two spadixes because on any one spadix the pistils mature before the stamens. Rub a spadix which has the anthers tipped with pollen against a spadix whose pistils are receptive, as evidenced by the minute drops of transparent fluid that the pistils exude. This procedure should be repeated once a day for several days. Two or three weeks after pollination the spadix will turn a dark green and increase in size. It will continue to increase in length and width. The seeds mature in four to nine months, depending upon the variety. When the seeds are ripe the berry which encloses them will change color and become so loose that it is easily removed. Remove the seeds from the berry and plant them right away. The seeds lose their viability in a relatively short time.

Caladium

There are about sixty species in this genus, mostly native to South America. The most important parent of our dozens of horticultural varieties is *Caladium bicolor*, a species that grows on hard-baked clay in the Amazon basin. The fancy-leaved caladiums are beautiful foliage plants with arrow-shaped leaves that are richly colored in shades of green, red, pink, and white in a great variety of patterns. They are at their peak of beauty during the summer.

Rhizomes may be purchased for delivery from January on. Plant the rhizomes from January through spring in 3- or 4-inch pots. Pot them so that the rhizome is about an inch below the surface of the soil. Or, if you prefer, start the rhizomes in a flat of sphagnum moss, and then, after the roots have developed, move them into pots. Caladiums thrive when potted in soil composed of equal parts of loam, peat, and sand. When the plants in 4-inch pots have made sufficient growth, shift them into 6-inch ones, a size which will carry the plants through the season. During the rooting period, they should be watered sparingly, but once they are established the soil should be kept moist. Caladiums need shade, high humidity, and a night temperature of 65 degrees. They benefit from periodic applications of a liquid fertilizer.

The leaves generally begin to dry up in October. At this time gradually decrease the waterings. In about one month's time the leaves will be completely dried and the plants ready for storage. The pots are kept dry at 60 degrees. Instead of storing the rhizomes in pots, you can remove them from the pots, shake them free of soil, cut off the dried leaves, and store them in sand at a temperature of 60 degrees. Caladiums can be increased by dividing the rhizome, and from seeds. The seeds germinate readily and the seedlings are easy to grow. The first five or six leaves of a seedling are generally green; the later ones are colored.

There are many named varieties of caladiums, among them Candidum, which has white leaves and green veins; John Peel and Crimson Wave, both with red leaves; Avalon Pink and Pink Cloud, with pink leaves; and Mrs. Arno Nehrling, Vivian Lee, and Fascination, all with varicolored leaves.

Calla Lily

From South Africa, a region of great plateaus and steep slopes, come the white calla (*Zantedeschia aethiopica*), the yellow calla (*Zantedeschia elliotiana*), and the pink calla (*Zantedeschia rehmannii*). They are favorite greenhouse plants, each producing about six long-lasting flowers during the season. Callas grow well with a night temperature of 60 to 65 degrees when potted in a mixture of half loam and half peat moss. Pot the tubers so that there is an inch or two of soil above them. Until growth begins, water sparingly; then ample water should be given until the rest period begins. During their period of active growth, callas benefit from biweekly applications of fertilizer or a solution of ammonium sulfate.

Tubers of the white calla are planted in August or September. The plants should be watered sparingly until growth begins, then copious waterings are called for until June, when watering should be stopped. The pots should then be stored in a dry place. In August the tubers are repotted and started into growth.

In contrast to the white calla, which flowers during the winter, the pink and yellow callas flower in the summer. They should be potted from January to April. When flowering is through withhold water and keep dry until time to repot again at the beginning of the year.

Fig. 13–3. Upper, the beautifully colored arrowhead leaves of caladiums make an attractive display. Lower left, *Dieffenbachia picta*, spotted dumb cane. Lower right, *Nephthytis*.

Dieffenbachia

Dieffenbachia picta is known as Dumb Cane because it contains an irritant that causes the tongue and mouth to swell when it is chewed. In the warm, humid Amazon basin it grows in well-drained red clay in company with slender palms, climbing ferns, selaginellas, vicious insects, and snakes. The stem of the Dumb Cane is somewhat succulent and bears at its top a cluster of large glossy grass-green oval leaves that are variously mottled or striped with white, yellow, or greenish brown. Other dieffenbachias that are cultivated include *Dieffenbachia bowmannii* (Colombia), *D. sequina* (Puerto Rico, West Indies), and *D. velutina* (Colombia).

The plants thrive at a temperature of 60 to 65 degrees and are potted in a mixture of equal parts loam, peat moss, and sand. If a plant becomes too leggy, you can cut off the top, retaining a considerable piece of the stem, and root it in moist sand. Thick roots will develop in about two weeks and the new plant may be potted. Or you can air-layer it by cutting half way through the stem, slanting upward. Insert a toothpick to hold the incision open slightly and then wrap the area with moist sphagnum moss held in place by polyethylene film fastened with string or Twist-Ems. In about a month the moss ball will be filled with roots. Cut the stem below the new roots and pot the new plant. You can save the old plant, or the stem may be cut into pieces about 2 inches long, each with one or more eyes. Plant the segments horizontally in a mixture of sand and peat. Each will develop roots and a shoot. Pot the cutting with its shoot in a 5-inch pot.

Hydrosme

Hydrosme rivieri, the Devil's Tongue, comes from Indochina and is a true curiosity of the plant world. In the spring, when no foliage is present and without an external supply of water, the large tuber will develop a monstrous flower spike 3 to 6 feet tall, topped by a huge calla-like green and purple spathe that surrounds a large reddish spadix. It emits an extremely foetid odor that attracts insects but is offensive to us. The flower stalk then dies down. After flowering, and even during it if you prefer, water the plant to encourage vegetative growth. When growth is completed the plant resembles a small tree with a naked rose-marbled stalk terminated with three or more spreading branches bearing many leaves. The plant grows well in a mixture of loam and peat moss. Cease watering in October. The top growth will then die. After the stem has dried remove it, thus revealing the start of the next season's flower stalk. The stalk will begin to grow in March.

Nephthytis

There are about a half dozen species in this genus, but only one, *Nephthytis afzelii*, is frequently cultivated. This species has arrow-shaped leaves borne on a slender creeping stem. The plants prefer shade and a warm moist atmosphere. They grow well when potted in a mixture of equal parts of sand, loam, and leaf mold with the addition of some rotted manure and bone meal.

Philodendron

The philodendrons are often grown in greenhouses for their ornamental foliage, and they are in demand as foliage plants for the

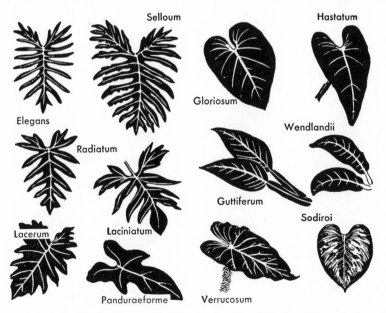

Fig. 13–4. Philodendrons. (Ladislaus Cutak and the Missouri Botanical Garden)

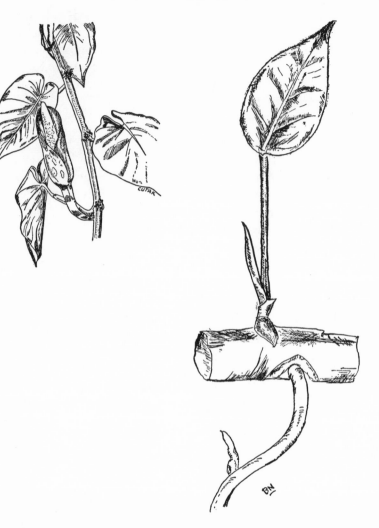

Fig. 13–5. Left, *Philodendron cordatum* in flower. (Ladislaus Cutak and the Missouri Botanical Garden). Right, stem cutting of *Philodendron pertusum*.

home. Their beautiful leaves and ability to thrive in the home make them deservedly popular. The genus includes about 250 species, but only a few are commonly grown and readily available. With the increased interest in this genus in recent years new varieties have been introduced and others have been developed by hybridization.

If you have known philodendrons only as house plants, you will be surprised at their greater size when grown in ample rich soil in a greenhouse. For example, *Philodendron cordatum* (more correctly *Philodendron oxycardium*) has leaves about 3 inches long when grown in a a 4-inch pot in the house. If it is planted in a bench of rich soil in the greenhouse, the leaves may be 16 inches long and the plant may attain a height of 20 feet or more if given support.

Most species are climbers, but a few are self-heading plants. In their homes in tropical America the climbers use trees for support. The name *Philodendron* comes from the Greek words meaning *tree-loving*. The nonclimbers generally grow mounted on trees as epiphytes. However, there are some nonclimbers that grow on the ground.

Among the climbing types are such favorite species as *Philodendron cordatum, P. dubium, P. hastatum, P. panduraeforme, P. sodiroi*, and *P. pertusum. Philodendron pertusum*, more correctly *Monstera deliciosa*, is a *cut leaf* species, with large leaves looking as if portions of the leaves had been cut out. *P. sodiroi* has beautiful silvery leaves with darker green areas. *Philodendron panduraeforme* has green fiddle-shaped leaves; *P. hastatum*, dark green arrow-shaped leaves; *P. dubium*, green, deeply lobed leaves; and *P. cordatum* bright-green heart-shaped foliage. All of the climbing species require support. Totem poles made of fern fiber, or of wire frames stuffed and covered with sphagnum, are ideal for this purpose. Roots are produced along the stems of the climbing species; these attach themselves to or can be trained onto the totem pole. More artistic supports can be devised according to your own ingenuity. An unusual piece of driftwood can be used, plain or with sphagnum moss tucked into hollow places.

The rosette or nonclimbing species (also called self-heading philodendrons) do not require a pole. Some of the rosette types, such as *P. speciosa* and *P. eichleri*, are too large for the small greenhouse, but *P. wendlandii* and *P. undulatum* keep within bounds. *P. wendlandii* is a nice compact plant with oblong leaves about 2 feet long. *P. undulatum* has heart-shaped leaves which form a wavy cup.

Both the climbing and rosette types prefer acid soil, occasional feedings, ample water, high humidity, shade, and a temperature between 60 and 65 degrees. A suitable compost for philodendrons consists of equal parts of sand, loam, and leaf mold. Good drainage should be provided so that the plants may be watered freely without danger of waterlogging the soil.

Fig. 13–6. *Spathiphyllum candidum* in flower. Notice the white spathe, which is a modified leaf, and the spadix, which bears many flowers.

The climbing types are readily propagated from stem cuttings planted in sand or in a mixture of sand and peat. They root quickly when the bottom temperature is 70 to 75 degrees. If your plants become too tall, cut off the top part of the stem and lay it on a mixture of moist sand and peat, or cut the stem into segments, each with at least one joint, and lay these on sand. Then cover the stem or segments with moist peat. In a short time a new shoot with roots will appear at each joint. Remove the stem and cut it so that each piece has a young plant. Pot each piece. Of course all species may be started from seed. Seeds germinate well when planted on sphagnum moss. Move the seedlings from the seed pans into 2½-inch pots. The seedlings grow well in peat moss, provided they are given liquid fertilizer every two weeks.

Scindapsus

Scindapsus aureus, the Devil's Ivy, comes from the Solomon Islands, and in the trade is sometimes called Pothos. The heart-shaped leaves resemble those of *Philodendron cordatum* but are much thicker; they have a dark green background flecked with yellow. The Devil's Ivy requires the same general treatment as the climbing philodendrons.

Spathiphyllum

The spathiphyllums, like certain anthuriums, have exotic long-lasting flowers as well as handsome leaves and beautiful red berries. Spathiphyllums can be grown in osmunda fiber, bark, or in a mixture of half loam and half leaf mold. The plants grow well with moderate shade, an even supply of moisture, and a humid atmosphere.

Spathiphyllum wallisii, from Colombia and Venezuela, has shiny, dark green leaves, 5 to 6 inches long and 1 to 1½ inches wide, with pointed tips. The spathes, formed from spring to autumn, are white and form the conspicuous parts of the flower heads. *Spathiphyllum cannaefolium* (Venezuela, British Guiana) bears dark green, leathery, corrugated leaves and a spathe which is green on the outside and white inside. *Spathiphyllum candidum* may be a large form of *S. floribundum* (Colombia); the leaves are satiny green, oblong and pointed and the spathe is white.

14

Begonias

The great variety of remarkably beautiful plants in the genus *Begonia* makes it a fascinating one for collectors. Many persons enjoy this diversified group of plants and have formed societies to further their interests. There are more than 40 branches of the American Begonia Society with several thousand members.

The genus *Begonia* is the only one of horticultural value in the family Begoniaceae. The other genera in the family, *Symbegonia*, *Begoniella*, and *Hillebrandia*, have not found favor as greenhouse plants. Some begonias are raised primarily for their exotic foliage, others because they bear myriads of beautifully colored small flowers, different ones because they produce large, elegantly formed blooms. There are over 1200 species in the genus *Begonia* and thousands of varieties which have been developed by hybridizers.

Begonias vary in size from miniatures, 2 inches high, to tall forms, 6 feet in height or more, and in growth habit from herbs to vines to shrubs to tree-like forms. They also vary in their habitats. In our travels in Central and South America we have collected begonias from rich humusy soil, from cliffs, and from branches and trunks of trees where they were growing as epiphytes in the accumulation of humus. All begonias share certain features. They have separate male and female flowers on the same plant. The female flowers have a three-winged ovary on top of which the petals are borne.

The collection of begonias from the wilds has had a long history and from the first they have been much admired. The first species were discovered in Santo Domingo by Charles Plumier, who named

Fig. 14–1. A begonia growing epiphytically among lichens, mosses, and ferns in the Andes Mountains of Peru.

them after his patron Michel Begon. Since then collectors have been continually exploring the tropics for new species. *Begonia rex* with its brilliantly colored and tapestry-textured foliage was discovered in Assam in 1856. The first tuberous begonias, which led to the development of the magnificent ones of today, were found in the Andes in the 1860's. From Africa came the maple-leaf begonias; from Brazil, the original *Begonia semperflorens;* and from Mexico, the first rhizomatous species.

Although in nature some begonias, *Begonia semperflorens* for example, grow in full sun, most grow in shaded locations. Hence, in greenhouses most begonias should be shaded except during the dull months of winter. Those that have come from the warm tropics grow best with a night temperature of 60 degrees with a 10-degree rise during the day. The humusy soil of their natural habitats may be imitated with various soil mixtures. A general one, which may be modified for certain varieties, consists of one part loam, one part leaf mold or peat moss, and one part of coarse sand, vermiculite, or perlite. If well-rotted cow manure is available you may prefer a mixture of two parts loam, one part leaf mold or peat moss, one part well-rotted manure, and one part sand. Many begonia fanciers prefer a soilless mix consisting of one part peat moss, two parts chopped sphagnum moss, and one part perlite; for each bushel add a handful of wood ashes and a 3-inch pot of bonemeal. Newly potted plants will not require feeding for a few weeks. Thereafter they should be fertilized every three weeks with an organic fertilizer such as fish emulsion or an inorganic one used half strength.

Most begonias can be grown from seed and many from leaf cuttings and stem cuttings. The seeds are minute, about 2 million per ounce, and, hence, they must be left uncovered on the surface of the soil. The soil may be a mixture of sand and peat moss or just leaf mold. For the latter prepare the usual seed bed by adding drainage to a seed pan or flat and covering this with a 1-inch layer of well-decayed, moist leaf mold. Then add a thin layer of finely screened moist leaf mold, level it, but do not press it down. The surface of either medium must be spongy so that when the seeds germinate the roots can easily penetrate it. Place the pans in shallow water to subirrigate them. When the surface is moist, sow the seeds thinly. Seeds may be sown directly or they may be mixed with fine sand in a salt shaker from which they are distributed over the surface of the soil. Cover the pan with a pane of glass and keep it in a shaded place at a night temperature of 65 to 70 degrees. Light is necessary for seed germination, which occurs in two or three weeks. During germination keep the surface of the soil moist. Even a slight drying of the surface is fatal to young plants. If you keep the surface overly wet, however, damping-off may be troublesome. Seeds of a few begonias, *Begonia evansiana* for example, will not germinate when the days are only nine hours long, but they will germinate promptly when days are twelve or more hours long.

Begonia specialists often group the kinds into three main categories: tuberous begonias, having tubers; rhizomatous, with a creeping rhizome; and fibrous rooted. For our purpose we will consider them as tuberous, winter-blooming, foliage, fibrous rooted, and miscellaneous.

Tuberous Begonias

The perfect form, large size, and crispness of the flowers of tuberous begonias have a compelling beauty. The flowers vary in size from 3 inches to 8 inches in diameter. Some varieties bear single flowers, but more popular are those with double flowers, some of which resemble the rose, the carnation, or the camellia. The flowers come in many colors, apricot, scarlet, pink, white, rose, and yellow.

Fig. 14–2. The exquisite shape of tuberous begonias makes them ever appealing.

Two kinds of flowers, male and female, are produced on each plant, the male or staminate flower being flanked by two less attractive female or pistillate ones. The male flowers are large and showy, and in double varieties most of the stamens have been transformed into petals. However, in those formed in the latter part of the season many petals revert to stamens, bearing pollen. It is then that you can collect pollen from the male flowers and transfer it to stigmas of female flowers to produce seed. To obtain the choicest and largest blooms some growers remove the buds of the female flowers, thus diverting more food to the male blossom which encourages it to grow to a larger size.

You may wish to start some tuberous begonias in your greenhouse for bedding outdoors. Others you will wish to raise as pot plants for flowers in the greenhouse from June through October. Tuberous begonias will flower in the winter if they are grown with more than fourteen hours of light each day. Days are easily prolonged by turning on electric lights at sundown and letting them stay lighted until about 10 P.M.

Fig. 14–3. Some varieties of tuberous begonias thrive in hanging baskets. (Vetterle and Reinelt)

Cut flowers last five to six days when floated on water. When cutting them take only half the stem. The remaining half will dry up and then fall off, leaving no open wound for the entrance of fungi.

In addition to upright forms of tuberous begonias, there are beautiful pendant ones that are profusely floriferous. These should be raised in hanging containers or in pots which stand on pedestals. Some of the pendulous varieties have stems 4 or 5 feet long and one plant may produce as many as 400 flowers.

Tuberous begonias are readily started from tubers, usually planted from January to March. Do not plant the tubers until pink growth buds appear on the upper concave surface. The appearance of the buds indicates that the rest period of the tuber is over. If they are planted and watered for a considerable time before growth is active, they may rot. Tubers which have been stored at 40 or 50 degrees during the fall months may be moved to a warm dark place to encourage sprouting. When the sprouts are evident, plant the tubers with a spacing of about 2 inches in a shallow pot or flat containing a mixture of leaf mold and sand. If you do not have any leaf mold

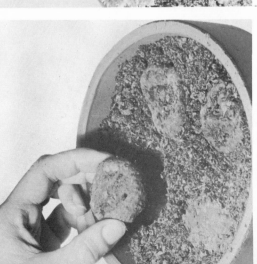

Fig. 14–4. Growing tuberous begonias from tubers. Plant the tubers in a shallow pot (upper left) or flat containing a mixture of leaf mold and sand, or in peat. When the shoots are well developed (upper right), remove the plants (lower left) and pot them (lower right).

Fig. 14-5. Stages in the growth of tuberous begonias from seed. Sow the seed on loose soil. Upper left, the seedlings here are magnified from their actual height of one-fourth inch. They are ready to be moved from the seed pan to a flat or community pot. Upper right, well developed seedlings in a community pot. Lower left, moving seedlings from community to 2½ inch pot. Lower right, when they have made good growth, shift them on into 4- or 5-inch ones.

you can start them in peat, which is not so desirable as leaf mold. They should be completely covered, leaving only the tips of the sprouts showing, and then watered. Keep the growing medium moist, not wet, and maintain them at a temperature of 60 to 65 degrees at night with a 10-degree rise during the day. When the shoots are well developed and the root system is extensive, about four or five weeks after planting, move them into 5-, 6-, or 8-inch pots, depending on their size. Pot moderately firmly, not hard. After potting, water well; then wait until the soil shows dryness before watering again. Throughout the growing season, avoid over-watering, which may bring about a rotting of the tuber.

Upright varieties of tuberous begonias are best grown with one main stem. If more than one shoot develops from a tuber remove the weaker ones and permit the strongest one to remain.

Hanging varieties (pendant types) are best grown with several shoots from each tuber. For best results one should use large tubers, as they will have more shoots than smaller ones. If only one or two shoots develop, pinch off the top of the stem when flower buds begin to form. Pendant types should be grown in large containers, 8 inches in diameter for small tubers, 10 inches for large ones. Azalea pots are ideal. Wire baskets lined with sphagnum moss and then filled with soil can be used, but the plants will not grow to the same degree of perfection as those raised in pots. Pots can be hung or set in hanging baskets for the same effect.

Tuberous begonias do not thrive in full sun. When the days become bright in the spring it will be necessary to shade the greenhouse. They do well in a greenhouse with a light intensity of about 2000 foot candles, which is about one-fifth full sunlight. Too heavy shade produces abundant leggy growth but few flowers; too much light results in dwarf plants with thick, shiny, curled leaves and burned flowers. You should seek the happy medium, neither too little light, nor too much. When actively growing, tuberous begonias benefit from monthly feedings of liquid fertilizer, either fish emulsion or commercial fertilizer. Staking is usually necessary. When danger of frost is over you may wish to move some of your plants to shaded parts of the garden. The plants may be knocked out of their pots and planted in humus soil about 1 foot apart, or the pots may be plunged in the garden. If the days are not extremely hot during summer in your locality, they will flower nicely in the greenhouse. On the other hand, if the summers are hot, the plants will do better in a lath house or in the garden than in a greenhouse.

Plants started from tubers will generally begin to flower in June. When the first crop of blossoms is over, a second may be obtained by resting the plant for three weeks. Keep the soil on the dry side during this period. When new shoots appear near the base of the stems, cut the old stem back. Permit two or three of the strongest shoots to remain and remove the rest. Then give the plant fertilizer. During autumn, when the second flowering is over and the foliage shows signs of dying, withhold water gradually, but not by any means suddenly, to induce dormancy. When the stem has dried, remove it. The tubers which have been growing in pots should then be stored in the pots at a temperature of 40 to 50 degrees. Those planted in soil in the garden may be dug after the first light frost. Remove the stem when it can be pulled off easily and shake the soil from the roots. Then store the tubers in dry peat or sand at a temperature of 40 to 50 degrees.

Tuberous begonias start readily from stem cuttings. If you wish to increase a favorite variety, make stem cuttings of it. Sometimes several shoots grow from one tuber of an erect variety. The erect varieties are best grown with just one shoot. Hence, when the extra ones are sufficiently large they can be cut off next to the tuber and used for cuttings. Pot the cuttings in a mixture of sand and peat and then plunge the pots to their rims in peat contained in a box or propagating frame. Cover with glass and, if possible, use bottom heat of about 70 degrees. With this technique, the cuttings will root rapidly and flower the first summer.

Tuberous begonias may be grown from seed. Plants grown from seed sown in January, or better in February, will flower during the summer and fall, generally later than those started from tubers. The seedlings will yield fine tubers by November. The next season's plants will be superb.

Prepare a seed bed and sow as described earlier. When the largest leaves are about the size of a dime transplant the seedlings into flats or pans containing two parts of peat moss or leaf mold and one of sandy loam. When they begin to crowd each other, pot them singly in 2½- or 3-inch pots. Later shift them into 4- or 5-inch ones, in which containers they will flower.

Throughout the growing period, shade the plants from bright sun and keep them in a moist atmosphere. After flowering is finished, withhold water gradually, store at 40 to 50 degrees until January or February, when the tubers may be shaken free of soil and started.

Fig. 14–6. Left, a Lady Mac begonia in flower. Right, a young plant developed from a leaf cutting. (Roche)

The tubers will be good for several years, but will make the best plants in their second year.

Begonias grow well and flower nicely when proper conditions are maintained. When the environment is not right they may drop their flower buds. During the summer months, when the temperature soars above 90 degrees, buds and flowers may drop off. When the days become cooler toward autumn the buds will develop properly. Poor drainage, very dry air, and overwatering may also cause bud drop.

Tuberous begonias are susceptible to powdery mildew. If the plants are dusted with sulfur at the beginning of plant growth and at biweekly intervals up to flowering time, this disease will not be a problem. Red spiders and thrips may be troublesome at times. These may be controlled with Malathion.

Winter-Blooming Begonias—Gloire de Lorraine Series

These begonias, with their compact masses of flowers, add beauty to the greenhouse during the winter months, when it is most appreciated. The winter-blooming begonias originated in 1891, when Lemoine in France flowered a hybrid of *Begonia socotrana*, a bulbous species, and *B. dregei*, a semi-bulbous species. This hybrid was called Begonia Gloire de Lorraine. Since then additional hybrids have been developed, among them Lady Mac, Glory of Cincinnati, Melior, and Marjorie Gibbs.

The winter-blooming begonias are increased by leaf cuttings made from December to March. Cut the leaf stalk close to the stem, shorten the leaf stalk to about 1½ inches, and insert it in a mixture of one-third peat and two-thirds sand. Plant the cuttings so that they do not touch each other and in such a manner that the leaf blade is not in contact with the rooting medium. Cuttings should be kept in a moist place, in a propagating frame, or in a box covered with glass. Use bottom heat of 70 degrees. The cuttings will root better and more quickly if the days are prolonged by turning on electric lights at sundown and letting them remain on until 10 P.M.

When a young plant is evident on a cutting, pot the cutting in a 2½-inch pot in a mixture containing considerable sand and leaf mold or peat moss. You need not separate the young plant from the leaf stalk. The pots should be plunged in moist peat. In June the plants will be ready to shift into 4-inch pots, and by September into 6- or 7-inch ones. Watering with a solution of fertilizer at biweekly intervals promotes vigorous growth. A solution made up of one ounce of 15–30–15 fertilizer in 3 gallons of water is ideal. Pinching is necessary to get stocky plants. Even so, it will be necessary to stake the plants. The plants cannot tolerate bright sun, so they must be shaded during the bright months of the year. This group of begonias thrives with a night temperature between 58 and 60 degrees.

The Foliage Begonias

Begonia rex is a noble species which has been the principal parent in the development of many varieties with ornamental foliage, called the rex begonias. The rex begonias do flower, but their real beauty lies in the brilliant, iridescent coloring of the leaves, characterized by pink, bronze, crimson, or silver tones overlying the green, and by their fascinating shapes.

Rex begonias may be started from seed or from leaf cuttings. Several seedmen sell seeds of hybrids, from which many different kinds can be expected. Seed may be sown on a fine mixture of equal parts of sand and peat moss. Best results are obtained by sowing in the spring. The seed should be scattered thinly so that the resulting seedlings can grow to a height of an inch or two without crowding. The seedlings are potted in 2-inch pots, later shifted into 3-inch ones, and then into larger ones when necessary.

Choice varieties are increased by leaf cuttings. One of the easiest ways is to remove a large and well-matured leaf (retaining the leaf stalk). Cut through the principal veins on the undersurface and insert the leaf stalk in sand, letting the lower surface of the leaf rest on the moist sand. It can be kept in contact with the sand by placing a few pebbles on it. A small tuber, which in time will form a new plant, develops near each cut place. The small plants are separated from the leaf and potted singly. Another method is to cut the leaf into triangular pieces, each with V-shaped main veins, and to insert each piece vertically in a mixture of sand and peat.

The plants should not be exposed to bright sun, but instead they should be grown in a shaded greenhouse. They grow well with a night temperature of 60 degrees. Rex begonias are frequently grown in pots, but they may be grown in benches or pockets of soil. Some choice varieties are Magnifica, Marie Louise, Louise Closson, Crimson Glow, Pacific Sunset, Dawn, Our Indian, Calico, Lavender Glow, Black Star, Autumn, and Emerald.

Fibrous-Rooted Begonias

There are many varieties of fibrous-rooted begonias, a good number of which are classified as *Begonia semperflorens*. It is convenient to divide the fibrous-rooted begonias into three classes, based on the height of the plants—dwarf varieties, 6 to 8 inches high; plants of medium height, 9 to 11 inches; and tall varieties, with heights of 12 inches or more. A few choice dwarf varieties are Pink Pearl, Red Pearl, Ball Red, Ball White, and Fire Sea. Some of medium height are Carmen, Indian Maid, Luminosa, Prima Donna, Scandinavia Pink, Scandinavia Red, and White Pearl. Tall varieties include Christmas Cheer Red, Ile de France, and Masterpiece. The fibrous-rooted begonias are useful pot plants for flowering during winter in the greenhouse. They are also good bedding plants.

Fig. 14–7. Angel Wing begonia. (Wilson Brothers)

The fibrous-rooted begonias are generally started from seed sown in the fall or early winter for good-sized flowering plants in May or June. For winter flowering, seeds are sown in spring. The plants will flower most of the winter if the seed pods are picked off. These begonias are also easily propagated from stem cuttings. Cuttings made in the spring will yield fine plants for late winter and spring flowering. A mixture of equal parts of loam and leaf mold or peat moss suits them. They grow well at a night temperature of 55 to 60 degrees. Like other begonias, the fibrous-rooted ones should be shaded from the direct rays of the sun.

Other Begonias

To add variety to your collection you may wish to include several species such as those which follow.

Begonia boweri, from Chiapas and Oaxaca, Mexico, is known as the "eyelash begonia" because the leaves are edged with fine white hairs. The variety Nigra Magda is a miniature rhizomatous plant with dark green leaves, 1 to 2 inches long, that have black markings. The flowers are pale pink.

Begonia coccinea (Brazil), called Angel Wing Begonia, develops cane-like stems, 6 to 9 feet tall, that bear glossy green leaves spotted silver and edged red. The coral red flowers, borne in drooping clusters, are produced throughout the year. The species is readily propagated from stem cuttings taken from spring to autumn.

Begonia foliosa (Colombia) is known as the fern-leaved begonia because of its tiny bronze-green leaves which are borne on delicate drooping stems. The small white flowers appear in late winter. It is specially attractive when grown in a hanging basket.

Begonia fuchsioides (Mexico), bears fuchsia-like red flowers in drooping clusters during summer and autumn. The flowers contrast beautifully with the glossy, vivid green leaves that are 1½ inches long. Stem cuttings taken in late summer will develop into plants that will flower the following year.

Begonia haageana (Brazil), also known as *Begonia scharffii*, is noted for its attractive foliage and beautiful flowers. The plant bears pale-pink blooms, 1 inch across, in hanging clusters during all months, but more profusely during summer and autumn. Like most, it is easily propagated from stem cuttings.

Begonia kenworthyi (Chiapas, Mexico) has fleshy five-lobed ivy-like leaves, up to 10 inches long, with plum colored bases and a coating of white powder. From December to March the plants are decorated with myriads of pink flowers.

Begonia manicata variety *aureo-maculata* (Mexico), called the leopard begonia, bears fleshy light green leaves that are blotched rose or yellow. The petioles bear collars of fleshy red hairs. Small, pink flowers appear in the spring.

Begonia metallica (Bahia) has large olive green leaves with a metallic sheen which are beautiful throughout the year. The veins are purple. The plant grows 2 or 3 feet tall and bears showy pink flowers during summer and autumn.

Begonia ricinifolia is a vigorous hybrid of Mexican origin with large bronzy-green leaves that resemble those of the castor-oil plant. The petioles are ringed by red hairs, especially near the apex. Large clusters of pink flowers appear during winter and early spring.

Pests and Diseases of Begonias

Red spiders, mites, thrips, aphids, white flies, and mealy bugs are some of the pests which may attack begonias. The semituberous and fibrous-rooted varieties are occasionally attacked by nematodes. Brown spots surrounded by water-soaked margins on the leaves are symptoms of this pest. The nematodes feed on the inner tissues of the leaves but emerge when moisture is present and move from one place to another. Syringing plants hastens the spread of nematodes. Control involves use of soil free of the pests, adequate spacing of plants, and removal and burning of infected leaves.

A wilt disease, verticillium wilt, may attack winter-blooming varieties. Use of disease-free soil and burning of diseased plants are control measures. Roots of seedlings are subject to black root rot, caused by the fungus *Thielaviopsis basicola*. Damping-off fungi may also attack seedlings. Raising seedlings in sterilized soil will prevent such injury.

Stem rot, caused by *Pythium intermedium* and by *P. ultimum*, is characterized by soft watersoaked lesions extending lengthwise on the stem. To control this disease, use sterile soil and avoid excessive humidity. Begonia blight, caused by the fungus *Botrytis cinerea*, may be serious at times. Diseased areas on the leaves or stem turn black, and then a brownish-gray mold becomes evident. To control begonia blight gather and destroy all plant parts that are affected. More ventilation and a lower humidity will reduce the incidence of this disease. Bacterial leaf spot (caused by *Xanthomonas begoniae*) may appear on tuberous begonias and fibrous begonias. This disease may be controlled by removing affected plant parts, decreasing the humidity, and by giving the plants more space and better ventilation.

Spotted wilt is a destructive virus disease of begonias. The virus is spread from one plant to another by thrips. Control consists of eliminating thrips and removing and burning all diseased plants. Sterilize all cutting tools after use on one plant before using on another to avoid spreading the virus.

15

Bromeliads

If you like the unusual, you will find fascination in the bromeliads, for this group includes beautiful and bizarre plants that are good companions for aroids, begonias, gesneriads, and orchids—plants that bring a tropical atmosphere into our greenhouses. The bromeliads are in the family Bromeliaceae, the pineapple family, which includes about 1,800 species in 46 genera. They are at home in tropical and subtropical regions primarily in the Americas from Mexico to Argentina and at elevations ranging from hot and humid sea level to a chilly 10,500 feet above sea level. If you visit a rain forest or a cloud forest in the tropics you will invariably see bromeliads perched on the trunks and branches of trees. These epiphytic bromeliads are adapted for a life in the trees by having their leaf bases arranged to form water-tight containers. The rain water that accumulates in their living vases is their main supply. In nature many aquatic animals make their homes in the aquaria of the bromeliads, among them larvae of mosquitos and other insects, salamanders, tadpoles, snakes, and even fish. Some of the larger bromeliads may contain a gallon of water and unless one is careful in removing the plants from a branch he may become doused with water. Vertical, solid rock cliffs, such as those near Machu Picchu, Peru are often covered with bromeliads, some with bright red leaves. As with the tree dwellers these are also tank plants. Some bromeliads are terrestial, growing in the ground in tropical forests.

Bromeliads are a diverse group and they make an intriguing hobby. The sturdy leaves vary in shape, in the presence or absence

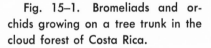

Fig. 15–1. Bromeliads and orchids growing on a tree trunk in the cloud forest of Costa Rica.

of spines, and in color. In some species the leaves are uniformly colored green, bluish green, or red whereas in other species the leaves are brightly banded or mottled. Even when the plants are not in flower they are interesting and attractive. In many species the flower cluster emerges from the center of the rosette of leaves. The stalk may be tall or nestled within the rosette where it may be surrounded by brilliant red leaves. Contrasting colors of red, blue, pink, purple, yellow, or green in the flower cluster yield dazzling effects which in the jungles serve to attract their pollinators—hummingbirds, night moths, and bees. By thoughtful selection of species one may have some plants in flower the year around. In a greenhouse they can often be induced to flower prematurely by enclosing the plant along with an apple in a polyethylene bag. The ethylene gas given off by the apple will induce flowering.

The bromeliads are rugged plants and easy to grow. They can withstand long periods of drought, but, of course, make better growth when water is uniformly available. Much of their water is absorbed by the basal part of the leaves, instead of the roots which serve primarily for anchorage. Hence, keep their vases filled with water as they are in nature. They grow vigorously and flower with a night temperature of 60 degrees, and with half shade except during the darkest months. Too intense sun will burn the foliage.

Fig. 15–2. The leaves of many bromeliads form water-tight containers.

The plants thrive when potted in a porous material such as shredded tree fern fiber (in Hawaii called "hapuu"), fir bark, redwood bark, or osmunda fiber. They also may be grown with a mixture of equal parts of sand and leafmold or a mixture of three parts peat moss and one of sand. In potting, first add crock for drainage and then hold the plant in position and firm the previously moistened potting medium around the roots, taking care not to injure them. Established plants should be fertilized with an organic or inorganic fertilizer used at half the recommended concentration, at biweekly intervals when active, or monthly when inactive. The solution may be sprayed over the foliage which will readily absorb the nutrients.

You may prefer to grow some on slabs or attractive pieces of driftwood, thus simulating their native homes. Wire pieces of osmunda fiber to the driftwood and then wire the plant to the fiber or make pockets of bark in which the roots will grow.

In all bromeliads the parent plant eventually dies, about a year after flowering. In the meantime, however, one or more side shoots develop. When they are about 4 inches high they can be cut off, cutting them cleanly as close to the base as possible. If the offshoot has roots, pot it using osmunda fiber or bark. Some growers fill the pot two-thirds full of a mixture of equal parts of sand, peat moss, and osmunda fiber and then top this with a layer of osmunda fiber. The tightly packed osmunda fiber furnishes good support for the offshoot. If the offshoot lacks roots, insert the base of it in a mixture of equal parts of sand and sphagnum moss, until rooted, and then pot it. A number of cryptanthus species produce many suckers which naturally fall off. These are easily rooted in sand. Offshoots generally attain flowering size in one or two years. Instead of separating offshoots you can culture the whole clump either in the old pot or in a new, larger one. Bromeliads should not be overpotted; they grow well in small pots. Newly potted plants should be kept somewhat on the dry side until root action begins.

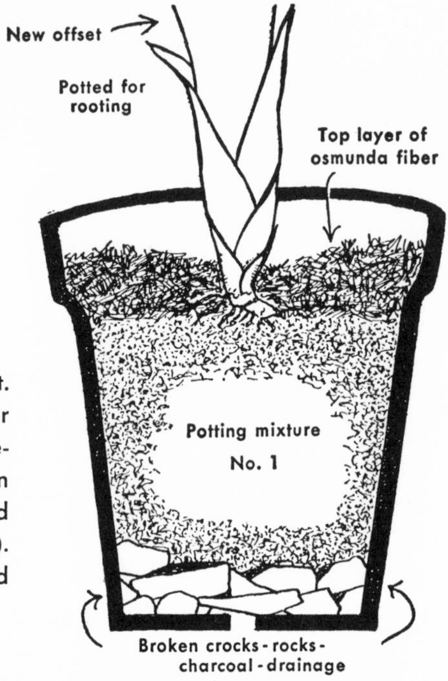

Fig. 15–3. Potting on offshoot. The upper layer of osmunda fiber holds the offshoot securely. The remainder of the pot is filled with an even mixture of sand, peat moss, and osmunda fiber (mixture No. 1). (Mulford B. Foster and the Bromeliad Society *Cultural Handbook*)

Bromeliads may be raised from seed. If you want your plants to produce seed, you will probably have to pollinate the flowers by hand. In their native homes they are pollinated by hummingbirds, night moths, and certain ants and bees, pollinating agents which may be lacking in our greenhouses. Seeds are viable for only a short time, between three and five months. Secure fresh seeds and plant them right away. The seeds of some bromeliads are dry and have feathery or winged appendages, for example those of *Tillandsia* and *Vriesia*. The seeds of *Billbergia, Aechmea,* and certain others are encased in a gelatinous substance, which should be washed from the seeds before they are planted. The dry seeds with appendages do not require cleaning. Seeds are best sown in pots furnished with drainage and filled with a mixture of peat moss and finely chopped

Fig. 15–4. Bromeliads. Upper left, *Aechmea fulgens* (South America). Upper right, *Billbergia vittata* (Brazil). Lower left, *Guzmania zahnii* (Panama). Lower right, *Neoregelia tristis* (Brazil). (Ladislaus Cutak)

Fig. 15–5. Bromeliads. Upper left, *Tillandsia butzii* (Mexico). Upper right, removal of an offshoot from a bromeliad growing in osmunda fiber. Lower left, a hybrid Vriesia (*Vriesia Mariae*). Lower right, *Vriesia splendens* (French Guiana). (Ladislaus Cutak)

sphagnum moss. Don't cover the seeds, because they need light for germination. After sowing, keep the pots in a moist, shaded place where the temperature is about 75 degrees. Another way is to sow the seeds on a chunk of peat about 8 inches long and 4 inches wide. The piece of peat should be cooked about two hours; wet it, wrap it in foil, and steam it in an oven at 225 degrees. Then place it in a glass or plastic container which has a small volume of water in the bottom. When the peat is cool, sow the seeds and cover the container with a piece of glass. The time for germination varies considerably with the species. Seeds of *Aechmea* germinate in about a week; those of *Vriesia* require three or four weeks. When the seedlings are about half an inch high they may be watered weekly with a dilute fertilizer solution.

When the seedlings are large enough, transplant them to flats containing a one-to-one mixture of peat and sphagnum, or a fine grade of bark (⅛ to ¼ inch), or osmunda fiber. Keep them in a moist, shaded place and feed them with liquid fertilizer. When they are eight to twelve months old, the seedlings can be moved into 2½- or 3-inch pots. Later they can be shifted into 4-inch ones. Well-grown seedlings flower when they are three or four years old.

Bromeliads are remarkably free of pests and diseases. However, seedlings may damp off. Watering with a fungicide and good cultural conditions will minimize the loss from this disease. Two scale insects (*Gymnaspis aechmeae* and *Diaspis bromeliae*) may attack bromeliads. Malathion is used for control. Seedlings may be attacked by thrips, which can be controlled with Malathion or with a rotenone spray.

Aechmea

There are about sixty species in this genus but only five are generally grown. *Aechmea chantinii*, from Venezuela and the Amazon of Peru, bears olive green leaves decorated with pinkish-gray crossbands. The salmon colored bracts, tipped yellow, are the most colorful part of the flower cluster.

The leaves of *Aechmea fasciata* (Brazil) (sometimes called *Billbergia rhodocyanea*) are beautifully marbled with silver-gray crosslines, and they radiate from the urn-shaped rosette. The flower stalk is about a foot tall and bears several erect, attractive, pale red bracts as well as attractive sky-blue flowers, with petals about three-quarters of an inch long.

Aechmea fulgens (Pernambuco) produces large numbers of flowers characterized by blue-tipped petals surrounded by rich red sepals. The pale green leaves spread from a basal rosette. This is a strong-growing species which produces many side shoots. *Aechmea marmorata* (Brazil) is distinguished by its artistic vase-like form, which has led to the common name Grecian Vase. Its stiff, recurved mottled leaves hold a considerable amount of water and the plant can actually be used as a vase. The pink and blue flowers generally appear in May.

Aechmea miniata discolor (Brazil) has satiny leaves, green above and pink-violet below. The flower clusters bear red bracts, within which the blue flowers are tucked.

Billbergia

These plants are closely related to aechmeas, and they should be included in every choice collection of bromeliads. They are named for F. B. Billberg, a Swedish botanist. The flower cluster rises from the center of a rosette of long leaves whose clasping bases are arranged to hold water. The colored bracts of the flower cluster are usually very showy and the flowers are interesting and beautiful.

Billbergia nutans, a favorite species from Brazil, Uruguay, and Argentina, has handsome linear leaves, 1 to 2 feet long. The flowers have green petals edged with blue, and attractive, long, golden stamens. The conspicuous red bracts of the flower cluster complete the color harmony. An unusual and beautiful plant is *Billbergia vittata* with silver-banded, leathery, olive to purplish-brown leaves.

Cryptanthus

The name *Cryptanthus* comes from the Greek and means *hidden flower.* The flowers are not especially decorative and are borne on a stalkless, dense head somewhat hidden in the cluster of leaves. However, these plants have superb and distinctive foliage. The low, flat plants have their leaves crowded in a rosette, recurved and spreading, with bizarre markings.

There are about a dozen tree-perching species, native to South America. Two of the favorite species are *Cryptanthus bivittatus* and *C. zonatus.* *Cryptanthus bivittatus* has a rosette of leaves with undulating margins. The leaves are striped with bars of brownish green and rose. The horizontal, spreading leaves of *Cryptanthus zonatus* have markings somewhat like those of a pheasant feather. The leaves are crinkled and marked with transverse bands of white, green, and brown. It is indeed a distinctive plant.

Guzmania

This is a group of about seventy-five tropical American species, some of which are choice foliage plants. The flowers are borne on nearly stalkless clusters among the foliage. *Guzmania zahnii*, from Colombia and Panama, is a favorite species. It has recurving leaves a foot or two long which are artfully arranged in a rosette. The lengthwise pencilings of bronze and red on the leaves add interest to the foliage. The branched inflorescence bears pink to yellow bracts and white flowers.

Neoregelia

There is quite a mix-up of names in this group of bromeliads. In some catalogs you may find what we are going to call *Neoregelia* going by the name of *Aregelia* or *Nidularium*. The members of the genus have the leaves arranged in a rosette, and the flower cluster is a dense head borne among the inner leaves of the rosette.

Neoregelia marmorata, *N. tristis*, and *N. spectabilis* are attractive species. The charm of *N. marmorata* lies in its delightfully mottled foliage. The six to twelve symmetrical leaves of the rosette are marbled with red. The pale violet flowers are produced in the center of the rosette. The red spot at the tip of each leaf of *N. spectabilis* has given this species the common name of Painted Finger Nail. The leaves are about a foot long, undulated along the margins, and barred on the back with narrow bands of silvery hairs.

Tillandsia

Tillandsia is a large genus of epiphytes; nearly all are native to tropical America, but a few enter the United States. One of them, Spanish moss, is a familiar sight throughout the southeastern United States. Spanish moss has long stringlike stems and threadlike leaves.

It is not commonly grown in greenhouses, but other species with large leaves and beautiful flowers make choice greenhouse specimens, for example *Tillandsia fasciculata*, and *T. lindeniana*. *Tillandsia fasciculata* has leaves about a foot long originating from a stem about two feet high. The flower cluster has greenish bracts tinged with red, and beautiful blue flowers.

The leaves of *T. lindeniana* form a rosette and they are about a foot long. The flower cluster is large, with showy carmine bracts and large bluish-purple flowers, making a decorative color scheme.

Vriesia

In this genus, native to tropical America, there are several striking species which deserve greater popularity. *Vriesia carinata*, often known as the Painted Feather, develops a rosette of shiny grass-green leaves out of which there emerges a feather-shaped flower cluster, bearing bracts that are scarlet at the base and yellowish at the tip, and flowers of a yellowish-hue. The flower cluster lasts extremely long, up to six months.

Vriesia hieroglyphica is noted for its handsome foliage and beautiful yellow flowers. The leaves are arranged in a rosette, and they are banded dark green above and brown-purple below. This species adds beauty to any greenhouse, even when it is not in flower. *Vriesia duvalliana* is a striking plant that is easily grown. Leaves attractively banded with brown characterize *V. splendens;* the flower spike is flaming orange and bears small yellow flowers.

16

Ferns

Ferns could be a hobby by themselves for there are about 9,000 species and varieties. However, many of us are content to have a few ferns to use as a background for other plants and to use for greens in making arrangements. Ferns are raised for their lovely leaves, which we call fronds. They are flowerless plants, reproducing by spores instead of seeds.

Ferns and their allies populated the earth long before the seed plants came into being and even though they are more primitive they still flourish. Although ferns grow from sea level to mountain tops and from the arctic to the equator on all continents most of those grown in greenhouses come from the warm and humid rain forests and cloud forests of tropical and subtropical climes. Here they thrive in humusy soil of the forest floor, on fallen logs, or as epiphytes on trunks and branches of trees. These ferns grow well in a greenhouse maintained at a night temperature of 60 degrees and with high humidity. They should be shaded from early spring to late autumn, and in bright regions during the winter as well. Ferns like ample water. Never let the soil become completely dry; also avoid water-logging the soil.

The tree-dwelling ferns thrive when potted in shredded firbark or osmunda fiber and they may also be grown on driftwood along with bromeliads and orchids. The terrestrial ones may be grown in a mixture of one part loam, one part peat moss or leafmold, and one part sand or perlite. Spring is a good time to repot ferns. Provide good drainage and firm the soil moderately. Established plants are fed at intervals with a liquid fertilizer used at half strength.

Well-grown ferns are usually not afflicted by insects. However, on occasions they may be attacked by the white fern scale, the large brown scale, mealy bugs, and, rarely, aphids. A solution of Malathion powder, used at 20 per cent of the recommended strength, may be used with caution. Some preparations of Malathion have kerosene-like carriers which may be injurious to ferns.

All ferns can be grown from spores which at certain seasons develop in clusters of spore cases, called sori, on the undersurfaces of the leaves. These are reddish or brownish, somewhat furry looking spots arranged in lines down the center of the leaves, or located at the edges, or in some kinds scattered. When the spores are shed on moist ground, each spore develops into a little, flat, green heart-shaped structure called a prothallium. On the undersurface of the prothallium sperms and eggs develop. If a fern plant is to develop, at least one egg must be fertilized by a sperm. Water is necessary to enable the sperms to swim to the eggs and fertilize them. When an egg is fertilized, it remains attached to the prothallium and is nourished by it while it develops into a young fern plant. It takes about six months from the time the spore germinates until the young fern plant attached to the prothallium is ready for an independent life. By that time its roots are long enough to furnish it with water and nutrients, and its leaves are large enough to make its own food.

Growing your own ferns from spores is a delightful experience.

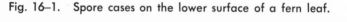

Fig. 16–1. Spore cases on the lower surface of a fern leaf.

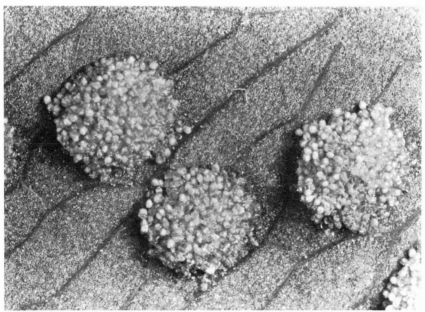

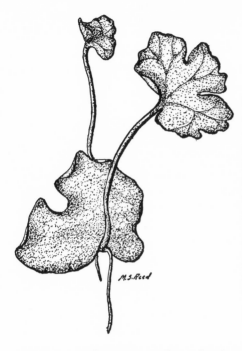

Fig. 16–2. A spore develops into the heart-shaped prothallium, on which sperm and egg cells develop. A fertilized egg, still attached to the prothallium, develops into the fern. Here is a young plant still attached to the heart-shaped structure. At this stage young ferns are ready to be transplanted to a flat. In time the heart-shaped plant will shrivel and die, but the fern that developed from the fertilized egg will continue to grow, and eventually produce spores in its turn.

Fill a pot with soil to within a half inch of the top, and over this put a layer of crushed flower pot (with the powdery bits screened out). It is best to sterilize the prepared pots by pouring boiling water through them. Pieces of fern leaf on which the spore cases are ready to open can be laid flat on the moist surface, and the spores will be shed onto the broken bits of pot. You may want to collect the spores beforehand by placing the leaves in a paper bag and storing in a dry place. The powder shed from the leaves is the spores. Spores can also be purchased from seed companies. After the spores are dusted over the prepared surface, cover the pot with a pane of glass and put it in a saucer of water to insure its being kept damp. After a few weeks the surface will be covered with tiny heart-shaped prothallia, and in a few more weeks the little fern plants will make an appearance from under their edges. Lift a prothallium and you will see that the fern plant attached to it is in the process of forming its first roots and leaves. The young fern plants can be transplanted, still attached to the prothallia, first to a flat, and later to individual pots. Keep the young ferns in a shaded spot.

An intriguing experiment would be to try your hand at making hybrid ferns by sowing spores from two species (preferably of the same genus) on the same pot. If they produce sperms and eggs at the same time and are compatible, you may have some very interesting results.

Ferns can also be increased by dividing the clump or rootstock. Spring is the best time to divide plants. Pot the divisions in pots just slightly larger than the clump. Avoid overpotting and keep the crown level with the surface of the soil.

The Boston fern, as well as some others, can be increased by runners. This fern produces many runners when grown in a bench. Ferns benched in early summer will produce many runners by fall. Separate the runners from the stock plants and pot the runners, one to each 2½-inch pot. Move them into larger pots as needed.

Bird's-nest Fern (Asplenium nidus-avis)

This fern grows perched on trees and inhabits vast areas, stretching from Madagascar to India and Indonesia, and including Australia and the islands of the South Pacific. Their leaves are arranged to form baskets and in their native lands birds lay their eggs in them. The undivided leaves are wavy-margined, light green in color with black veins, and they are about 2 feet long on an old plant, smaller and more attractive on a young one. They radiate from a short central core of stem. Do not water in the crown, for this may induce a rotting of the leaves. The roots have a spongy texture that retains water. They thrive when potted in bark or osmunda fiber. Plants are generally started from spores.

Boston Fern (Nephrolepis exaltata)

There are a great many varieties of *Nephrolepis exaltata*, of which the Boston fern is one. The species ranges from Florida to Brazil, Africa, South Asia, and Australia. The native home of the Boston fern is the West Indies. It is the old-time favorite, with drooping fronds that reach three feet in length. Its leaves are simply pinnate. Many new varieties have appeared, some more compact, many with leaves divided and re-divided so that they appear quite ruffled. Some are large, majestic forms, others are dwarf. Among the large forms are *piersonii, whitmanii,* and *rooseveltii. Scottii,* Dwarf Boston, and *wagnerii* are dwarf varieties. As previously mentioned,

Fig. 16–3. Upper, Bird's-nest fern, *Asplenium nidus-avis*. Lower, Staghorn fern, *Platycerium bifurcatum*. (Longwood Gardens)

Boston ferns are readily propagated from runners. They do not respond well to division.

Creton Brake Fern *(Pteris cretica)*

You will find many uses for these small attractive ferns, native to Florida, Ethiopia, Natal, Iran, India, and Japan. The fronds are about a foot long. Among the fine varieties are Ribbon Brake, Riverton Brake, May's Brake, Wilson Brake, and Wimsett Brake. The brake ferns are generally started from spores sown in the spring.

Holly Fern *(Cyrtomium falcatum)*

As the name suggests, the holly fern, native to Japan, China, India, Celebes, and Hawaii, has firm glossy leaflets (pinnae) which are holly-like in general appearance. There are several good varieties, among them *Rochefordianum*, which grows to a height of about 1½ feet, and *Compactum*, a smaller variety. The holly fern is a good choice for the cool greenhouse, since it prefers a night temperature of 45 to 50 degrees.

Maidenhair Fern *(Adiantum)*

Maidenhair ferns inhabit mild, damp climates in many parts of the world. Two species of *Adiantum*, *A. cuneatum* (and its many varieties) and *A. farleyense*, both native to South America, are delicate, lacy ferns, perhaps the most graceful and attractive of all. They are useful in making corsages and flower arrangements as well as for lending beauty to groupings of plants in the greenhouse. Like most other greenhouse ferns the maidenhair prefers a night temperature of 60 degrees and a humid atmosphere. The plants are propagated by division of the crowns and by spores. The divisions should be fairly large and potted in 3- or 4-inch pots. Spores may be sown at any time of the year, but preferably in the spring. A temperature of 65 to 70 degrees brings about rapid germination of the spores. The young plants are grown in community pots or flats with a spacing of 1 inch by 1 inch. Later, about eight months from sowing time, they are put in small pots, and, when sufficient growth has been made, into larger ones. Don't let the plants become potbound.

Fig. 16–4. Repotting a Boston fern. (Genereux)

Rabbit's Foot Fern *(Davallia fejeensis)*

The golden furry rhizomes of this fern, a native of the Fiji Islands, resemble rabbit's feet. It is a beautiful plant, of easy culture, that bears graceful, durable, lacy fronds. The fern thrives when grown in a hanging basket which will in time become surrounded by the interesting rhizomes.

Staghorn Fern (Platycerium bifurcatum)

The leathery, forked, grayish-green fronds of this decorative and long-lived fern somewhat resemble in shape the horns of the European reindeer. In humid regions of Australia, New Guinea, and New Caledonia it grows on the branches and trunks of trees. This epiphyte is best grown on a chunk of osmunda fiber wired on a board or on a slab of fern fiber. Even a small plant is decorative and eye-catching, and a large specimen is a true showpiece. There are many other species of *Platycerium;* the genus spreads all through the tropics of Asia, Africa, and South America. Instead of bearing their spores in sori, the staghorns produce sheets of spore cases on their undersurface that look like brown velvet.

Selaginella

Selaginellas are not true ferns, but are allies of ferns. Like the ferns, selaginellas reproduce by spores. The spores are formed in cones borne at the tips of the branches. *Selaginella emmiliana* (South America) is a compact plant about 6 inches tall, whose branches are clothed with tiny leaves. Another good species, somewhat dwarf and more compact, is *S. kraussiana browni* (Azores), which resembles a cushion of bright green moss. They thrive in quite moist places and, if they overflow a pot, will spread rapidly in the soil of the bench. Small rooted clumps can be broken off from the main plant and potted separately. The familiar "resurrection" plant sold in novelty shops is *S. lepidophylla.*

17

Gesneriads

The family Gesneriaceae (referred to as gesneriads) can bring the tropical and subtropical world into your greenhouse with beautiful plants from Central and South America, Madagascar, East Africa, South Africa, India, Malaysia, and others. The family includes eighty-four genera, five hundred species, and innumerable hybrids. Most familiar are achimenes, African violet, columnea, episcia, gesneria, gloxinia, kohleria, smithiana, and streptocarpus. Many cultivated gesneriads have remarkably beautiful flowers and handsome foliage. They are good companions for each other, thriving with a night temperature of 60 degrees and with diffused light, not full sun, and a high humidity. Many thrive when the light intensity is between 1,000 and 2,000 foot candles, that is, between one-tenth and one-fifth of full sun light.

In the wilds gesneriads grow in varied habitats. The African violet grows in shaded rock crevices where soil has accumulated. *Streptocarpus saxorum* clings to vertical cliffs in the Usambara Mountains of East Africa. Other gesneriads grow in rain forests and cloud forests, some on the ground and others along with orchids, ferns, and begonias, on trunks and branches of trees. Even though they occupy different niches, in greenhouses they thrive when potted in a similar soil. Most kinds do well in a mixture of one-third loam, one-third peat moss or leaf mold, and one-third coarse sand, vermiculite, or perlite with the addition of one cup of superphosphate to every bushel of mixture. Some growers prefer a mixture with a greater proportion of organic matter, prepared by mixing

Fig. 17–1. Gesneriads may be increased from seed, stem cuttings, and leaf cuttings. Upper, left and right, seeds may be mixed with fine sand in a salt shaker and then scattered over the surface of the soil. Lower left, a stem cutting of episcia. Lower right, a leaf cutting of gloxinia; a half-inch of the petiole (leaf stalk) was inserted into sand. Notice the tuber that has formed at the base.

one part loam, to two parts of peat moss or leaf mold, and one part sand, vermiculite, or perlite. Well-established and actively growing plants should be fed biweekly with a half-strength solution of a soluble fertilizer.

When watering gesneriads make certain that the temperature of the water is about the same as that of the greenhouse. If the leaves are wetted with cold water they may become spotted. Except during the dormant period the soil should be kept moist, but never soggy.

With few exceptions gesneriads may be increased by leaf cuttings and a few by tubers. All can be started from seeds. The seeds of gesneriads are dust fine and just one ounce may include a million seeds. The seeds germinate promptly on a sterile medium such as a mixture of one-half milled sphagnum moss and one-half vermiculite. Another suitable medium is one-half peat moss and one-half vermiculite. Moisten the medium and then scatter the seeds evenly over the surface. Do not cover the seeds. Place a pane of glass over the container or enclose it in a polyethylene bag; keep it continually moist, warm, and shaded. The seeds will germinate in about two weeks. When the seedlings become crowded transplant them to flats or small pots. Then pot in larger containers as necessary. Most will flower during the first year.

The most serious pest of gesneriads is the cyclamen mite (*Tarsonemus pallidus*), a mite so small that you need a powerful hand lens to see it. The damage, however, is obvious; the plants are dwarfed, the new growth is distorted, and the flowers are malformed. Periodic spraying with Kelthane gives good control and may be used to prevent infestation. Gesneriads may also be attacked by mealy bugs, white flies, aphids, and thrips, insects that may be controlled with Malathion.

Achimenes

If you are raising African violets and gloxinias you may wish to include these less well-known relatives which are native to tropical America. Achimenes, popularly called Cupid's Bower or Magic Flower, furnishes a grand display of velvety, petunia-shaped flowers throughout the summer and autumn at little expense. The flowers are upwards of 2 inches across. The cultivated achimenes are for the most part hybrids derived from *Achimenes gloxiniaeflora, A.*

Fig. 17–2. Achimenes is easy to grow and will make a fine display through the summer and into fall. (Antonelli Brothers)

longiflora, and A. *patens*, which bear white flowers, and A. *picta* and A. *coccinea*, with scarlet flowers. There are many named varieties in shades of red, rose, orange, blue, purple, and white.

You can obtain a succession of blooms by starting tubers at intervals from February until the end of May. The plants flower eight to ten weeks after planting. The tubers resemble miniature pine cones. Plant the tubers about half an inch deep; six or seven in a 5-inch pot or nine or ten in a 6-inch one, keeping varieties separate. Instead of potting the tubers directly in the pots in which they will flower, you can start them in flats filled with a mixture of sand and peat moss. Water should be applied sparingly until the tubers begin to grow, after which the soil should be kept moist and never be allowed to dry out. When the plants in flats are about 2 inches high, move six uniform ones into a 6-inch pot. Achimenes may be grown in baskets as well as in pots. For this culture, line a wire basket with wet sphagnum moss. Insert plants so that the shoots extend out through the sides. Then fill the basket with soil and plant a few on the surface. When well rooted give biweekly applications of liquid fertilizer. Keep thrips, red spiders, and aphids under control.

After flowering is through and the plants show signs of resting, allow them to dry off gradually. The rest period may come on quite suddenly, and the entire plant may turn brown within a week. When the foliage is withered, remove the tubers, shake off the soil, and store them in sand at a temperature of 45 to 50 degrees. In addition to growing from tubers, Achimenes may be propagated readily from stem cuttings or leaf cuttings taken in the spring, or from seeds.

Aeschynanthus (formerly *Trichosporum*)

From the rainforests of Java come several interesting epiphytes, *Aeschynanthus javanicus*, *A. lobbianus*, *A. pulcher*, and *A. speciosa*. *Aeschynanthus javanicus* is known as the lipstick plant because the blossom resembles dark red lipstick emerging from the case. The foliage is light green. The tubular flowers are scarlet with a yellow mouth and the case-like calyx is purplish red. *Aeschynanthus lobbianus* has fleshy leaves and clusters of hairy, red flowers, about two inches long; the calyx is blackish purple and about one inch long. *A. pulcher* bears hairless vermillion flowers with a green calyx. *A. speciosa* has four-inch long, flame-orange flowers.

Aeschynanthus thrives in hanging baskets lined with sphagnum moss and filled with a mixture of sand, leaf mold, and loam or with fir bark. Like other gesneriads they prefer shade. They are propagated from stem cuttings or seeds.

African Violets—*Saintpaulia*

African violets are native to Tanzania in Africa, where they are found growing in pockets of humusy soil, in crevices of limestone and gneiss rock, always in shaded habitats. The one we know by this nickname is *Saintpaulia ionantha*. *Saintpaulia* commemorates

Fig. 17–3. The African violet, upper, is easily propagated from a leaf cutting, lower. Five plants developed at the base of the petiole (leaf stalk) which was inserted in sand. Each plant will be potted separately.

the family name of the discoverer of this fine genus. The genus was named after Baron Walter von St. Paul-Illaire, whose son discovered it in Africa. The species name *ionantha* is from the Greek meaning *with flowers like a violet.* Actually, of course, African violets are no kin of the violets which are in the family Violaceae.

African violets are indeed choice plants with their well-proportioned form, attractive foliage, beautiful flowers, and extended blooming period. Some varieties bloom continually, others periodically. Through hybridizing and the selection of mutations we now

Fig. 17–4. Here are some interesting and beautiful gesneriads. Upper
left, *Aeschynanthus pulcher*. Upper right, *Columnea gloriosa*. Lower left,
Lipstick vine, *Aeschynanthus lobbianus*. Lower right, *Episcia*. (Upper figures,
Addisonia, New York Botanical Garden. Lower left, W. Atlee Burpee Co.)

have hundreds of varieties of diverse types of foliage and of flower colors, and many new ones are introduced each year. The color range includes white, near blues, purples, pinks, and bluish reds. Most varieties have single flowers, but certain ones have double flowers. We suggest that you obtain catalogs for descriptions of the hundreds of varieties that are now available.

Among the newest introductions are miniature African violets which are less than 6 inches in diameter and which can be grown and flowered in 3-inch pots. In a small area many miniatures can be grown.

The enchantment of African violets lures a grower to an increasingly large collection. Many fanciers started their African violet collections in their homes, but soon found that the home could not accommodate all of their plants, so they built a greenhouse.

It is certainly easier to grow African violets to perfection in a greenhouse than in a home. In a greenhouse, the light, the humidity, and the temperature may be more easily adjusted to meet the needs of the plants. The ideal night temperature is 60 to 65 degrees. The day temperature should be 10 degrees higher, although higher seasonal temperatures will do no harm. A relative humidity of 60 to 70 per cent suits African violets. Damping down of walks and benches during the day will keep the humidity up, as will a humidifier.

African violets grow and flower well with a light intensity about one-tenth to one-fifth that of full sunlight; in other words, with light intensities between 1,000 and 2,000 foot candles. You can tell whether your plants are getting the proper amount by their appearance. If the petioles are long, the foliage dark green, and the flowers scarce, they are not getting sufficient light. On the other hand, if the leaves are small and with a yellowish cast or are burned, the light intensity is too high. If most of the winter days are cloudy in your locality you may not need any shade on the greenhouse from December to February. In February shade the glass lightly, and as the days become brighter toward spring apply heavier shade.

Fig. 17–5. Breeding African violets can be fun. These steps show how it is done. Above, the flower selected as the female parent. First its anthers and petals are removed. Center, the anthers from the male parent are broken open and some of the pollen obtained with a brush. Below, the pollen is brushed on the stigma of the female parent.

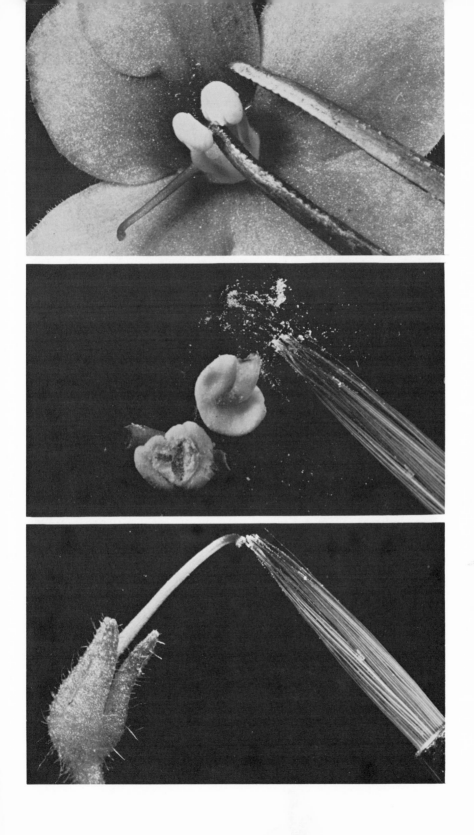

Beginning in October or November, depending on the locality, the shade may be gradually reduced.

The plants do not thrive in soil that is either water-logged or bone dry. Water thoroughly and then let the surface become dry before watering again. As is true of all gesneriads cold water splashed on the leaves causes yellowish or whitish spots, rings or streaks to develop on the foliage. This trouble does not develop when the water is moderated to greenhouse temperature, and the plants grow better.

African violets are easily propagated from leaf cuttings. Cut through the leaf stalk close to the crown. Then shorten the leaf stalk to about an inch and a half, dip in a rooting hormone, and insert the leaf stalk in sand or vermiculite. Keep the cuttings in a moist place, preferably with bottom heat of 65–70 degrees, and keep them carefully watered. In about four to eight weeks, the new plants, which form at the base of the leaf stalk, will have grown well above the rooting medium. The leaf, with the attached plants, may then be removed, and the young plants may be separated from it and potted in 2½-inch pots. After the plants have become fully established in 2½-inch pots, they may be shifted to 4- or 5-inch pots, in which containers they will flower. Of course, the miniatures may be allowed to remain in 2½-inch pots or be shifted to 3-inch ones. It takes about nine months from the time the cuttings are made until they flower; for example, those propagated in April will flower in 4-inch pots at Christmas.

Large plants should be potted annually. If you wish multiple-crown plants merely shift them into larger pots. However, an exhibition plant is a one-crown plant. When growing a plant for show, remove young shoots as they develop on the crown. Large plants can be divided at potting time. To do this, let the soil become slightly dry and then knock the plant out of the pot. Break up the root ball, shake the soil from the roots and separate the crowns, keeping as many roots as possible on each. Pot each division.

African violets can be increased by offsets which develop from the main stem. When the larger leaves of an offset are 2 or 3 inches long, cut off the offset near the main stem. The offset is treated as a stem cutting. Root it in a mixture of sand and peat, contained in a pot.

These gesneriads can also be grown from seed. Growing plants to maturity from seed requires about the same time as growing them from cuttings. Usually the plants grown from cuttings are exactly like the parents, but you can expect a variety of types in a group raised from hybrid seed. Some may be outstanding. There is suspense when you raise plants from seed. The seeds will germinate in about three weeks if kept at a temperature of 60 to 65 degrees. When the seedlings are about half an inch high they may be transplanted to flats and later to pots.

You might wish to try your hand at hybridizing African violets and growing plants from the resulting seed. About two weeks after pollination, a small seed pod will begin to form and will ripen in about six to nine months. You may wish to cross one variety of *Saintpaulia ionantha* with a different variety, or if you are adventurous you may try crossing a variety of *Saintpaulia ionantha* with a different species of *Saintpaulia*. As yet few, if any, crosses between species are on the market.

Some species you may wish to add to your collection and to use in breeding work are *Saintpaulia amaniensis, S. diplotricha, S. Grotei, S. magungensis,* and *S. tongwensis.* All are native to Tanzania and except for *S. diplotricha* they grow at an elevation of about 3,000 feet in the Usambara Mountains. *S. diplotricha* is a rock-dweller from Maweni near low coastal Tanga.

Saintpaulia amaniensis. This species, a close relative of *S. Grotei,* grows trailing on the ground. The leaves are oval in shape with petioles about 3½ inches long. The flowers are about an inch across, of violet-blue color.

Saintpaulia diplotricha. This species resembles *Saintpaulia ionantha* but has both long and short hairs on the leaves, whereas in *S. ionantha* they are of uniform length. Moreover, *S. diplotricha* has long and curved seed pods; *S. ionantha* has short ones. The flowers are violet in color and about 1¼ inches across. The leaves are pale green on the upper surface and nearly white underneath.

Saintpaulia Grotei. This has a long creeping stem bearing glossy, almost-round leaves, pale green above, whitish below. The flowers are pale blue-violet in color. *S. Grotei* can be trained in the same manner as an ivy or philodendron. Climbing house plants which flower are quite rare, which gives this species a special charm. It is also excellent for hanging baskets.

Saintpaulia magungensis. This species resembles S. *Grotei,* but the leaves are smaller and have shorter petioles. The flowers are a darker blue-violet.

Saintpaulia tongwensis. This species resembles S. *ionantha* but has elliptical, shiny, nonquilted leaves. The seed capsules of S. *tongwensis* are densely hairy, and longer than those of S. *ionantha.*

Mealy bugs, thrips, and mites may attack African violets. Light spraying with nicotine sulfate or Malathion will control insects and Kelthane is effective against mites.

One of the worst afflictions of African violets is *root knot,* caused by tiny parasitic worms called *nematodes.* The worms invade the roots and cause pulpy enlargements, called *nodules,* to form on the roots. After invasion, absorption of water is interfered with and the foliage begins to droop and appears dull. The best control consists of using only sterilized soil and disposing of infected plants.

African violets are susceptible to a few fungus diseases, among them gray mold (*Botrytis*), bud rot, crown rot, and mildew. Plants that are chilled, overwatered, not properly ventilated, or given inadequate light are especially susceptible. Proper attention to good cultural conditions will minimize the incidence of disease. Never crowd plants. Give each one sufficient room for its proper development. Spraying with Fermate or light dusting with sulfur is also helpful.

Chirita

The lavender chirita (*Chirita lavendulacea*), a native of tropical or subtropical Asia, is a choice erect greenhouse plant about 2 feet high. The tubular flowers are delicate lavender in color, except for the throat and the outside of the tube, which are white. The flowers, 1½ inches long, are produced during the winter months.

Chirita is of easy cultivation and prefers a soil rich in humus. They should be given ample water and be grown in shade. Plants are propagated from seed or by stem or leaf cuttings.

Columnea

The scarlet columnea (*Columnea gloriosa*), a native of Costa Rica, bears bright scarlet flowers, 2 or 3 inches long, during the summer months. The plant grows to a height of about 2 feet and bears fleshy leaves of a reddish hue. In nature it grows pendant on trunks of trees. Columnea is successfully cultivated in hanging baskets or in pots placed on pedestals. However, it may be grown erect by staking the stems.

Another interesting species from Costa Rica is *Columnea hirta,* an epiphyte with creeping, hairy, red stems and vermillion-red flowers marked with orange. The leaves are oval shaped, satiny, and red.

Episcia

These gesneriads, natives of the American tropics, develop beautiful flowers, ranging from red to orange, yellow, white, and blue. The flowers are trumpet shaped, five-lobed and with frilled edges. Unlike African violets episcias have a limited flowering season, but even when not in flower their beautiful foliage is adequate compensation. They come in a variety of leaf patterns and textures, and some varieties have a copper luster, others bronze or silver. The surface may be velvety or furry. Their popularity is increasing as they become better known and as new varieties are introduced.

Episcias can be propagated from leaf cuttings and stem cuttings. Because leaf cuttings root slowly, stem cuttings are generally preferred. Stem cuttings inserted in a mixture of peat moss and sand or vermiculite will root in two to four weeks.

A number of species grow well in a greenhouse, among them *Episcia chontalensis. E. coccinea, E. cupreata, E. dianthiflora, E. melittifolia,* and *E. tesselata. E. chontalensis* has darkish green leaves, each with a narrow silver-colored center vein, and bears light blue blossoms. *E. coccinea* has dark metallic green leaves, is free-flowering, and bears scarlet flowers. *E. cupreata* is suitable for pot or basket culture. The blooms are scarlet and the foliage is a striking coppery hue. *E. dianthiflora,* a species with a trailing habit, grows well in a hanging basket. The leaves are oblong and velvety green. The large white blossoms have a delightful fringed margin. *Episcia fulgida* is a handsome creeping plant with oval shaped, copper colored leaves with green veins. The flowers are bright red. *E. melittifolia* has an upright growth habit, shiny dark green leaves, reddish stems and cerise flowers that appear over a long season. *E. tesselata* also grows upright and has glossy purplish brown leaves and yellow flowers. Plants grow to a height of about two feet. There are many named varieties of episcias; among the newer ones are Pink Haga, Ember Lace, Firebird Red, Antique Velvet, Tropical Topaz, Ruby, and Cleopatra.

Gesneria

The family gesneriaceae takes its name from this genus. The most popular species is *Gesneria cuneifolia,* a native of Cuba, Puerto Rico, and Hispaniola. It is an evergreen plant with a rosette of shiny green leaves, 4 inches long. The flowers are red, somewhat bottle shaped. The plants are readily increased by leaf cuttings.

Gloxinia

Gloxinia (correctly, *Sinningia speciosa*) was discovered in Brazil in 1785 and named in honor of P. B. Gloxin of Strassburg, Germany. Later, however, it was found to belong in the genus *Sinningia.* The name Gloxinia is still commonly used. Gloxinia is a superb greenhouse plant which bears large, velvet-textured, tubular flowers with colors ranging from blue to purple, red, pink, carmine, and white. Some varieties have solid colors, others are bicolored, and some are beautifully spotted. The velvety sheen of the foliage is also handsome. New varieties become available each year. Among the newest introductions are miniature gloxinias that may be grown in 3- or 4-inch pots. A mature miniature measures about 7 inches across and blooms over a longer period than the standard varieties. The directions which follow are for the standard varieties. If you are growing miniatures simply use smaller sized pots than those indicated.

The easiest way to start a collection is to purchase dormant tubers, available from about December on. Store the tubers in dry peat at a temperature of 50 degrees until the buds begin to develop. Some tubers start growing before others. At intervals, examine them and plant those which show signs of growth. If tubers have become considerably shriveled during storage, pot them even though they do not show new growth. However, be careful not to overwater them. By starting the tubers at intervals you will get a succession of blooms. Tubers which are about 1½ inches across are

Fig. 17–6. Upper, gloxinia seedlings ready for potting. The larger ones will go into 4-inch pots, the smaller into 2½-inch ones. Lower, potting a seedling into a 4-inch pot.

planted in 5-inch pots, larger ones in 6-, 7-, or 8-inch pots, depending on their size. Small tubers of seedlings may be potted in 3-inch pots and later shifted into 5-inch ones. Prepare the pot by placing crushed charcoal, pebbles, or pieces of broken pot in the bottom for drainage. Nearly fill the pot with soil, firm moderately, and then place the tuber on the surface. Then add more soil and firm it moderately so that the top of the tuber is level with the surface of the soil. You can also start tubers in flats containing a mixture of equal parts of peat moss and sand which is kept damp. When the shoots are an inch or two tall, remove the plants from the flat and pot them.

After the tubers are potted, water thoroughly, but thereafter water sparingly until active root growth begins. If the soil is kept continually wet before roots are present to absorb the water, the tuber may rot. Throughout the growing period, water carefully. Use water which is at the same temperature as the greenhouse, or slightly above. Avoid wetting the foliage with cold water. If cold water is splashed on the leaves, they are likely to become spotted. At each watering, water thoroughly; then don't water again until there are signs of dryness at the surface, for gloxinias do not thrive in waterlogged soil. They grow best when the air is humid. If you do not have a humidifier, you should wet the walks and the ground under the benches several times on bright days. After the plants are well established, biweekly applications of a dilute liquid fertilizer promote sturdy growth.

The plants should be raised in a shaded part of a greenhouse maintained at 60 degrees during the night. The day temperature should be about 10 degrees warmer. The appearance of your plants will tell you whether they are getting the correct amount of light. If burned spots appear and the leaves become yellowish, apply more shade. If the plants become leggy or spindly, give them more light.

The largest tubers will flower about four months after they are planted, the smaller ones later. You can often have plants in flower from spring through summer and fall. We used to believe that the plants should be dried off after their first flowering, but now we know that many will bloom a second time if regular watering is continued. If only a few leaves turn yellow and die after the first blossoming, continue to water the plants as before. Soon you will notice new leaves, and within a few weeks a number of flower buds. These will give you a second display. Don't try to get a third flowering. After the second flowering, when the leaves begin to die, gradually withhold water to induce dormancy. Finally cease watering. The tubers may be stored in the pots. If storage space is limited, you can remove the dormant tubers, shake them free of soil, and store them in dry peat. The tubers should be given a rest period of at least two months. Beginning in January, make periodic examinations and repot those which are beginning to grow.

If all of the leaves become yellow and die after the plants have flowered the first time, cease watering immediately. Let the tubers become dormant and store in the manner just described.

If you wish to increase a choice plant, you may do so by leaf cuttings. Cuttings always come true. Remove a medium-size, healthy leaf by cutting through the leaf stalk close to the main stem. Insert the stalk of the leaf in sand, vermiculite, or peat moss. Keep the cuttings in a moist atmosphere and continue to water until the parent leaf dies. In time, a tuber will develop at the base of the leaf cutting. When the parent leaf turns yellow and dies, the tuber that has formed is ready for potting. Leaves rooted in June will have tubers $1\frac{1}{2}$ inches across by November. Gloxinias can also be increased by cuttings made from the blade of a leaf. The leaf segment is placed vertically in sand. In time a tuber forms near the midrib.

Gloxinias are readily grown from seed. If you plant high quality hybrid seed, you have a thrill awaiting you. From such seed a great variety of plants may be obtained. Perhaps no two will be exactly alike; an occasional one may be very outstanding. The suspense of waiting for the seedlings to flower can be exciting. Many growers prefer to sow seeds in February, but you may, if you wish, plant them at any time. Plants grown from seeds sown in November will flower in May and June; those from seed sown in February, during the summer months.

The seedlings grow rapidly at first, and then growth almost ceases. The slow growth of the top coincides with the development of a small tuber below the surface of the soil. If the plants are not crowded in the seed pot, you can let them remain there until they are an inch or so high, when they can be moved into $2\frac{1}{2}$-inch pots. If they are crowded, move them into flats or large shallow pots and space the young plants about 2 inches apart in rows with 2 inches between. Later, these can be potted. As the plants become larger, shift them into 4-inch pots, a size suitable for their first flowering.

Even more thrilling than raising plants from purchased seed is

Fig. 17–7. A gloxinia seedling in flower during late summer.

the adventure you can have by hybridizing your own best plants, collecting seed, and sowing it. Select the parents carefully, considering color, marking, size, and substance, with the idea of combining the best traits of one with the best of the other. With a match stick or brush secure pollen from one parent and transfer it to the stigma of the other. The best time to do this is when the flowers have been open about five days, at which time the stigma will be sticky and receptive. If pollination is successful, the petals will fall off the seed parent in a day or two, and shortly thereafter the seed pod will begin to enlarge. In six to eight weeks the seed pod will be fully formed and the seeds ripe. Remove the seed pod and place it upside down in a dish. As the pod dries, the seeds will be liberated. The seeds may be planted in about a week, or you can save them for later plantings. Seeds remain viable for at least three years.

Thrips, mealybugs, aphids, and the cyclamen mite are some pests that attack gloxinias.

Kohleria

Kohlerias are noted for their velvety leaves and brightly colored tubular flowers, usually spotted with a deeper or contrasting shade. There are about 65 species and many hybrids. Two favorite species are *K. amabilis* and *K. eriantha*. *K. amabalis*, a native of Colombia, is a dwarf plant with silvery green leaves that have a red-brown pattern along the veins. The small pink flowers are dotted carmine red and are produced over a long period with a peak of flowering from late winter through spring. *Kohleria eriantha* is distinguishd by its deep green, ovate leaves bordered by reddish hairs. The flowers are orange-red and spotted blood-red. It is beautiful when grown in a hanging basket or when staked upright.

Like achimenes, kohlerias are grown from scaly rhizomes. Plant 3 or 4 rhizomes in a 5-inch pot covering them with one-half inch of soil. Water sparingly until growth is active and then keep the soil uniformly moist. Fertilize at biweekly intervals with a dilute solution of a complete fertilizer. Kohlerias tend to remain evergreen and not go completely dormant. When the plant appears to be resting apply less water and cease giving fertilizer. Soon thereafter the plant may be removed from the pot and the new rhizomes collected. Kohlerias may be grown from seed and stem cuttings. Such plants will flower in less than a year.

Rechsteineria

Rechsteineria cardinalis, from Central America, is a low, shapely plant with downy emerald green, heart shaped leaves. The scarlet tubular blooms, about 20 per stem, appear in the summer. The culture is like that of gloxinias. Plant tubers in winter, water sparingly until growth commences, then keep uniformly moist until flowering is over. The plant rests after flowering, but you can keep the attractive leaves green through the winter by sparsely watering the plant. Rechsteineria is readily increased by stem cuttings and from seeds.

Another beautiful plant is *R. leucotricha* that grows natively on cliffs near waterfalls in Brazil. The flowers are rosy coral covered outside with silky white hairs. The glistening silvery foliage is most attractive. After flowering this species has a six-month resting period at which time watering should cease.

Smithiana

Smithianas, commonly called temple bells because their flowers resemble Oriental temple bells, are native to the mountains of southern Mexico. They were named for Matilda Smith, a botanical artist employed by the Royal Botanical Garden at Kew, and have been cultivated since 1840. They are among the most beautiful of greenhouse plants with exquisite flowers and handsome foliage. The upright compact plants bear large, velvety, heart shaped leaves which are uniformly green in some varieties but variegated with purplish-red markings in others. From early summer to winter, with a peak in autumn, beautiful, nodding, bell shaped flowers in shades of red, yellow, pink, orange, and white are produced. There are five species and many hybrids. The most popular species are *S. cinnabarina, S. fulgida, S. multiflora,* and *S. zebrina.* Among the beautiful hybrids that were developed at Cornell University by crossing *S. fulgida* and *S. zebrina* are Abby, Cathedral, Cloisters, Vespers, Capistrano, Carmel, Santa Barbara, and Santa Clara; those named after early missions in Mexico and California have red leaves, the others green leaves.

Smithianas are most easily grown from scaly rhizomes which resemble miniature pine cones. Pot the rhizomes in March when they show signs of sprouting. Lay one to three rhizomes horizontally on moist soil contained in a 4- or 6-inch pot and then just barely cover them. Once growth is initiated keep the soil moist, not soggy, until flowering is through. After blooming is completed gradually withhold water to induce dormancy. After the tops have withered remove them. The rhizomes may remain in the pot or they may be removed and stored in dry vermiculite contained in a polyethylene bag. Smithianas can easily be grown from seed which may be sown any month of the year. Flowering plants are produced in six to eight months.

Streptocarpus

Streptocarpus, also known as the Cape primrose, has many species, chiefly native to South Africa. Most of those popularly grown are hybrids, stemming from such species as *Streptocarpus Dunnii,* a rose-flowered kind; *S. Wendlandii,* which bears violet-blue flowers; *S. Galpinii,* with mauve flowers; and *S. luteus,* a yellow-flowered species. Except for *S. luteus,* those mentioned develop only one large leaf. The species add interest to a collection, but they are not so beautiful as the hybrids, which have many leaves and bear flowers from 2 to 5 inches across. The flowers of the hybrids are often fringed and crested, and the color range is quite complete—with pink in all its shades, reds, blues, and whites with dark blotches. Well-grown plants are always admired (Fig. 1–3, page 8).

The Cape primrose is generally started from seed. By successive sowings from October to March, some plants will be in flower the year round. Plants grown from seed sown in January will begin to flower in August. The seeds are small and are sown in the same manner as those of African violets and gloxinias, using a planting mixture of equal parts of loam, leaf mold, peat moss and sand, which should also be used for the subsequent transplanting and potting. As soon as the seedlings are large enough to handle they should be transplanted into flats or pans with a spacing of about 2 inches. When they begin to crowd each other, move them singly into pots. Cape primroses should be grown in shade, not in bright sun, and they should not be allowed to dry out during their growing and flowering periods. In a greenhouse maintained at a night temperature of 60 degrees, they should be kept at the cooler end, especially when they approach flowering size. If you wish to grow the plants a second year, keep the plants slightly on the dry side (but not absolutely dry) from December until March. Then knock them out of the pots, remove some of the old soil, and repot in fresh soil. Plants with many crowns can be divided prior to potting. The Cape primrose may be increased by leaf cuttings. Use only the basal section of the leaf. Cut it into a wedge and plant in a mixture of sand and peat moss.

18

Orchids

Orchids are an amazing family of plants. With upwards of 30,000 species they have greater variety of form and habit than any other plant family. Some plants are taller than a man, others barely an inch high; flowers are from dinner-plate size to smaller than the head of a pin, of fantastic shapes and colors, and, with few exceptions, are long lasting. They range all over the world, from the cool high elevations to warm coastal areas; from dry cliffs to damp stream banks; from within the Arctic Circle to Tasmania and the tip of South Africa. Most of those grown in greenhouses come from the tropics and subtropics—the more equable temperatures in these regions, whether cool or warm, enable them to accept greenhouse conditions. However, the terrestrial orchids of cold or temperate climates are beautiful to see even though many resist efforts to move them to gardens, and require very special treatment in a greenhouse. In the United States, these are found from Alaska to Florida and they climb to 10,500 feet in the Rocky Mountains. So ubiquitous are orchids that they are entirely absent only in deserts and regions of permanent snow.

Some years ago only a few kinds were known by the general public—those used for corsages by florists. With increased travel people are seeing others in foreign lands and are sending them home to friends. Still the best known, however, and the kinds most amateurs choose for their first plants, are *Cattleya, Cymbidium, Phalaenopsis,* and *Paphiopedilum.* Even among these there are more sizes and combinations of colors than were dreamed of twenty years ago.

Lavender or white cattleyas now share the scene with recent hybrids that range from pink, yellow, and peach, to green, orange, and red, and the once-valued larger sizes are giving way to neater, more waxy, more perky hybrids, the smallest of which are sometimes called "cocktail" orchids. Cymbidiums can now be had in larger-than-ever standard types or the new miniature ones, and their colors are richly varied from white to pink, red, green, and yellow. Phalaenopsis, once generally known only in white or pink, are being hybridized to include yellow and subtle combinations of hues and some are striped or speckled. Paphiopedilums, the lady slippers (still commonly though incorrectly called cypripediums), now come in white and red as well as their accustomed yellow, brown, and green. Other kinds are becoming better known, among them vandas and dendrobiums, so often seen in leis in Hawaii but available as handsome hybrids in tremendous variety, and oncidiums, especially the "dancing doll" type. Hundreds of other kinds are available through dealers who specialize in the unusual.

It is easy to become a fancier of orchids, but they make congenial companions to other plants. One can have a few to add variety to a general collection, or can have mostly orchids with some other kinds—bromeliads, gesneriads, aroids, ferns, for example—for added interest.

Orchids are not difficult to grow. Although their needs vary according to their habits and the climate in their native haunts, their requirements are not hard to learn. As far as temperature is concerned, they are divided into three main groups: a cool group from high elevation that requires nights of 50 degrees in cultivation; an intermediate group from areas of moderate temperatures for which nights of 55 degrees to 60 degrees are suitable; and a warm group from lower elevations which needs a night temperature of 60 degrees to 65 degrees. Day temperatures should run 10 degrees higher, and most kinds can take a greater rise during the summer. Each group offers a wide choice of kinds, but it happens that the largest number of popularly grown ones comes in the intermediate range. In any group some will need more or less water, or more or less light, but if they are compatible regarding temperature, these other needs can be met individually.

Only a few of the favorite greenhouse orchids grow on the ground in soil, among them paphiopedilums. Most are epiphytes (tree dwellers). They perch on branches or trunks where their roots ramify through mosses and lichens and intertwine with those of other epiphytes, clinging to the bark or hanging free in the air. Neither they nor the plants that grow along with them are parasites; their roots do not penetrate the tree or obtain nourishment from it. Instead, they obtain minerals from decaying organic matter—dead plant parts, bugs, bird droppings, etc.—accumulated among their roots, which is the equivalent of that which nourishes soil-growing plants. Some kinds are equally at home on rocks, thatched roofs, or old fence posts—where they find the same type of support and nourishment as in the trees.

The epiphytic habit assures orchids of good air circulation and good light. In the trees some prefer the higher branches where the light is brighter; some live on the lower branches and have more shade. All have better light than they would if they lived on the forest floor, although the light is modified by the moving leaves of branches above them. In greenhouses these orchids need plenty of air circulation and good light. They cannot take full sun during our seasons of hot weather and long days, however, so the light must be lessened for them from spring through fall by shading on the glass. Winter sun is less strong and the temperatures are then cooler, so that in many regions they can have full sun. In areas where the winter sun is bright, however, some shade may still be necessary.

Epiphytic orchids do not have access to a continual supply of water as do ground-growing plants. They are subject to periodic drying—for as short a time as the interval between rains or as long as several months in regions where there are wet and dry seasons. Even in a season when there may not be a drop of rain there may be heavy dews, and frequently the atmosphere is quite humid. In what are called the "cloud" forests there are mists rising up the sides of valleys that keep the air charged with moisture, and plants in such forests hardly know drought as such. Yet in all such regions the tree dwellers are equipped to withstand drying. They have thickened stems and fleshy leaves which store water, and their roots are covered with a stiff, spongy material, called velamen, that soaks up water quickly and transmits it to central conducting cells that carry it to all parts of the plant. The thick plant parts store food as well as water.

The perfect drainage offered by a tree branch, the free aeration of the roots, and the periodicity of the water supply all point to three important principles for cultivating orchids: (1) the potting

Fig. 18–1. Many orchids are epiphytes, growing on trees. Above, collecting orchids from a branch extending over a tributary of the Amazon in Peru. Right, orchids growing on a tree trunk in Costa Rica.

medium must be open to allow good drainage and aeration, yet it must be firm enough to hold the plant in position and give the roots something to cling to both for support and for absorbing water and minerals; (2) water should be applied carefully so as to wet the medium thoroughly, yet not allow it to stay wet too long or become waterlogged; and (3) air within the greenhouse must be kept in motion by a fan—it is not enough merely to have ventilators open, although they should be opened for fresh air whenever the weather permits. Moving air, circulated briskly from one end of the greenhouse to the other, is a must for all orchids.

As different as orchids are in appearance one from another, they are all built on the same basic flower pattern. The three outer parts are the sepals. Within the sepals are three petals, one of which has been so transformed in shape and coloring that it has been given another name, the lip or labellum. Within the lip, standing with its back to the dorsal sepal, is the column, hallmark of the orchids. It is formed by the fusion of the reproductive parts. The column is a fleshy, more or less club-shaped organ, which bears the anther at its tip. Within the anther are the pollinia, waxy masses of pollen. Below the anther and separated from it by a little partition, is the stigma, the female receptive organ, a sunken area containing a sticky fluid. Most orchids are constructed so that a visiting pollinator receives the pollinia as it leaves the flower, thus ensuring that the pollen will be carried to another flower, effecting cross-pollination. The column is continuous with the ovary, which forms the "stem" of the flower, and which develops into the seed pod or seed capsule.

There are two general types of growth habit in orchids. One is the sympodial type, in which new growths are made seasonally from a ground stem or rhizome. It is found in cattleyas, cymbidiums, oncidiums, in fact in the largest number of species. The other is the monopodial type, in which the plant does not have a rhizome but instead a single stem, at whose tip new leaves are formed continually. Occasionally branch stems come from leaf axils, but not from the base. Vandas, phalaenopsis, and a number of others are of this type.

Using a cattleya as an example of the sympodial type, the illustration on page 283 shows its parts. The rhizome grows just at the surface of the potting medium. The upright stems, called pseudobulbs (they are not true bulbs) arise at intervals from the rhizome. Each comes from a bud at the base of the pseudobulb made the

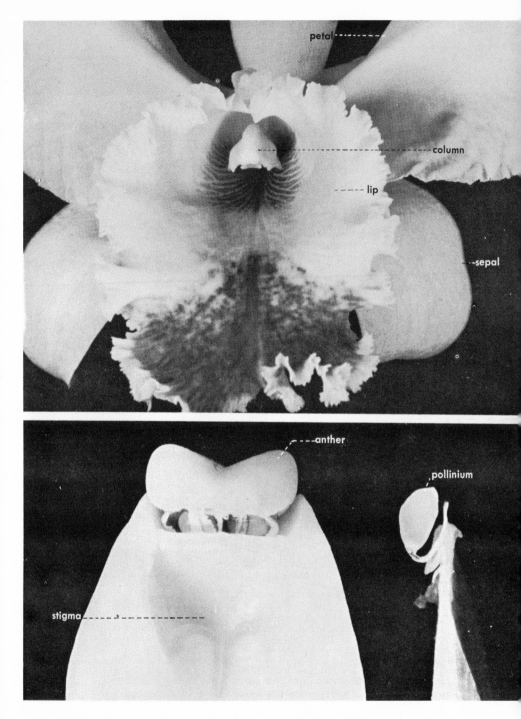

Fig. 18–2. Structure of an orchid flower, a cattleya. Above, notice the large lip (labellum) that surrounds the column, the two broad petals, and the more slender sepals. Below, details of the column. The anther cap has been tipped back to reveal the pollinia within it. The sunken area below it is the stigma. A pollinium is stuck to a sharpened matchstick at the right.

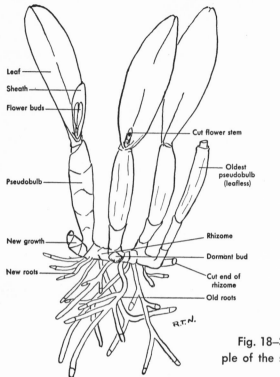

Fig. 18–3. A cattleya plant, example of the sympodial type.

previous season. When the growing season starts, the bud or "eye" swells, grows horizontally for an inch or so, and then curves upward. The horizontal part becomes an extension of the rhizome, while the upward-growing part produces the stem and leaf, and eventually the flowers. The growing end of the plant is called the lead or lead growth. Sometimes two buds break from the same pseudobulb, or buds on the older parts may become active, giving a plant with several leads.

When the developing lead is 4 to 6 inches tall, the true leaf emerges from the thinner sheathing leaves, and as it grows and expands, there can be seen within it a sheath, a closed green envelope. The flower buds develop from the tip of the pseudobulb, grow up within the sheath, and as they reach the top break out through it. The stems elongate, the buds grow larger, and the flowers open in two to six weeks.

Not all sympodial plants are shaped like cattleyas. Some have

Fig. 18–4. A vanda plant, example of the monopodial type.

round or flat, conical or pear-shaped pseudobulbs, others have stems that are cane-like, and some have no pseudobulbs at all. Some have many leaves to a growth, and they may be broad and thin (not fleshy) with prominent veins, or cylindrical and pencil-like. In oncidiums, cymbidiums, and many others the flowering stem comes from the base instead of the top of the pseudobulb, and in dendrobiums and still others, flowers come from the leaf axils near the tip of the stem or along most of its length.

A monopodial plant is illustrated by a vanda. It grows very tall, as do many other monopodials, with several leaves forming from the top each year. Roots come from the stem between the leaves, and are very thick. Flowering stems arise from the leaf axils, sometimes several times a year, or several at the same time. Side branches occasionally form, and make their own roots. A phalaenopsis plant does not grow as tall as a vanda, forming only one or two new leaves a year, and these are broad and rounded. Among the monopodials, just as in the sympodials, there are a great many kinds, from large to small. Nearly all are native to the Pacific area, Asia, and Africa.

Plants can be bought from growers who specialize in orchids. Many hybrids are available in almost every group, and species can be had either raised from seed or newly collected and imported. It is usually suggested that your first orchids should be mature plants, although this is not really necessary. Husky seedlings approaching maturity are just as easy to care for as mature plants. Younger ones require somewhat damper conditions, a bit less light, more frequent repotting, and an alert lookout for damp-off or other fungous infections. The younger the seedlings are the less they cost, so a larger number can be had for the same money. Age is related to pot size; those in 2½- or 3-inch pots may be three or four years old, while those in "community pots" may be anywhere from one to two years old. The community pot is used to grow the very young seedlings just out of the flask, and holds from 10 to 20 little plants. You need not buy a whole community pot; dealers will sell any number you desire.

Seed is sown in flasks on an agar jelly to which nutrient salts and sugar have been added. After first growth is made, they are transferred to a fresh flask, and when they are large enough to be on their own, to community pots. They may be purchased in the flasks if you wish a large number of the same kind.

There is great satisfaction in raising plants from seedling stages, and a good deal of anticipation in waiting for hybrids to bloom. One can never predict exactly what a hybrid will be like, for in any cross there is bound to be some variation among the offspring— sometimes they are quite alike, sometimes very different from each other. A grower always hopes that the good qualities or desirable features of the parents will be combined in the seedlings. Sometimes unusual combinations result, perhaps beautiful, possibly not. So the seedlings are a gamble, but a delightful one.

When you get the urge to make your own crosses and sow the seed yourself, we suggest that you obtain detailed instructions from books specializing in orchids. It is not a difficult process but one for which present lack of space prevents doing it justice.

Another process for multiplying plants, called meristem or tissue culture, is a recent innovation. Minute portions of a stem tip are removed from a desirable plant and aseptically transferred to flasks containing appropriate nutrients. With the proper treatment one stem tip will yield many new plantlets, all exactly like the parent. Meristem plants are available at low cost, and since only fine ones are worth meristemming, you can get duplicates of the best for very little.

Potting

Plants should be repotted when they have outgrown the ones they are in, or when the medium has broken down and begun to get soft or mushy.

The best time to repot any orchid is just when new roots are forming. Most kinds make new roots from the young growth, so it is easy to watch for this stage. Cattleyas usually form them from the base of the previous year's pseudobulb, coinciding with the flush of new growth. Those which have this habit should be potted promptly. You will notice that old roots form branch roots at the same time. However, some plants may start new growth and new roots while making flowers. If the flower buds are still small so that the plant can be handled without injuring them, they can be repotted. If the flowers are opening or the stems too long to make it possible to handle the plant, you will have to wait. In such a case, wait until the new roots are six inches or more in length; if the new roots are injured when they are still very short they will grow no more that year, whereas those that have grown longer will themselves form branch roots along with the older ones, so that injury by handling is not so serious.

Orchids can be grown in ordinary flower pots, or in hanging pots or baskets, or they may be mounted on slabs of tree fern or hardwood or cork bark, or on decorative pieces of driftwood. Osmunda fiber was for a long time the standard potting medium. Although it is still used for special purposes, and although some growers adhere to it entirely, it is time-consuming and difficult to handle, and is also very expensive.

Practically all orchids thrive in chopped fir or Douglas fir bark, which is much simpler to use and less costly. In Hawaii chopped tree fern trunk, called "hapuu," is popular. Some dealers offer their own special mixes, consisting essentially of chopped fir bark, perhaps some redwood chips or fiber, perlite, or other ingredients. Lightweight aggregate such as Holite, Solite, etc., is often used where orchids are grown outdoors in wet climates. The choice of medium is a matter of preference, and preference comes with experience, but since all are handled alike in the potting process, we will use bark as an example.

Bark comes in grades according to the size of the pieces. The finest is 0 to ⅛ inch and is used for seedlings just out of the flask. The next grade is ⅛ inch to ¼ inch for seedlings a bit larger, followed by a medium grade of pieces ½ inch, with some a little smaller and some a little larger, for older seedlings and mature plants. A coarse grade, ¾ to one inch, is used for vandas and other types with thick, heavy roots. Most growers prefer to soak the bark before use, and then pour off the water. It can be settled in the pot more firmly and is easier on the hands when it is damp.

The once-preferred clay pot is giving away to plastic, but either may be used. If they have been used before they should be washed and soaked in Clorox, one part to ten of water, to sterilize them, then be thoroughly rinsed and aired. Never cut a plant with an unsterilized tool. When you are finished with one plant, flame the knife, or razor blade, or clippers before using on the next plant.

Figure 18–5 (pages 289–91) gives the method for potting a mature cattleya. After wetting the plant to loosen its roots from the pot, remove it and gently shake out as much as possible of the old bark. Separate the roots and tease out the rest with your fingers. Trim off any rotten roots clear to their base, and cut healthy ones back to a two- to three-inch stub. The stubs will give rise to branch roots, whereas if they are left long they will rot.

A plant that has but one lead with perhaps seven or eight pseudobulbs in a line behind it should be divided to give two parts, a front half of three or four vigorous pseudobulbs, and a back half. The oldest, shrivelled pseudobulbs can be removed and discarded. Dormant buds will break on the back half to give a second flowering division. A plant that has several leads need not be divided; you can keep it intact, removing only the oldest pseudobulbs, to give a plant with many flowering leads. However, if you divide it, keep three or four pseudobulbs together on each part.

Choose a pot that allows room for two years' growth, estimating it on the basis of distance between growths. Put an inch or more of drainage material in the bottom (gravel, aggregate, or pieces of broken pot), and add a couple of handfuls of bark. Hold the plant or the division with its older end touching the side of the pot and the rhizome slightly below rim level and horizontal. Scoop in more bark, working it in among the root stubs. Tap the pot firmly on the bench to settle the bark, and then add more up to the top. Tap the pot again on the bench, and press the bark down with your thumbs or a blunt potting stick (metal, so that it can be sterilized). The final level of the bark should be a half-inch or an inch below

A. Remove the plant from the pot and work off the old bark.

B. Cut the rhizome and separate the two parts.

Fig. 18–5. Potting a cattleya plant.

the rim, and should be packed rather solidly to give the roots a firm foothold.

Push a metal stake deep into the bark and tie each growth to it, aiming for a natural vertical position. Growths that have strayed from vertical can be gently brought upright, but be careful not to

C. After preparing the pot, put enough bark in it to hold the plant at the proper level. Then, holding the older end against the side, fill with bark, thumping the pot occasionally to settle it.

D. Press the bark down with force to firm it.

Fig. 18–5 (Cont.).

E. Fasten a stake to the rim, or drive one into the center, and tie each growth to it.

Fig. 18–5 (Cont.).

break them. Tie a label to the stake or the plant, giving date of potting along with the name.

Newly potted plants should be kept on the dry side for a couple of weeks to let the cut roots heal without rotting. Keep them in a shady spot and give them a daily mist spray unless the humidity is high. When the new roots and branch roots are growing rapidly, begin to water regularly. New bark does not hold water as well as that which has been in use for a few months, so watering may have to be more frequent, always with care not to keep it too wet. When the roots are well established, remove the extra shade.

You may wish to grow cattleyas or other kinds, particularly those that require brightest light or which have drooping flower sprays, in a hanging position. Pots can be suspended by means of wires or hooks. Baskets are available made of closely set strips of redwood. Bark can be used in these. Other baskets made of widely spaced bars of wood or wire would allow bark to spill out, and osmunda fiber is best. It should be soaked and drained so that it is damp and soft, then torn into pieces. Place pieces in the bottom and around

Fig. 18–6. Seedlings are started in a flask containing agar jelly plus nutrients and sugar.

the sides of the basket. Prepare the plant by tucking pieces among its roots to form a good ball, and then settle it in the center. To tighten it all up, push pieces of fiber between the sides of the basket and that which is already in place. Hanging plants, particularly those in the open baskets, must be watered more frequently than those on the bench.

To mount a plant on a piece of tree fern trunk, place a thin pad of damp sphagnum moss on it first, and then tie the plant with its roots spread out by wrapping nylon fishing line around it and the piece of tree fern. The same method is used to mount a plant on driftwood or a slab of bark. Instead of fishing line, fine plastic-covered wire may be used. This method of growing is especially suitable for many little species, particularly those that have a climbing habit or like to become dry between waterings.

Seedlings must be shifted on into larger pots whenever their size merits it. Small ones need not be removed from the bark—merely be moved on in the intact ball with fresh medium added. Larger seedlings can be handled the same way if they have been in their pots for only a year or so. In other words, the roots of seedlings need not be cut back, nor the old medium removed, each time they are put into larger pots.

Monopodial plants require a different technique, since they grow

Fig. 18–7. Seedlings from a community pot ready for individual pots.

upward with a single stem. As the plant grows taller, basal leaves wither and fall. On a vanda plant the leaves sometimes remain green for ten to fifteen years; thus, the plant can attain a height of several feet with leaves still on the lower part. Such a plant can be simply moved on into a larger pot without much disturbance, replacing most but not all of the bark. You cannot hope to keep all of the roots in the pot—they will wander out, and will grow outward from the stem. It is often possible to bend some of them around to go into the medium, however. When a plant has lost many basal leaves, resulting in a bare stem for some distance, the top, leafy part should be cut off and put into a fresh pot. Always leave a few vigorous roots on the upper half. Partially fill the new pot with bark, settle the base of the stem into it, placing the roots therein if possible, and bring the bark level to within an inch of the rim. For large plants, a three-fourths height pot is best, and for still larger ones an even more shallow pot but of larger diameter, such as a bulb pan of ten inches or more.

A phalaenopsis is repotted in the same way, except that there will not be so much of the old stem base to remove. Just break off the part that has been down in the bark, along with the older roots growing from it, leaving the younger roots attached to the upper section. Settle the base of the upper stem into the new bark, with the younger roots just under or upon the surface.

Side branches develop on vandas from time to time. When one has made roots of its own it can be removed and be potted separately. Occasionally this will happen on the old part left in the pot after the upper section has been removed. Let the old part stay, water it regularly, and wait to see if new growth develops.

Flask seedlings of all kinds of orchids can be removed from the flask by pouring in water at room temperature, swirling, and pouring out water and seedlings together. Those that remain fastened in the agar can be lifted out with a long spoon. The little plants should then be put in a bowl of fungicide solution (Natriphene is good), and from this into pots or small flats of fine bark. Settle each one gently and push bark up around its roots. Try to keep them sorted as to size so that they will make approximately equal growth in any one container.

The community pots or flats must be kept damp. They can be set in a wooden box with a glass cover. The cover should be opened part of each day for ventilation. They need to be shaded so that they have 200 foot candles of light at first, increasing to 500 foot candles in a couple of months. They grow faster with nights of 70 degrees but can be kept in a warm spot in the intermediate house. When they go into individual pots they can have more light—1,000 foot candles at first, gradually increasing to 1,500 foot candles. They still need to be kept damp in the pots but do not need the glass cover. With the next shift into larger pots they can be given the same light and temperature as mature plants but should still not be allowed to dry out. From four-inch size on, they are treated as mature plants.

Fertilizer, Light, and Water

Orchids in bark or any of the mixes require regular applications of soluble fertilizer. This should be of a high nitrogen content, in the proportions 30–10–10, since bark contains little nitrogen. Special formulations are available from growers, and these usually contain iron chelate and trace elements. Organic fertilizers such as fish emulsion can also be used, or alternated with the chemical ones.

Directions will be given on the package, usually calling for ½ to one teaspoon per gallon of water, to be given at every other watering. Orchids are sensitive to salts that can build up in the medium. Therefore, pots should be flushed thoroughly at each watering. Don't just dribble water into the pot—let the hose run in it long enough to allow water to pour out the bottom, moving the hose around over the surface to be sure all the medium is soaked. When fertilizer is to be given, water the plants in the same way and then follow it immediately with the fertilizer solution.

No one can give an exact schedule for watering. Pots of different sizes dry out in different lengths of time, and an actively growing plant will use water faster than one in a resting state. A general rule can be made, however, to let the medium become almost dry before adding water. The bark should feel slightly cool when you put your fingers into it, but should not be so damp as to wet your fingers. Certain kinds need to be allowed a really dry period during their dormancy.

Leaves can burn when they have too bright light. Most orchids, cattleyas among them, do well with one-fourth to one-third of full sun in spring, summer, and fall—in other words, during seasons of warm weather. Where winters are dull they can have clear glass, but in regions of bright winter sun they may still require some shade. A few kinds need less light than cattleyas, and some need more, individual differences stemming from their native conditions. In general, leaf color indicates whether a plant has the right amount. Too dark a green shows they are not receiving enough; yellow or yellow-green color, or scorched areas, too much.

Pests and Diseases

The usual greenhouse pests attack orchids, particularly mites, scales, mealy bugs, thrips, aphids, slugs, and snails. Never use a strange insecticide until it has been proven for orchids, and never use an aerosol pressure spray. Always follow directions carefully because too strong a solution, or using it under the wrong conditions, can damage the plants. We cannot recommend systemic insecticides in general—they have been used on a few kinds successfully, but have not been proven safe for very many.

When scale insects are seen, they may be scrubbed off with a brush dipped in Malathion, using rubber gloves and taking care not to inhale strong fumes. This should be followed by spraying. Mealy bugs that are seen can be killed with alcohol on a cotton swab, but since large populations can hide under the covering leaf sheaths, etc., when their presence is known the whole plant should be dipped in Malathion solution to which has been added a few drops of dish-washing detergent. Aphids and thrips can ruin the flowers, the former making punctures surrounded by a watery halo, the latter by chewing and scarring the parts. (Orchids do not have extra petals that can be removed, as do roses and many other flowers, when some are spoiled!) Malathion, rotenone, or nicotine sulfate will control them.

A special warning is necessary against false spider mites, mites so small they cannot be seen with a magnifying glass of less than 10 power. These smallest of mites wreak terrific damage to the leaves, causing pits and scars, and even causing leaves to die. Dimite, Kelthane, or chlorobenzilate will control these as well as the two-spotted mite and red spiders, and should be included in a regular spray program. Any of these can be mixed in the sprayer with Malathion.

Slugs chew root tips, young leaves, and flowers. Snails, a small, flat-coiled variety, feed on root tips. Both are controlled with Metaldehyde. Various formulations are available from orchid dealers, and come as powder, granules, or liquids. Use them according to directions. Never use a bait containing arsenic on orchids.

Diseases include various fungous, bacterial, and virus infections. It is not easy to tell them apart. Soft brown spots should be smeared with a paste of Tersan, or sponged with a solution of Natriphene. When a rot attacks any plant part and is not stopped by this, the diseased area should be cut out, making the cut well down into clean tissue. Then the whole plant should be immersed in a Natriphene solution for an hour or two, and be allowed to remain dry afterward for a week or more. Viruses cannot be cured; a plant with a known virus infection must be discarded. Laboratories that test for viruses will perform tests on samples sent to them. Virus infections usually show up as mottling or streaking of the foliage, often with distortion, or as color break and distortion in the flowers.

Some Kinds to Grow

A selection of kinds to grow could include hundreds, for there are almost limitless possibilities. We suggest that you visit commercial ranges, and amateur greenhouses, and also obtain illustrated catalogs. Those we will give here can be a mere introduction to the most popular genera.

Many kinds are grown as species, but in some genera you will find mostly hybrids available. A distinctive feature of orchids is the ease with which species and even genera can be crossed. A hybrid may have a dozen species in its ancestry, from as many as three or four genera. Those that will interbreed with each other are closely related genetically, of course, but they are often quite different in appearance. In the group to which *Cattleya* belongs, hybridizers have crossed the genera *Cattleya, Laelia, Brassavola,*

Sophronitis and *Epidendrum* with each other to form *Laeliocattleya, Brassocattleya, Epicattleya, Sophrocattleya, Brassolaelia, Epilaelia, Sophrolaelia,* and so on for the other combinations. These have been combined to give trigeneric hybrids such as *Brassolaeliocattleya* (abbreviated Blc) and *Sophrolaeliocattleya* (Slc). By the time four genera are combined, using the generic names in combination becomes too awkward so the multigeneric hybrids are named after people; for example, the hybrid combining the first four of the genera above is called *Potinara.*

The following pedigree illustrates the making of a hybrid:

Cattleya mendelii ⎱ *Laeliocattleya* ⎱		
Laelia purpurata ⎰ Canhamiana ⎰		*Brassolaeliocattleya*
		Mount Everest
Brassavola digbyana ⎱ *Brassocattleya*		
Cattleya dowiana ⎰ Mrs. Leeman		

All seedlings from a hybrid cross go by the same name, even though they may be quite different from each other. And if the cross is repeated using the same species or hybrids, the same name must be used again. For example, every plant resulting from crossing *L.* Canhamiana × *Bc.* Mrs. Leeman is named *Blc* Mount Everest. A particularly fine plant (clone) of a species or a hybrid may be singled out with a varietal name put in single quotes, for example a desirable individual of the above might be called *Blc* Mount Everest 'Pearl.'

Most large cities have an orchid society and you would enjoy belonging. The American Orchid Society is international in character. Membership brings with it the *American Orchid Society Bulletin,* a monthly publication full of informative articles and the advertisements of commercial growers and suppliers. Another good publication is the *Orchid Digest,* published by a corporation of societies in the western states.

Cattleya and Its Relatives

This group ranges through the American tropics and subtropics, from Florida and Mexico on through Argentina. They grow well with a night temperature of 55 degrees to 60 degrees or slightly warmer, and with 2,000 to 3,000 foot candles of light. The medium should approach dryness between waterings.

Cattleya

Almost any collection should include a few cattleyas for the sake of their large, showy, often fragrant flowers, which can last up to six weeks on the plant. Blooming plants can be brought into the house and enjoyed for a month or more. Cut flowers are wonderful for corsages and arrangements.

The large ruffled species are known as the "labiata" type, among them *Cattleya labiata, C. mossiae, C. trianaei, C. gigas,* and *C. mendelii,* all various shades of lavender, and *C. aurea,* yellow. Until the advent of the hybrids, these species were the showiest orchids known. They are less frequently seen now, hybrids having taken their place, but are still prized by collectors. Their plants bear a single leaf to the pseudobulb and are therefore often called unifoliates.

Another group of species are the bifoliates, plants with two or more leaves to the pseudobulb, which have smaller, more waxy flowers of many colors, often decorated with bars and spots. The hybrids resulting from crossing these with each other and with the labiata group tend to be smaller, more waxy flowers of many colors, usually with a greater number to the stem. Among the bifoliates the species are very popularly grown, as well as the hybrids. Delightful for any collection are *C. aclandiae,* greenish sepals and petals spotted with brown, and a pink lip; *C. aurantiaca,* orange; *C. bicolor,* brownish green with a pink tongue-shaped lip; *C. bowringiana,* brilliant rose-purple, occurring in clusters of ten to twenty to a stem; *C. granulosa,* green or brownish green, with a yellowish lip; *C. guttata,* green, spotted with deep purple; *C. loddigesii,* light rose-lilac (there is also a white form much used to make dainty white hybrids); *C. skinneri,* bright cerise, national flower of Costa Rica; and *C. walkeriana,* rich rose color with the odd habit of producing the flowering stem from the rhizome between the pseudobulbs.

Laelia

Laelias are very much like cattleyas. While some have large flowers, many of them are small and star-shaped, of brilliant colors, and often have large numbers of blooms on a tall stem. They are crossed with cattleyas, enhancing the hybrids with their bright hues and often modifying their shape. The species are delightful in themselves. *Laelia anceps* and *L. autumnalis* have tall stems topped by clusters of large rosy or lavender flowers. Star-shaped and also with many to a stem are *L. flava*, bright yellow; *L. milleri* and *L. cinnabarina*, brilliant red or red-orange, and *L. harpophylla*, soft orange. *L. lundii* is a miniature with little light lavender, cattleya-like blossoms. *L. purpurata* is the most famous and has been much used in hybridization for its richly colored lip and large size.

Brassavola

Brassavola digbyana and *B. glauca* (both also called *Rhyncholaelia*) are different from each other and both are used in hybridization. *B. digbyana* is a huge greenish-white flower with a fantastically fringed, very broad lip. The lip size and shape, but not often the fringe, carry over to its hybrids. *B. glauca* is used to make hybrids with small, perky flowers, often in tones of yellow. Another species, *B. nodosa*, which has white, spidery flowers with a rounded lip, is called "lady of the night" because it sends forth its fragrance in the evening to attract night-flying moths.

Sophronitis

The little species *Sophronitis coccinea* must be included because of its role in the creation of red and near-red hybrids, but it requires cool conditions and is not easy to keep alive. The plants are miniature in size, and the flat red, one and one-half inch flowers are large in proportion.

Epidendrum

Epidendrums are easy to grow and flower profusely. There are hundreds of species, some showy and well known, some insignificant and rather colorless. Some have true pseudobulbs while others have reed-like stems. Among the former are *E. atropurpurem* (or *cordigerum*) which has graceful two-inch greenish brown flowers with a large lip; *E. ciliare*, white with a pointed lip with fringed side lobes; *E. cochleatum*, with a shell-shaped lip that is green with purple stripes, blackish on the back, and *E. fragrans*, another with a shell-shaped lip, but of cream with red stripes; *E. prismatocarpum*, which has star-shaped, cream colored flowers spotted with purple; and *E. tampense*, a native of Florida which has delightful little greenish flowers. Among the reed-stemmed species, *E. ibaguense*

(or *radicans*) has long been popular. It has tall (reaching six feet) leafy stems topped by a round head of red one-inch flowers with a fringed lip. It has been hybridized with similar types to give shorter plants, better suited to small greenhouses, and flowers of cream, salmon, pink, yellow, orange, and red. A reed-stem becoming well known is *E. pseudepidendrum*, medium tall plants with a cluster of striking flowers in "psychedelic" colors—green, with a waxy orange lip with a purple band at its base.

Cymbidium

Cymbidiums, native to Japan, Asia, and the Pacific Islands, are graceful plants with grassy, lily-like foliage and egg-shaped pseudobulbs. Most familiar are the large flowered hybrids called "standards" which are winter blooming plants with tall stems holding ten to twenty or more large, waxy flowers in a wide array of colors. The species from which they are made are native to high elevations of the Himalayas and they require rather special conditions for blooming. Recently being created are smaller hybrids, the smallest of which are called "miniatures," and the medium sized ones "polymins." These embody species from warmer climates and may be raised along with cattleyas. They flower several times a year.

The plants are semi-terrestrial and have fleshy roots. They are grown in a soil-like medium consisting of sand, loam, fine bark, leaf mold, sometimes with screened peat moss or Perlite added. Commercial growers who specialize in their culture usually offer their own type of potting mix for sale. The plants should not be allowed to dry out, yet must have perfect drainage so that the medium does not stay sopping wet. Fertilizer should be given at every other watering.

The standard cymbidiums are so spectacular and their flowers so long lasting (up to three months on the plant) that many amateurs try to grow them under less than ideal conditions. They are best grown in a cool, bright greenhouse. Night temperatures of 45 degrees to 50 degrees from fall through winter, and summer nights of

Fig. 18–8. Upper, *Dendrobium densiflorum*, with many flowers to a spray. Lower left, cymbidiums are waxy and long lasting. This is a hybrid. Lower right, *Oncidium splendidum*.

60 degrees or under assure good growth and flowering. An evaporative cooler is essential in most areas to control summer day temperatures. Initiation of flower spikes takes place in late summer or early autumn, and at this time the nights should be as cool as possible. In warm climates growers are often able to get them to bloom by putting them outside under light shade from spring until frost threatens. A switch from a high nitrogen to a low nitrogen–high phosphorus fertilizer in late summer also helps to bring about blooming.

Although they require bright light this does not mean that they can take full sun in a greenhouse; a thin shading of the glass is necessary during the warm months to keep the foliage from burning or yellowing, and when the plants are in bloom shading will help keep the flowers fresh for a longer time. The yellow and green ones need a bit more shading than other colors to keep them from getting a brownish tinge.

Miniatures and polymins can be grown with cattleya conditions, but they will also grow well in a cool greenhouse. The miniatures are small plants with many flowered spikes of delightfully colored, small, pert flowers. The polymins, being crosses between miniature and standard forms, are often larger and have larger flowers. Except that they are more tolerant of warm temperatures, and do not need as much light, they are cultivated in the same manner as the standards.

Cymbidiums thrive when they are left undivided for as long as possible. They can be put in larger pots until they reach an unwieldly size, or until they have a large number of leafless pseudobulbs, when dividing becomes necessary. Divide the plant by cutting through the rhizome between clumps of three to six pseudobulbs, then gently work the divisions apart, taking care not to injure the roots. Roots that are rotten or broken may be trimmed off, but some can be left intact. Pot the plant as you would any soil-growing kind, having the base of the pseudobulbs just slightly below soil level. Leafless backbulbs may be removed and inserted in damp sphagnum moss. They may give rise to new growths from dormant buds. When the new shoot is two to three inches tall, the backbulb should be potted in regular mix. New roots will come from the new shoot when it is about four inches tall.

Red spiders and false spider mites are particular enemies of cymbidiums. They injure not only the leaves, feeding on the under sides, but also attack the flowers from the moment they emerge as small buds.

Dendrobium

The tremendous genus *Dendrobium* has many delightful types with various habits, and among them are both cool- and warm-growing species. They occur all through Asia, Australia, Papua-New Guinea, and the Pacific Islands. Those you are likely to find in catalogs have a cane-like stem. Some produce long stems of flowers from the upper leaf axils; others give clusters of flowers from nodes all along the cane. They are potted in the same materials and watered in the same manner as cattleyas, except that they do better in small pots and need not be repotted as frequently.

Dendrobium nobile and its hybrids with similar types are beautiful and satisfying. They can be grown with cymbidiums all year around, or can be kept with cattleyas during the growing season and moved to the cool greenhouse for flower-bud formation. The canes lose their leaves the second year, and during this time clusters of flower buds form at the nodes. No water should be given from early fall until the flower buds are well formed. If they are kept too warm, or are watered during this period, small plantlets may form instead of flowers. Watering should be resumed as soon as it is ascertained that the buds are present. The velvety flowers are sweetly rounded, and their colors range from white with lavender markings to purple and pink. Other deciduous types that are equally lovely are *D. parishii, D. pierardii, D. primulinum,* and *D. adrasta,* all of which like cattleya conditions, but with a dry period before flower formation.

Among the so-called evergreen types, which keep their leaves for several years, are *D. thyrsiflorum* and *D. densiflorum,* closely related kinds that have lantern-shaped pendant sprays of blooms, white with a yellow lip in the former and pure golden yellow in the latter. These are cool-growing, but do not require restricted water at any time. They need somewhat more shade than cymbidiums, however. Their 15-inch stems are thickened upwards and bear several broad shiny leaves.

In a class of their own are *D. phalaenopsis* and the many hybrids between it and related kinds. These are cane types eighteen inches to two feet tall that retain only the upper few pairs of leaves. The long arching flower stems come from the upper leaf axils. According to the particular hybrid or species, the flowers range from light lavender to rich red-violet, occasionally white, and are velvety in texture. They grow with cattleyas and keep their leaves for several years. Old canes can flower a second and third time. One caution should be carefully observed. From the time flowering is finished and until the new growth is making its own roots, *absolutely no water should be given in the pot.* The new growth is very touchy and can be killed if the potting medium is kept wet. The plants can be given an occasional mist spray, however.

Oncidium and Its Relatives

Oncidiums and their relatives together offer over 1,000 species. The interbreeding of *Oncidium, Odontoglossum, Miltonia,* and *Brassia* has led to additional hundreds of hybrids, and in *Miltonia* the hybrids are more familiar than the species. In the others the species are desirable and available, and are probably more commonly grown. The group is native to Mexico, Central and South America, and the Caribbean Islands.

Oncidium

Incredible variety is found in this genus. Many are good companions for cattleyas, others are cool-growing. Even the smallest species makes a delightful show, and the large flowered ones are spectacular. A charming feature of most is the fancifully carved and decorated lip crest. All can be grown in bark or the mixes and some can be mounted on slabs. Whether warm- or cool-growing, they are watered like cattleyas and take about the same amount of light. New roots come from the newly forming lead. Most have a somewhat compressed conical or rounded pseudobulb and flat, rather thin leaves.

The "dancing doll" type is so called because its lip is round and skirtlike, while the sepals and petals are much abbreviated and stand up around the tip of the column, giving it the appearance of a doll's head with a headdress. Of several species of this type, *O. varicosum* and *O. ampliatum* are well known, and give dainty, bright yellow flowers. Then there are kinds with a less large lip but which also have multi-flowered sprays sometimes five feet long, of vari-colored flowers, usually with spots or bars on the sepals and petals. Among these are *O. sphacelatum* (yellow and brown); *O. leucochilum*, green with brown bars and a white lip; *O. ornithorhyncum* and *O. incurvum* (both pink, the latter cool-growing); and *O. cheirophorum*, yellow, almost a miniature. Two handsome ones with a huge yellow lip and brown-barred sepals and petals, but with very different vegetative parts, are *O. tigrinum* from Mexico, which has large conical pseudobulbs and broad rather thin leaves, and *O. splendidum* from Central America which has a single stiff, thick leaf shaped like a burro ear attached to a pseudobulb that is hardly more than a swelling at its base. Other burro-ear species have a quite different type of flower—small, with a tiny lip, and ruffled sepals and petal, all very waxy. Among these are *O. cavendishianum*, *O. luridum*, and *O. carthagenense*.

Oncidium papilio and *O. kramerianum* are distinctive for their huge brown and yellow flowers that open one at a time atop a tall stem, looking exactly like big butterflies. The dorsal sepal and the petals are drawn out to form slender "antennae," while the broad lateral sepals and rounded lip give the impression of wings. Their foliage is green mottled with brown or red-brown.

Another group of huge brown and yellow flowers comes from the Andes of Ecuador and is cool-growing. These have long vining flower stems, reaching 12 to 20 feet, which bear large numbers of blooms. *Oncidium macranthum* and *O. lamelligerum* are typical ones, a distinctive feature being the tiny lip, hardly more than a short necktie. The sepals and petals are large, wavy in *O. macranthum*, highly ruffled in *O. lamelligerum*.

There are many other types, but we shall mention only one more, the "equitant" species which have a little fan of leaves that are curiously formed. They look as if they had been folded together at the midrib and had grown together. Indeed, they have "grown together," for they cannot be unfolded. Some are perfectly flat, others are triangular in cross section. They range throughout the Caribbean Islands, and at least one species occurs in Central America. Among them are *O. triquetrum* with red and white flowers; *O. pulchellum*, with lovely round pink flowers; *O. desertorum*, yellow, with petals that are shaped much like the lip; and *O. pusillum*, the one that also occurs on the mainland, perhaps the most beautiful of all orchid plants with its almost round fan of bright green leaves and yellow flowers large for its size.

Odontoglossum

Some of the odontoglossums come from very high elevations and even when given cool conditions are difficult to grow. However, these have been hybridized to give what are called "crispum" types, named for one of their chief progenitors, *Odontoglossum crispum*, and these lovely star-shaped, ruffled hybrids can be more easily grown. Less difficult cool species are *O. rossii*, a delightful miniature with brown-barred sepals and petals and a pink lip, and *O. uro-skinneri*, a larger plant which has sepals and petals of green barred with brown, and a heart-shaped rose colored lip. Do not let any dry out at the roots.

For intermediate conditions, *O. grande* is the most famous, and is one of the most striking of orchids. It has five-inch flowers of waxy brown barred with yellow, a white lip with brown bars, and a crest that resembles an inflated rubber doll. It needs to be kept somewhat dry between flowering and start of the new growth. Another one to grow with cattleyas is *O. pulchellum,* the "lily-of-the-valley" orchid, which has slender stems of small fragrant white blossoms.

Miltonia

The flat, rounded flowers of *Miltonia* are called "pansy" orchids. Species are available, but for the most part it is the hybrids that are generally grown. They are of great beauty and come in colors from white, yellow, and cream to rose, pink, and dark red, all with a mask resembling a butterfly on the lip. They grow well with cattleyas, with a bit more shade, and should not be allowed to dry out. They do not like extreme heat and where summers are hot do better when an evaporative cooler is in operation.

Brassia

These flowers with their elongated sepals and petals (the sepals are the longer) are called "spider" orchids. Even the lip looks like the body of a spider. The flowers come in shades of brown and green, and the lip is usually white or pale green with spots of brown or green. Up to ten flowers grow to a stem, arranged in two rows, all facing forward. In *B. verrucosa* the sepals from tip to tip measure about eight inches; in *B. gireoudiana* ten to twelve inches; and in *B. longissima* fifteen inches or more. They are grown like oncidiums, and are rewarding conversation pieces.

Fig. 18–9. Upper left, a miltonia hybrid. Upper right, a paphiopedilum hybrid grown with many leads gives a wealth of blooms. Lower left, the fly orchid, *Trichoceros parviflorus*. Lower right, a phalaenopsis hybrid.

Paphiopedilum

The lurid beauty of *Paphiopedilum*, a genus of terrestrials that ranges natively from Asia to Indonesia and New Guinea, has drawn about it a real cult among orchid growers. These are the "ladyslippers," which have a pouch-shaped lip, a large striped or spotted dorsal sepal, and slender, extended petals often decorated with hairs or warts. The lateral sepals are united and lie behind the lip. The waxy flowers are long lived, much used for corsages and as cut flowers. The plants are terrestrial, without pseudobulbs, and the leaves spread fanlike in each growth. A single flowering stem comes from the center of each new growth bearing one or several flowers according to the kind. Colors range through the spectrum; some flowers tend toward green, brown, or yellow with suffusions of red or purple, while others are mostly red, and some are white. The species are delightful, the hybrids equally so.

Fig. 18–10. Small plants on pieces of tree fern, hanging on a driftwood "tree."

Kinds with plain green foliage, for example *Paphiopedilum in-signe, P. fairieanum,* and *P. spicerianum* and their hybrids, grow best with a night temperature of 50 to 55 degrees. Those with mottled foliage such as *P. lawrenceanum, P. villosum,* and *P. barbatum* and their hybrids require a night temperature of 60 degrees. Hybrids between the plain and mottled leaved ones do well at night temperatures of 55 to 60 degrees, and some even at 65 degrees.

From March or April to early November they grow well with a light intensity of 1,000 foot candles or less. In the winter, when light is less strong, they can be given a higher intensity, and where winters are quite dull they may get along without shade on the glass. They grow well in a cymbidium mix but many growers offer their own formulation for sale. Their roots are fleshy, and covered with hairs; they should not be allowed to dry out. They are best repotted soon after they have flowered, every second year. They can be grown into large plants with many growths, or may be divided into plants with a single lead and the two growths backing it up. They are sensitive to salts in the medium, and require less frequent applications of fertilizer than other orchids—once a month or six weeks is sufficient.

Phalaenopsis and Vanda

For serene beauty, *Phalaenopsis* rivals *Miltonia.* The breathtakingly lovely white hybrids and the plain pink ones, that range from light to dark tones, are open, flat flowers of velvety texture. Newer hybrids in yellow, peach, pink, or white, with suffusions of other colors, a lip of a different hue, and even with spots or stripes, may be smaller flowers, often star-shaped, sometimes of waxy texture. The species come from the Philippines and other South Pacific Islands, and are less often seen than the hybrids in amateur collections. *Phalaenopsis equestris* and *P. leuddemanniana* are two exceptions—they are delightful small species. The former is light rosy lavender. The latter, a bit larger, has many color forms. After the first flush of flowers on a spray, most of the hybrids form additional buds at the tip of the stem. Also, after flowering is finished, if the stem is cut below the node that produced the lowest flower, a branch stem may form to give a second complete flowering. Sometimes plantlets form on old flower stems, and these can be removed and potted.

Fig. 18–11. Left, *Cycnoches*, the swan orchid. Right, *Catasetum macro-carpum* (note the trigger within the lip).

Phalaenopsis grows well in medium grade bark, although grow-ers have their favorite mixes. They like a rather constantly damp medium, a fairly high humidity, and fresh moving air. Tempera-tures should not go below 60 degrees at night. They need some-what more shade than cattleyas, particularly in the summer.

Vanda is related to *Phalaenopsis*, but is tougher, requires much brighter light, in fact the brightest spot in the cattleya house, and while it becomes a more lush plant at temperatures above 60 de-grees will also do well if the nights drop to 55 degrees. The species are native to tropical Asia and the Philippines, and a few are popu-larly grown. Such are *Vanda coerulea*, the blue vanda, which likes a somewhat cooler spot than the rest; *V. dearei*, which has fragrant white and yellow flowers; and the most handsome of all, *V. sanderi-ana* (now called *Euanthe sanderiana*) which has huge flowers whose upper parts are white and rose, and lower parts are green, netted with brown. These three and many others have been crossed to produce an array of beautiful hybrids.

Other lovely monopodials are *Angraecum, Aerides,* and *Ascocen-trum*. There are many intergeneric hybrids in the group, among them a type that is becoming very popular, *Ascocenda*, a cross be-tween *Vanda* and *Ascocentrum* that gives charming little plants with round, brightly colored flowers.

Other Orchids

While there are many other desirable kinds, we'll end with three that will become conversation pieces in your collection.

The Swan Orchid (familiarly known as *Cycnoches chlorochilon*, but whose real name is *Cycnoches ventricosum var. warscewiczii*) is a sheer beauty. The very wavy fragrant flowers have chartreuse sepals and petals and a white swan-shaped lip. The slender arching column completes the illusion with its resemblance to the neck and head of a swan.

Catasetum has many species that are pollen shooters—they are equipped with triggers which when touched cause the pollen-bearing apparatus to shoot out with great force, adhering to whatever it happens to land upon, in nature the pollinating insect, in a greenhouse your finger or a nearby plant. The flowers have various shapes and colors, some of them quite lurid in appearance. A few species are *Catasetum macrocarpum, C. viridiflavum,* and *C. integerrimum,* all of which have helmet-shaped lips, and come in shades of green or yellow, with varying amounts of spotting; and *C. pileatum,* a beautiful clear yellow with a saucer-shaped lip.

Both *Catasetum* and *Cycnoches* are deciduous. The broad, thin leaves fall as winter approaches and the thick spindle-shaped pseudobulbs remain naked through the winter. During this period the plants should be kept dry. New growth starts in the spring, and when their roots begin to form watering should be resumed. Flower spikes come from the base of the pseudobulbs in *Catasetum* and from the upper leaf axils in *Cycnoches,* after the growth is mature or while it is maturing, and often not until the leaves are ready to fall.

Stanhopea has strangely shaped flowers that look somewhat like a bird of prey. The flower spikes bore down through the growing medium and the plants must, therefore, be grown in open hanging baskets. When the large egg-shaped buds burst open the greenhouse is filled instantly with a spicy perfume. The yellow, tawny, or white flowers have widely flaring sepals and petals, spotted in most kinds. The lip is intricately carved and contorted, and bears a pair of horns at the end. Together with the downward arching column it forms a chute through which a visiting insects falls when it loses its footing on the waxy base of the lip. As the insect falls through the chute it comes in contact with the sticky disc of the pollinarium and flies off with it attached to its back. The plants are evergreen, keeping their broad leathery leaves for several seasons. The plants come from many different habitats in nature—some that have a dry period and some that are constantly wet. In a greenhouse they do best when they are allowed to just approach dryness between waterings, and are thoroughly wetted by soaking in a bucket at watering time. They are grown in osmunda fiber and do not require feeding. Most familiar species are *Stanhopea wardii* and *S. oculata*. The flowers last only three days, but that's long enough to call in the neighbors to see the weird spectacle, and a plant with several leads will flower over a period of weeks.

19

Cacti and Other Succulents

Deserts are fascinating places with their blue skies, bright days, interesting animals, and strange plants. The plants are exposed to scorching sun interrupted only occasionally by heavy rains. Following a rain the plants plump up, grow, and flower. Many of the desert plants have extensive root systems and small leaves or none at all. After a rain, the extensive roots absorb water which is then stored in fleshy stems or fleshy leaves. The small leaf area cuts down evaporation, and results in a slow rate of foodmaking and therefore of growth, enabling such plants to grow for many years in small pots. Plants with fleshy stems or leaves or both are called *succulents*.

The strange and varied forms of the succulents, the rare beauty of some of their flowers, and their remarkable adaptations for desert life make them appealing plants. Building up a collection of these interesting plants has become almost a mania for some greenhouse gardeners. There are those who have designed desert landscapes of great charm in their greenhouses, even devoting the whole greenhouse to their collection. You may wish to make these plants your hobby and use your greenhouse only for them. Or perhaps you will want just a few. You can raise them in pots. Then if you want a more natural setting you can plunge the pots in sand or gravel so that the pots do not show. A few attractive rocks artfully spaced will add to the naturalness of the scene. If you wish, you can move the plants outdoors in the summer and have a desert arrangement in part of your garden. Of course, you can plant cacti and other succulents directly in a bench where they can remain year after year.

Deserts are not the only places we find succulents. Strangely enough, some succulents grow in tropical rain forests which are always humid and moist. Here they grow on trunks or branches of trees or on rocks, where they are shut off from a supply of ground water. Plants which grow perched on trunks or branches of trees are called *epiphytes*. They are rooted in small accumulations of debris. During a rain and shortly thereafter water is available, but soon the scant debris in which they are rooted dries out and the plants are subject to drought. In the interval between rains, however, the plants use the water stored in their fleshy stems or leaves. Among the cacti which are epiphytes are the orchid cactus, the Christmas cactus, and the Queen of the Night.

Cacti, with one exception, are all native to the western hemisphere and are the most abundant succulents of our deserts and those of South America. But there are plants other than cacti which have the succulent habit, and in the deserts of India and Africa they are the dominant plants. We know that in the animal world unrelated animals have evolved mechanisms that enable them to carry on similar activities. Thus insects, birds, and bats can fly. Unrelated plants have evolved similar forms and structures which enable them to cope with desert conditions: thus we find plants of a succulent habit in the cactus, lily, amaryllis, crassula, milkweed, and spurge families.

In our greenhouses we should not try to simulate exactly the environment of a desert. On the desert the day temperatures may exceed 100 degrees on many days, yet the plants will thrive better in a greenhouse if day temperatures are kept down to 70 degrees. A night temperature of 60 degrees is ideal for many. In their native homes most succulents withstand the full glare of the sun, but in our greenhouses full sun during the summer might burn them. To avoid excessive temperatures in summer, light shade is needed.

We have learned that a soil with more humus than desert soils contain makes for better growth. Except for the epiphyllums and other epiphytes, cacti and other succulents thrive when potted in a mixture of equal parts sand, loam, and peat moss or leaf mold. Another suitable mix consists of 8 parts loam, 4 parts peat moss, 3 parts coarse sand, and one part of crushed brick. The epiphytic

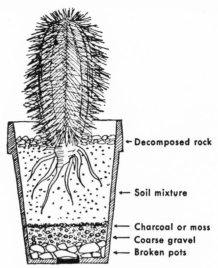

Decomposed rock

Soil mixture

Charcoal or moss
Coarse gravel
Broken pots

Fig. 19–1. A correctly potted cactus plant. (From *Cactus and Succulents*, by Scott E. Hasleton; Abbey Garden Press)

cacti prefer a mixture with a higher content of organic matter. They can be potted in firbark or in a mixture of 1 part loam, 2 parts leaf mold, 1 part well-rotted manure, and 1 part of ¼ to ½" bark.

Cacti and other succulents are relatively free of insect pests. They may be attacked by mealybugs, scales, and even aphids; a periodic spraying with Malathion will keep the plants free of insects.

The Cactus Family—Cactaceae

You have only to visit a greenhouse of a cactus fancier to realize the great variety of cacti. Some, such as the Saguaro cactus, grow to great heights; others, the Peyote for example, to less than an inch. The stems of certain species are globular in shape; those of others are cylindrical, triangular, quadrangular, or flattened. The stems may be smooth, channeled, or tubercled. The flowers vary in color, time of opening, and in size. The night-blooming cereus has flowers a foot long, while those of the mistletoe cactus are only a quarter of an inch across. The spines are interesting, too. Some cacti are formidably armed; others lack spines. Even though cacti are diverse in shape, size, and spine pattern, they all have a number of features in common. None have expanded foliage leaves, and foodmaking is carried on by the green stems which also store water.

The flowers of all cacti are alike in many ways. With only one exception, they are borne singly. The flowers of all cacti have many petals and many stamens; both the petals and stamens arise from the top of the ovary.

January to March is a good time to pot most cacti. Some kinds may need to be repotted annually, but others can go for several years without repotting. If the plants are thriving, don't be too anxious to repot them—let well enough alone. Small cacti will thrive in 3- or 4-inch pots.

When potting, put pieces from a broken pot over the drainage hole and then a layer of gravel, followed by some charcoal or moss. Then pot the plants with the mixture suggested previously, over which you may place a layer of fine gravel. You had better wear leather gloves or use a paper loop or tongs when you handle the plants.

Although cacti survive long periods of drought in their native homes, when grown in pots they may be injured if their roots remain dry for a long time during the growing season. In winter most cacti are dormant; during this season let the soil become nearly dry before watering again. A weekly watering is sufficient for most kinds. Overwatering during winter can be harmful, because it may bring about a soft watery rot that may be fatal. When spring comes, growth will start and then the plants should be watered more frequently. In the summer when the plants are actively growing, give them ample water and do not permit the roots to become dry.

Cacti are increased by offsets, by stem cuttings, and by seeds. Some kinds produce offshoots which may be removed and placed on sand until they root, after which they are potted. Stem cuttings root quickly. If the plant is a branching type, break or cut off a branch at the socket. If the variety does not produce offsets or branches but only a single stem, you can cut off the upper 2 or 3 inches of the stem and root it. After the cuttings are made, allow the cut or broken surface to dry for a few days until a corky layer forms. Then insert the base of the cutting in sand with the base just below the surface. If the cutting is slender and floppy, fasten it to a wooden stake with rubber bands. Water the cuttings sparingly at first, just enough to keep them from shriveling. When they are rooted, move them into small pots.

Many fanciers of cacti start plants from seeds and are always hoping that some unusual form will appear among the offspring.

Add drainage material to a pot; then fill the pot to within an inch of the top with sterilized sandy soil. Firm the soil and sow the seeds. Then cover the seeds with a quarter-inch layer of a mixture of sand and pea-sized gravel. Damping-off is the greatest hazard to success in raising cacti from seed. We recommend the use of sterilized soil. After sowing, water with a fine spray. The pot should be covered with glass and paper until germination occurs; then remove them. The seedlings of most genera will appear in about ten days. When spines are evident on the seedlings, transplant them to flats. The plants may remain in the flats from one to several years, depending on the rapidity of growth. Eventually the plants are moved into pots.

Many fanciers of cacti produce novel forms by grafting. For example, a ball-shaped cactus may be grafted on the top of a cactus which has a straight columnar stem, or even several different kinds may be grafted to the top of a stem. You may wish to graft a Christmas cactus on the top of some high-stemmed variety so that the flowers may be displayed more attractively. Grafting is easily done and nearly always successful; even distantly related cacti can be grafted together. We call the part above the graft union the *scion*, and the part below the union the *stock*.

One of the simplest methods is to cut the stock off horizontally at the desired height, and similarly slice off the scion. Place the cut surface of the scion on that of the stock. Use a few cactus spines to hold the scion in place, and then to keep the stock and scion firmly together stretch rubber bands over the top of the grafted plant and under the pot. Two rubber bands at right angles are necessary. You can use string if you prefer.

Another method is to cut a V-shaped piece out of the top of the stock and then bevel the lower surface of the scion to fit into the groove. The scion is held in place with spines and with string or rubber bands. This method is frequently used to graft scions of the rattail cactus onto a stock of *Selenicereus*. The grafted plant is quite attractive, with its upright stem of *Selenicereus* crowned at the top with pendant branches of the rattail cactus.

The pendant Christmas cactus makes a nice standard when it is grafted on to *Pereskia*. Cut off the top of the latter cactus and then make a slit about an inch deep. Into this slit insert a scion, one or two joints long, of the Christmas cactus. The basal part of the scion should be wedged shaped so that it will easily fit in the groove.

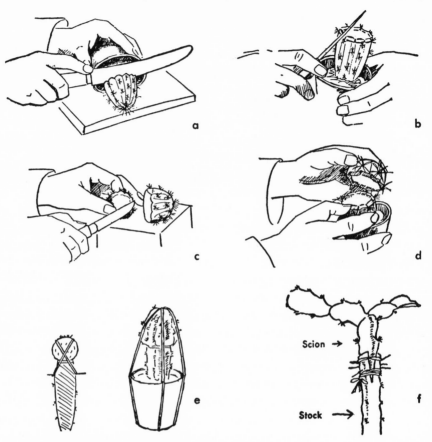

Fig. 19–2. Grafting cacti: a, cut the grafting stock; b, trim the rough edges from the stock; c, cut off a scion from the desired plant; d, place the scion on the stock; e, secure the two together with rubber bands anchored to a spine or extending under the pot. The sketch f shows how a Christmas cactus is grafted to a *Pereskia* stock. (From *Cactus and Succulents*, by Scott E. Hasleton; Abbey Gardens Press)

Pin the scion in place with a couple of cactus spines and then shade the grafted plant until the union is complete. If you wish you can use *Opuntia* for the stock instead of the shrublike *Pereskia*.

Varieties of Cacti

Because the cactus family is very large, including over a hundred genera and 1300 species, it is difficult to recommend varieties that you may want in your greenhouse. The more usual kinds may appeal to the beginner whereas the advanced grower may wish only the rare ones.

The space available will also influence your selection. Certain varieties are naturally dwarf; others grow to a considerable height. Among the kinds which do not get large are certain species of *Astrophytum, Chamaecereus, Echinocereus, Echinopsis, Gymnocalycium, Hematocactus, Lobivia, Lophophora, Mammillaria, Notocactus, Opuntia,* and *Rebutia.*

The bishop's cap cactus, *Astrophytum myriostigma,* is about 2 inches high, has an attractive form, and bears yellow flowers. The peanut cactus, *Chamaecereus silvestrii,* also grows to a height of about 2 inches, is covered with white spines, and produces orange-scarlet flowers as large as the plant. The hedgehog cereus, *Echinocereus delaetii,* grows to a height of 8 inches, is covered with white hairs, and bears pink flowers. The Easter lily cactus, *Echinopsis hybrida,* is noted for its white flowers and deeply ridged globe shape. The chin cactus, *Gymnocalycium damsii,* is a globe-shaped cactus with pink flowers. The strawberry cactus, *Hematocactus setispinus,* grows to a height of 8 inches, but may produce its yellow flowers with a conspicuous red throat when it is only 2 inches tall. A choice species of cob cactus is the scarlet-flowered *Lobivia cinnabarina.* The peyote, *Lophophora williamsii,* is a flattened globe, 3 inches or less in diameter, that produces pink flowers 1 inch across. There are many species of *Mammillaria,* the pincushion cactus, which make good greenhouse subjects, among them *M. bocasana, M. campotricha, M. carnea, M. elongata, M. fragilis, M. kewensis,* and *M. wildii.* Among the species of the ball cactus, *Notocactus,* that may appeal to you are *N. haselbergii* and *N. scopa.* The rabbit's-ear cactus, *Opuntia microdasya,* is suitable for the small greenhouse. *Rebutia minuscula* makes a globe about 2 inches in diameter and produces bright crimson flowers.

If you have plenty of space, you may wish to raise some large cacti, various species of *Aporocactus, Cephalocereus, Cleistocactus, Echinocactus, Lemaireocereus, Oreocereus, Selenicereus,* and *Trichinocereus.* The rattail cactus, *Aporocactus flagelliformis,* can be trained on a support, allowed to grow pendant, or grafted onto a straight stem of some other species; it is easy to grow and produces crimson flowers about 3 inches long. The old man cactus, *Cephalocereus senilis,* always attracts attention with its cylindrical stems covered with shaggy white hair. Scarlet bugler, *Cleistocactus baumannii*, grows to a height of 6 feet, has cylindrical stems about an inch and a half in diameter, and bears orange-scarlet flowers 3 inches long. One of the favorite barrel cacti is *Echinocactus grusonii*. This species grows to 4 feet high and 2 or 3 feet in diameter. The flowers are red and yellow. The organ pipe cactus, *Lemaireocereus marginatus*, grows to a height of 25 feet and has ribbed, pipelike stems; the flowers are red outside and greenish-white inside. Old man of the Andes, *Oreocereus celsianus*, grows to 3 feet and is covered with white hairs.

Queen of the night, *Selenicereus grandiflorus*, grows natively in the humus that accumulates on trunks and branches of trees in Jamaica and Cuba. The magnificent flowers, with a vanilla perfume, open as darkness comes and last only through the night. By morning the blooms are limp. The flowers are 6 inches across, salmon outside and white inside. Even larger flowers are produced by *S. macdonaldiae*, another night-blooming plant. The flowers are 14 inches across with white petals and reddish or yellowish sepals. Although the plants are trailing and ungainly in their growth habits, their spectacular blossoms make them worth growing. The white torch cactus, *Trichocereus spachianus*, grows to a height of 3 feet, has ribbed stems, and bears white flowers 6 inches across.

Epiphyllums. The epiphyllums come from tropical rain forests of Central and South America, where they grow as epiphytes. They are found with orchids, ferns and gesneriads and grow in large clusters on the branches of trees. Some open their glorious flowers at night, others in the day. Unlike other cacti, they require more shade during the bright months, a higher humidity, more frequent waterings, and they benefit from occasional syringings. The epiphyllums are more at home with orchids than with other cacti, and, like orchids, they thrive when potted in firbark, provided they are fed with a dilute fertilizer at biweekly or monthly intervals. Water newly potted plants sparingly for a week or two until the roots are established. When epiphyllums are actively growing give them ample water. During their dormant season keep them on the dry side but don't let the roots become completely dry. They grow well and flower regularly when the night temperature is 60 degrees.

The epiphyllums are easily propagated from stem cuttings, and they can be grafted on to *Pereskia* or some other stock. You may wish to start them from seed. It takes about three years to get

Fig. 19–3. Interesting cacti for the greenhouse. Upper left, *Astrophytum asterias* (Mexico). Upper right, *Echinocereus chisoensis* (Texas). Lower left, *Gymnocalycium mihanovichii* (Mexico). Lower right, *Mammillaria microcarpa* (Arizona). (Ladislaus Cutak)

Fig. 19–4. The flowers of *Epiphyllum oxypetalum,* "Princess of the Night," are fragrant and voluptuous. Single blooms last only one night, but the plant flowers over a long period.

blooming plants. An interesting experience would be to cross epiphyllums.

Choice species of epiphyllum are *E. strictum* (white orchid cactus), *E. oxypetalum* (Princess of the night), *E. ackermannii* (red orchid cactus), *E. crenatum.* The flowers of the white orchid cactus are about 6 inches long, opening in late evening and closing before dawn. Princess of the night, a huge rambling plant, has 6 to 7 inch white flowers, globe-shaped and with a heady perfume. The red orchid cactus blossoms during the day. The flowers are about 6 inches across and they are red with a greenish-yellow throat. *E. crenatum* is another attractive plant that flowers during the day. The flowers are delightfully fragrant and 6 to 10 inches long; the outer petals are greenish yellow, the inner ones white.

Many plants commonly called epiphyllums are in different genera, some being in the genus *Schlumbergera,* others in *Zygocactus. Schlumbergera gaertneri,* the Easter cactus, is a good greenhouse plant. This species bears scarlet flowers about 3 inches long. The culture is the same as the true epiphyllums.

Botanically, the Christmas cactus, also called crab cactus, is *Zygocactus truncatus* which grows on trunks and branches of trees in the moist jungles of Brazil. The flowers are beautifully translucent, about 3 inches across, and red in color. When grown with a

Fig. 19-5. Epiphyllums are easily propagated from cuttings taken at a joint. Tie the cutting to a label one or two inches longer than the cutting, then put the label into the soil until the base of the cutting touches the sand.

night temperature of 63 to 65 degrees the plant flowers about Christmas time. If grown at a night temperature of 55 degrees it may flower either during the short days of winter or during the long days of spring. When grown with a night temperature of 70 to 75 degrees it does not flower. The Christmas cactus may be grown in pots or in hanging baskets.

In addition to the various species of *Epiphyllum*, *Schlumbergera*, and *Zygocactus* there are thousands of named varieties with flower colors ranging from white through yellow, pink, lavender, and purple. The size runs from 1½ inches to 12 inches and the form from flat to cup to funnel. The varieties are fascinating plants that provide interest and beautiful color in the greenhouse during winter.

Fig-Marigold Family—*Aizoaceae*

Included in this family are a number of plants which always attract attention, among them tiger's-jaw, stoneface, and living rocks. These are admirably adapted for life on the rocky deserts of South and Southwest Africa where the plants mimic stones, a disguise that keep them from being consumed by thirsty and hungry animals.

When they burst into blossom their disguise is over, for their brilliantly colored, large, daisy-like flowers are conspicuous. The flowers have many petals and stamens. Some members of the family bear only two thick succulent leaves, in which water is stored. In some species the leaves are partially buried, leaving only the upper surface to act as a light-gathering window.

The members of this family grow well in a 60-degree greenhouse when potted in a mixture of equal parts of loam, sand, and leaf mold. Like all desert plants, they should be grown with good drainage and the soil should not be waterlogged. During the summer the plants require frequent waterings, but during the winter they should be kept on the dry side. Many of the fig-marigolds are slow growers and require only small pots. Members of this family are propagated by cuttings, by division, or from seed. Cuttings should be allowed to dry for a day or two before they are inserted into sand.

Among the genera of interest to greenhouse owners are *Conophytum* (cone-plants), *Faucaria* (tiger's-jaw), *Fenestraria*, *Glottiphylum*, *Lithops* (stoneface), *Pleiospilos* (living rocks), and *Titanopsis*. The cone-plants form rounded clumps, and each growth consists of two leaves joined together.

The leaves of the tiger's-jaw occur in pairs, and the upturned edges bear long soft teeth, giving a fanciful resemblance to the open jaws of a tiger. The flowers are produced in the fall and are stemless, bright yellow, and about an inch across. *Fenestraria* is a genus of only two species, *F. aurantiaca* with golden yellow flowers and *F. rhopalophylla* with white flowers, from the coastal sand dunes of southwest Africa. In nature they grow buried to their leaf tips, which bear translucent "windows," but in cultivation the leaves should not be buried. *Glottiphylum* has bright green leaves that feel cool, and bears yellow flowers 3 inches across.

Perhaps the best known and most available fig-marigold is the stoneface (*Lithops*), a plant which resembles pebbles on the ground. In the deserts of south and southwest Africa it grows partially buried with only the upper surfaces of the leaves exposed to the elements, the hot desert sun and the drying winds. Many of these also have translucent "windows" on their rounded tops to admit light. A Lithops plant consists of two conical succulent leaves attached to a short stem which grades into an extensive root system. Once a year two new leaves develop from the stem tip. As they increase in size the old leaves shrivel until finally the new

Fig. 19–6. Upper left, *Fenestraria rhopalophylla*. Upper right, *Lithops marmorata*. Lower left, the panda plant, *Kalanchoë tomentosa*. Lower right, partridge breast aloe, *Aloe variegata*. (Upper figures, Chester B. Dugdale)

leaves replace the old ones. In greenhouses many species flower during the autumn. The flower color varies with species. Species with white flowers are *L. framesii*, and *L. salicola;* those with yellow flowers are *L. divergens* and *L. turbiniformis.*

Two favorite species of living rocks (also called split rocks) are

Pleiospilos bolusii and *P. simulans*. Both resemble stones, and both bear yellow flowers about 3 inches across.

The leaves of *Titanopsis schwantesii* form small rosettes. The tips of the fleshy leaves are covered with white tubercles. The flowers are about an inch across and are produced in the spring.

Lily Family—*Liliaceae*

Several members of this family are adapted to desert life, among them *Aloe*, *Gasteria*, and *Haworthia*, plants native to the deserts of South Africa. They grow slowly and can be confined in small pots which are provided with good drainage. The soil mixture should be equal parts of sand, loam, and leaf mold. The succulents of the lily family require shade from April or May until early autumn. Water them freely in summer and moderately during winter. They may be increased from seed or more usually by offshoots or leaf cuttings. If you remove a leaf and lay it on sand, plantlets will develop which can be potted up.

Aloe. Aloes range in size from rosettes just a few inches high to trees towering to 60 feet. Certain species yield incense, medicines, and cord. A species suitable for our greenhouses is *Aloe variegata*, called tiger aloe by some and partridge-breasted aloe by others. When young, this plant has a compact form. The three-sided green leaves are banded with white and grow in a triangular rosette. In addition to their decorative foliage the aloe produces beautiful red flowers on a loose spike, about 1 foot high.

Gasteria. These plants are known as file aloes. They are dwarf plants with tongue-shaped leaves that form a dense basal rosette. *Gasteria acinacifolia* and *G. verrucosa* are favorite species. The first has dull gray leaves that are very fleshy and about 10 inches long and 2 inches wide. The flower cluster is up to 4 feet long, and has reddish flowers about 2 inches across. *Gasteria verrucosa* is characterized by the white warts on the grayish green leaves. The leaves are about 6 inches long and ¾-inch wide. The flowers are pink, about an inch long, and are borne on a cluster that is 2 feet tall.

Haworthia. Among the interesting species are *Haworthia cymbiformis*, *H. margaritifera*, and *H. arachnoides*. *H. cymbiformis* has pale, oblong, smooth leaves and produces a flower stalk about 1 foot tall. *H. margaritifera,* the "pearl aloe," has large pearly warts on the leaves and bears flowers on a cluster 2 feet high. *H. arachnoides* has three-sided leaves which are fringed. The flower cluster is about 1½ feet high.

Milkweed Family—*Asclepiadaceae*

Certain members of this family deserve a place in a collection of succulents, among them *Caralluma, Hoodia, Huernia,* and especially *Stapelia.* These odd plants superficially resemble cacti; they have thick fleshy stems and lack foliage. The milkweeds have unique flowers of intricate construction that are very different from those of cacti or any other family. The succulents of this family can be grown in small pots in an even mixture of sand, loam, and leaf mold. For best growth a night temperature of 60 to 65 degrees should be maintained. As with other succulents, they should be watered freely when they are actively growing and kept on the dry side during their dormant period, generally in winter. These succulents are easily propagated by breaking off sections of the stem and inserting them in moist sand.

Caralluma. All of the species of *Caralluma* are low-growing succulents with leafless, four-angled stems that have teeth on the ridges. The star-shaped flowers are borne near the top of the stem and they are purple, brown, or yellow, depending on the species. They vary in size from the eight-inch flowers of *Caralluma sinaica* to the quarter-inch ones of *C. nebrownii.*

Hoodia. The branches of these cactus-like plants bear spine-tipped tubercles. There are a dozen or so species, of which *Hoodia gordonii* is most frequently seen in collections. The flowers of this species are pale purple with greenish-yellow stripes, and they are about 3 inches in diameter.

Huernia. These dwarf succulents produce odd bell-shaped flowers. The flowers of *Huernia penzigii* are black-purple in color; those of *H. primulina* are cream-yellow.

Stapelia. The showy and distinctive flowers of the stapelias make them the most spectacular of the milkweeds. Because their appearance leads one to liken them to a starfish, they are sometimes known as starfish flower. The unpleasant odor of the flowers at close hand has led to another common name, carrion flower. These natives of Africa have thick, fleshy, four-sided, green stems without leaves. The flowers are grotesquely marked and barred with dull red, purple, or yellow. The petals are fleshy, and near their base there is a two-rowed crown that may be curiously colored. The flowers are large, 3 inches in diameter in *Stapelia verrucosa* and 12 inches in *S. gigantea*. The flowers of the former have red spots against a yellow background. The yellow flowers of *S. gigantea* are barred with many crimson lines. Other species that you may want in your collection are *S. variegata*, *S. grandiflora*, *S. patula*, *S. revoluta*. Unlike other species *S. variegata* is not unpleasantly scented; the flowers are yellow with purple markings.

Spurge or Poinsettia Family—*Euphorbiaceae*

The genus *Euphorbia* of this family includes a number of species which resemble cacti in several ways. Some of the succulent euphorbias are globular, others columnar, and still different ones are climbers. Some are very spiny. Unlike the cacti, however, all of the euphorbias have milky sap, which in some species is extremely poisonous. Cultural conditions suggested for cacti suit the euphorbias. They are propagated by stem cuttings. Allow the base of the cutting to callus somewhat before inserting it in sand.

One of the favorite succulents is the Medusa's head, *Euphorbia caput-medusae*, which has a globular main stem that bears many declining branches 1 to 2 inches thick. *Euphorbia pseudocactus* is gray-green in color and has upright three- to five-angled stems with spines along the ridges. Other species of interest to collectors are *E. cereiformis*, *E. meloformis*, *E. globosa*, *E. cooperi*, and *E. beaumierana*. Most of them have inconspicuous flowers.

The Stonecrop Family—*Crassulaceae*

This is a large family, including 900 species in twenty genera. The plants are noted mostly for their thick, fleshy leaves and interesting forms. However, certain kinds produce beautiful flowers. Members of the family prefer good light, a temperature of 55 to 60 degrees, and a dry atmosphere. A soil consisting of equal parts of sand, leaf mold, and loam is suitable for potting. The pots need not be large, but ample drainage must be provided. When the stonecrops are actively growing, the soil should be kept moist; when dormant, keep the plants on the dry side. They are easily raised from seed and by leaf or stem cuttings.

Among the genera that appeal to fanciers of succulents are *Crassula*, *Echeveria*, and *Kalanchoë*. In addition you may want to try *Cotyledon*, *Sedum*, and *Sempervirens*.

Various species of crassula are grown for their distinctive forms and some for their flowers. All species are from the Old World, and mostly from Africa. Among the favorites for greenhouse culture are the scarlet paint brush (*Crassula falcata*), princess-pine (*C. lycopodioides*), and the necklace vine (*C. rupestris*). The scarlet paint brush may grow to a height of 8 feet but the other species are quite dwarf and may be grown in small pots.

You may know the echeverias by their common name of hen-and-chickens. They grow in symmetrical rosettes, bear attractive orange-red or coral flowers, and most species have bluish-white fleshy leaves that are broad and flat. The genus is a large one of more than sixty species. Among those available for greenhouse culture are *Echeveria elegans*, *E. gibbiflora*, *E. glauca*, *E. setosa*, *E. secunda*, and *E. weinbergii*.

There are more than one hundred species in the genus *Kalanchoë*. They have interesting foliage and produce an abundance of attractive flowers. We have already considered *Kalanchoë blossfeldiana*, which is noted for its attractive flowers. One of the most common species is *K. pinnata*, which is known as the miracle leaf, air plant, and good luck leaf. Its main interest is its habit of producing small plants in the notches along the margin of the leaf. The plantlets appear at times when the leaf is on the plant, and will develop from a severed leaf. *Kalanchoë digremontiana* is another species which has this same capacity. The panda plant, *K. tomentosa*, is distinguished by its fleshy leaves arranged in a rosette. The leaves are covered with hairs; the hairs are white except for those near the tips of the leaves, which are rust-red or almost black in color. *Kalanchoë marmorata* is another interesting pot plant. It bears leaves about 6 inches long that are blotched with purple and has creamy white or yellowish flowers nearly 3 inches long. *Kalanchoë flammea* is also of interest, bearing flowers that are yellow and orange-scarlet.

20

Bulbs for Forcing

Bulbs are easy to grow, and furnish a succession of colorful blooms during winter and spring. Your efforts will be rewarded by beautiful flowers and pleasant fragrances.

Tulips, hyacinths, narcissi, irises, grape hyacinths, as well as others, may be forced in the greenhouse by starting bulbs in the fall. Order the bulbs early so that you will get a good selection of top-quality ones. Only the best grades of varieties especially suitable for greenhouse culture should be used; always remember that it takes as much work to flower an inferior bulb as one which produces flowers that you can be proud of.

It is best to plant the bulbs as soon as you receive them. If for some reason you cannot plant them promptly, store the tulip and narcissus bulbs at a temperature of 48 degrees and those of hyacinths at 65 to 70 degrees. Plant the bulbs in pots, or in flats (about 4 inches deep) if you are primarily interested in cut flowers. Standard 5- or 6-inch pots and 7- and 8-inch azalea pots can be used. In sizes above 6 inches, azalea pots are preferred because they are more stable and attractive than standard pots. Often a number of bulbs may be planted in a pot, spacing them about an inch or an inch and a half apart. A 7-inch pot will accommodate about six tulip bulbs or three or four narcissus bulbs. One hyacinth bulb is planted in a 5-inch pot or three in a 6- or 7-inch one.

Bulbs require good drainage, provided by placing several pieces of crock or pebbles in the bottom of the pot. A mixture of three parts loam to one of peat moss with the addition of superphosphate or bone meal is a good potting medium. Add soil to the pot. Then gently press the bases of the bulbs into the soil without turning them. Add more soil, firm it with your fingers, and then tap the pot on the bench to settle the soil. When the job is done correctly the soil level should be about half an inch below the rim and the noses of tulip and narcissus bulbs should be just protruding. The nose of a hyacinth bulb should be about half an inch below the soil surface. Place a label in each pot and water thoroughly.

It is best to plant only one variety in a pot. If bulbs of several varieties are planted together, growth and flowering will not be uniform.

After potting, labeling, and watering, the bulbs should be kept at a cool temperature, which favors root development and initiates the development of the shoot. The best storage temperature for tulips and narcissus is 48 degrees and for hyacinths 50 degrees. Lower temperatures are not harmful, but they slow development and necessitate a longer cool period. A refrigerator, cellar, or storage room where the temperature is between 40 and 50 degrees is suitable for storing the potted bulbs. The bulbs should remain in storage until the roots are well developed and the shoot is 2 or 3 inches high. Do not let the pots become dry during storage. Water them at intervals.

An excellent substitute for a storage room is a trench outdoors. In an out-of-the-way place in the garden dig a trench 15 to 18 inches deep. Spread about 2 inches of gravel in the bottom to provide good drainage. Then place the pots in the trench, leaving about an inch between them to facilitate their later removal. Since the bulbs can be brought into the greenhouse at intervals for a sequence of blooms, group together in first place those pots which will be first removed from the trench, those that come second in second place, and so on. Cover the pots with 2 inches of sand, which can be easily shaken off the shoots when the pots are removed. Fill the trench with soil and then add a 1-foot mulch of leaves or straw.

Instead of burying the pots in a trench they may be placed in a cold frame on a 2-inch layer of gravel and covered with leaves or straw, or better still with Propalite, a light, shredded, inexpensive styrofoam. After the frame is filled cover with a screen to keep the insulating material from being blown away. If Propalite is used the pots are easily removed without injury to the shoots and the material may be saved and used for many years.

After the bulbs have made good root growth and when the shoots are 2 to 3 inches high you can begin moving them from the storage site to the greenhouse. For untreated bulbs late December would be the earliest time to bring the pots into the greenhouse. The bulbs will not be injured by a longer storage. Hence you can bring bulbs into the greenhouse at intervals from late December on for a sequence of blooms.

When the plants are brought into the greenhouse, you can keep them under the bench until the rate of growth accelerates, after which they should be placed on a well-lighted bench. Hardy bulbs can be flowered at a temperature of 50 degrees or at 60 degrees. In a 60-degree greenhouse, tulips and narcissi flower in about four weeks and hyacinths in three weeks. At a temperature of 50 degrees, blooming will take a week or two more. The best way to force hardy bulbs is to grow them at 50 degrees at first and then gradually increase the temperature to 60 degrees. Do not grow bulbs at temperatures above 70 degrees, which may cause buds to blast and flower tips to turn white. Keep the plants well watered during the forcing period.

Hardy bulbs should not be forced a second time. However, you can plant them outdoors. If you wish to save the bulbs for planting in your garden, keep the plants watered after they are through flowering. Then let the foliage dry off gradually. When the soil in the garden is workable, plant the bulbs. They will not flower the first season outdoors but will the next year.

So far, we have considered the general methods for forcing hardy bulbs. Let us next talk about the varieties that may be forced and special techniques that may be used.

Hyacinths (Liliaceae)

The common garden hyacinths (*Hyacinthus orientalis*) come in a variety of colors and can be brought into bloom during winter. They add delightful fragrance as well as beauty.

The hyacinth, a native of Syria, Asia Minor, Greece, and Dalmatia, has been cultivated for nearly a thousand years. Omar Khayyam, the Persian poet, wrote about hyacinths in the eleventh century and the bulb has been in the commercial trade since the early 1600's.

Add crock for drainage, and some soil.

Space the bulbs, fill with soil.

Firm the soil.

Water thoroughly.

Place pots in trench.

When storage period is over, bring pots into greenhouse.

Fig. 20–1. Stages in forcing bulbs, illustrated here with tulips.

Hyacinth bulbs may be planted when received in the fall, or planting may be delayed until as late as January if the bulbs are stored in a dry place at a temperature of 65 to 70 degrees. Delayed planting is sometimes practiced to get quality blooms in early spring. Bulbs planted in the fall will flower from January on. Pot the bulb so that the nose is about half an inch below the surface of the soil. Store the pots in a cool place. The plants can be brought into the greenhouse when the buds are visible and the bulbs are well rooted, at the earliest in late December or early January. Do not let the plants get frozen or chilled while digging or transporting them to the greenhouse. If they are chilled the flower spikes may appear cut off or fail to develop.

Plants which are brought into the greenhouse during December or early January should be kept in a dark place at 60 degrees until the shoots are 4 inches high. It is a simple matter to rig up a box of canvas, black cloth, or paper to give them darkness, which results in the elongation of the leaves and flower stalk.

Plants kept in darkness should be given light gradually until the normal green color has developed, after which they can stand full sun. Bulbs brought into the greenhouse during mid-January or later do not require darkness. They can be grown directly on the bench. A temperature of 60 degrees is ideal for hyacinths.

Some varieties of hyacinth, their descriptions, and the earliest dates at which they may be brought into the greenhouse are shown in the following table. Of course you can bring the plants in at later dates to get a sequence of flowers.

Variety	Color	Earliest date to bring in
Bismarck	Light blue	December 22
City of Haarlem	Golden yellow	January 15
Edelweiss	White	January 15
Gertrude	Rose pink	January 1
Grand Maitre	Dark porcelain	January 1
Jan Bos	Scarlet	December 22
King of the Blues	Dark blue	January 15
La Victoire	Red	January 1
L'Innocence	White	December 22
Marconi	Rose pink	January 5
Ostara	Clear blue	December 22
Pink Pearl	Pink	December 22
Queen of the Blues	Azure blue	January 18
Queen of the Pinks	Rosy pink	January 15

Fig. 20–2. These hyacinths were maintained in a trench outdoors, brought in, and then placed under a darkened bench where it was warm. The plants have just been removed from the dark and placed on the bench.

Narcissus (Amaryllidaceae)

There are many species of narcissus which can be grown in the greenhouse. All are native to southwestern Europe. Narcissus is in the amaryllis family.

The daffodil or trumpet narcissus (*Narcissus pseudonarcissus*) is especially fine for greenhouse growing. The varieties of this species are yellow or cream in color, and the trumpet is as long as, or longer than, the petals. Among the choice varieties of this species are King Alfred, Aerolite, and Rembrandt.

King Alfred is superb and is frequently grown by commercial florists. You can have flowers at Christmas if you plant precooled, #1, double-nosed bulbs in late September or early October. (The "double-nosed" bulb is the mother bulb plus one or more daughter bulbs that are still attached and it produces two or more flowers. Precooled bulbs have been given cool treatment before being sold to permit early blooming.) After potting, keep the bulbs in cool storage until December 1, when the plants should be brought into the greenhouse and grown at 60 degrees.

Fig. 20–3. Left: three large, double-nosed King Alfred daffodil bulbs are ready to be covered with soil. They will be watered and placed in the trench. Right, shoots of King Alfred daffodil bulbs just after the pots were removed from the trench on December 23; these bulbs are ready for forcing in the greenhouse.

Precooled bulbs need not be used for flowering in mid-January or later. If you wish King Alfred flowers in mid-January, plant #1 size, double-nosed, regular bulbs in the fall and move them into the greenhouse from the storage place about the middle of December. Of course, pots can be brought into the greenhouse at intervals for a succession of blooms.

At a temperature of 56 degrees, allow five to six weeks for flowering, at 60 degrees four weeks. However, King Alfreds should not be grown at 60 degrees until the bud is visible. During the dark days of winter it is advisable to keep the temperature above 53 degrees, otherwise the petals may curve inward.

The poet's narcissus (*Narcissus poeticus*) has white petals and a small trumpet with a dark red edge. *Actaea* is a favorite variety with its pure white corolla and small, yellow, fiery-red edged cap. This variety is potted in the fall, kept cool until at least February 1, then forced in the greenhouse.

The poetaz narcissi are hybrids between *Narcissus poeticus* and *Narcissus tazetta* (the paper white). Early Perfection, a white and yellow variety, and Laurens Coster, with its white petals and orange cup, are good varieties. Early Perfection may be brought in from the cool place after January 1, whereas Laurens Coster should remain until at least January 20.

Unlike the species of narcissus previously mentioned, the paper white (*Narcissus tazetta*) does not require cool conditions for rooting. The bulbs of this group may be potted, flatted, or planted in a bench in the greenhouse during fall, and they will flower at Christmas or before. They will do well if kept continually in the greenhouse. However, root development is hastened if they are kept in a cool dark place for two weeks before being brought into the greenhouse. They grow well in dishes of pebbles kept wet with water. After the container is partially filled with pebbles, the bulbs are placed on them. Sufficient water is added so that the bases of the bulbs are just wetted. The ideal time to start the paper whites is from October 15 to November 15, but the plantings can be made from October 1 to March 1. You can get a succession of blooms by planting at about ten-day intervals. The Chinese sacred lily, *N. tazetta* var. *orientalis*, may be grown in the same manner as the paper whites.

Tulips *(Liliaceae)*

Tulips are in the lily family. A number of species are native to Asia Minor, China, and Japan. The species have been crossed and the hybrids recrossed until now we have a great number of varieties of beautiful form and beautiful color. Some varieties force well, others cannot be recommended. Certain ones can be brought into bloom early, others only later.

To obtain tulips in flower during January, precooled bulbs must be used. Precooled bulbs are those which have been stored at a temperature of 45 to 50 degrees before you receive them. They should be potted as soon as received, then watered thoroughly, and placed in cool storage.

Among the choice precooled varieties that are available and their colors are: Allround, scarlet; Bellona, yellow; Blizzard, white; Paris, orange-red; Peerless Pink, satiny pink; and Sulfur Glory, yellow. These varieties will have made a potfull of roots by December 15 and they can then be forced in the greenhouse where they will flower in about a month.

For flowering from February on, precooled bulbs need not be used. The following are varieties suitable for February flowering, varieties that will flower about five weeks after they are brought into the greenhouse: Bellona, yellow; Coleur Cardinal, red; De Wet, orange; White Hawk, white; Boule de Neige, white; Electra, cherry red; Golden Victory, gold; Peach Blossom, pink; Big Chief, rose; General Eisenhower, red; President Kennedy, yellow and rose; Blizzard, white; First Lady, purple-violet; Peerless Pink, satiny pink; and Prominence, deep red.

Among the choice varieties for March flowering are: Balalaika, red; Golden Age, yellow; Glacier, white; Insurpassable, lilac; Queen of Bartigons, pink; Queen of the Night, purple-black; Smiling Queen, rosy pink; Orange Favorite, orange; Red Parrot, red; Van Dyck, rose-pink. These will flower four or five weeks after they are brought into the greenhouse.

After the tulips are brought into the greenhouse, keep them watered. The foliage will be more attractive and the flowers of better color and texture if the plants are given a weekly watering with a solution of soluble fertilizer, made up according to the manufacturer's recommendations. Some growers like to use a fish fertilizer.

The most recent development in tulip culture is the treatment of bulbs in such a manner that they do not require any cold treatment. Instead the bulbs are planted directly in the bench, in a deep flat, or in pots from December 1 until February 1. The bulbs must be planted within 24 hours of receiving them. Among the varieties available from John Scheepers, Inc., 63 Wall Street, New York which do not require a cold treatment are Beauty of Dover, yellow dusted rose; Dover, poppy red; Gudoshnik, pink; Jewel of Spring, yellow-edged rose; Oxford, orange-red; and President Kennedy, yellow-flushed rose.

Other Hardy Bulbs for Winter Flowering

Tulips, narcissi, and hyacinths are the major bulbs which are forced. There are others, however, which are readily forced, among them Cape cowslips, crocuses, grape hyacinths, ixias, and scillas. Not only do they make a beautiful display but add charm and interest. In common language the term "bulb" includes not only true bulbs but also corms which superficially resemble bulbs. A bulb consists of fleshy scales that surround a shoot. A corm lacks fleshy scales and consists of a fleshy stem that bears buds.

Cape Cowslip (Liliaceae)

Early August is the ideal time to start the Cape cowslip (*Lachenalia*), a native of South Africa, which is one of the most beautiful of pot-grown bulbs. The bulbs are potted in 5-inch pots just

Fig. 20–4. Grape hyacinths in flower during late February.

below the soil surface and about 1 inch apart. They grow well in a rich loam. They may be kept in a shaded cold frame until growth begins, after which they are grown in a greenhouse at 50 degrees. If a cold frame is not available they may be placed under the bench in a 50-degree house. When growth appears bring them into full light. *Lachenalia Nelsonii* is a rich golden yellow, and *Lachenalia tricolor* is striking red. They will add color to your greenhouse from December through May. The nodding flowers, about 25 to a stem, remain attractive for two months. If the plants are dried off gradually after flowering, the bulbs may be used again the next autumn. The bulbs should be allowed to remain in the dry soil until August, when they are repotted.

Crocus *(Iridaceae)*

Plant eight to ten crocus corms, about 1 inch deep, in the fall in a 6- or 8-inch pot. Keep them in the trench or other cool place until February 1, by which time the plants will be well rooted and top growth started. Bring them into the greenhouse and grow them at a temperature of 50 degrees. They will bloom six or seven weeks after they are brought in.

Grape Hyacinth *(Liliaceae)*

The delicate spires of nodding, azure-blue, urn-shaped flowers of the grape hyacinth (*Muscari armeniacum*) make excellent cut flowers. The bulbs are planted in fall, kept in a cool place until early January, and grown on in a greenhouse. If the greenhouse temperature is 60 degrees they will flower in about six weeks; if lower, in a longer time.

Ixia *(Iridaceae)*

Ixia, the African corn lily, is a beautiful plant that comes from South Africa. The plant bears grass-like leaves and wiry stems, about 2 feet tall, that bear many flowers in shades of white, blue, yellow, or pink, depending on the variety. The flowers are long-lasting and are excellent cut flowers. The corms are planted in a sandy fibrous soil in September or October, five or six to a 5-inch pot or a larger number in a flat. The pots or flats are placed in a cool place, remaining there until December, when they may be brought into the greenhouse and grown at a temperature of 50–55 degrees. They flower in March and April. After they flower, allow the foliage to die down gradually. The corms may be saved and used again in the fall.

Scilla *(Liliaceae)*

Two species of *Scilla* make good greenhouse plants, *Scilla sibirica*, the Siberian squill, and *Scilla campanulata*, the Spanish bluebell or wood hyacinth. The variety, Spring Beauty, of the first species has large, brilliant blue flowers on graceful spikes 4 to 5 inches high.

The following are favorite varieties of *Scilla campanulata:* Alba Maxima, with pure white flowers; Excelsior, with beautiful porcelain blue blooms; and Rose Queen, a lovely lilac-pink variety. The bulbs are potted in September or October, placed in a cool place such as an outdoor trench or cool cellar until February or March, by which time they will be well rooted. They are then grown in a 50-degree house.

21

Bulbs Not Requiring Cold

The amaryllis, buttercup, iris, and lily families include many plants which will lend beauty and fragrance to your greenhouse, among them the amaryllis, clivia, Mexican fire lily, Persian buttercup, freesia, Dutch iris, lilies, and lily of the valley. These plants are grown from bulbs or similar underground structures such as corms and tubers. Unlike the plants discussed in the previous chapter these plants, and some of their relatives, do not require a cold period. Instead they are kept continuously in the greenhouse from planting through flowering. They will thrive in a mixture of equal parts of loam, peat moss, and sand or vermiculite or perlite. After the bulbs are planted, water sparingly until growth begins and thereafter keep the soil moist until the onset of dormancy when watering should be decreased.

Amaryllis Family (Amaryllidaceae)

The Amaryllis Family includes a number of choice plants, many of tropical origin, that grow well in pots in a greenhouse maintained at a night temperature of 60 degrees. Some are dainty while many have bold and showy flowers. Among the favorite kinds are *Amaryllis, Clivia, Eucharis* (Amazon Lily, Star-of-Bethlehem), *Haemanthus* (Blood Lily), *Polianthes* (Tuberose), *Sprekelia* (Mexican Fire Lily), *Vallota*, and *Zephyranthes* (Zephyr Flower, Fairy Lily).

Amaryllis—*Hippeastrum Vittatum*

The modern varieties of amaryllis, with their spectacular open-faced flowers and broad, iridescent petals, have been developed from the single species native to the Cape of Good Hope. The flowers may be as much as 8 inches across, of white, salmon, deep red, or orange color. A large bulb usually produces two, sometimes three, flower spikes, each bearing three or four magnificent blooms.

Special temperature treatment has been perfected to cause development of flowers within the bulb during the storage period. When these are planted in November, the flower spikes begin growth immediately and flowers are open for Christmas. You can purchase these specially treated bulbs for delivery in early November, enjoy their early flowers, and then, after carrying them through the year, treat them yourself for flowering the following Christmas.

Treated bulbs are those which have been stored for four weeks at a temperature of 70 to 75 degrees. Plant the bulbs singly in standard 6- or 7-inch pots using a mixture of one part soil, one part sand, and one part peat moss or leaf mold. A tablespoon of bone meal should be added to that quantity of soil needed for a 6-inch pot. Cut off any roots which are dead, but do not remove or injure any living roots. These living roots will later branch and increase the root area. Plant the bulb so that one-third of it is in the soil and two-thirds above. After potting, water thoroughly, but thereafter, until the shoot appears, keep the soil somewhat dry. When the flowers are developing, watering should be more frequent. Sometimes the flowering shoot develops before the leaves and in some instances the plant flowers even before the leaves emerge from the bulb. During other years the same bulb may produce leaves and blossoms at the same time, making a more handsome plant. After the flowers shrivel, cut off the flowering stalk about 2 inches from the top of the bulb.

Because the food necessary for next year's growth is made when the plants are through flowering, keep them actively growing by giving them ample water, frequent syringings, and liquid fertilizer at three-week intervals. The plants should be given full light except during the hottest summer months.

If you want flowers at Christmas, select only the large bulbs (at least 8 inches in circumference) and treat them as follows. Cease watering them on August 15. On September 10 pull off the leaves if they are shriveled, or cut them off if green. Store the bulbs in the pots until October 13 at a temperature between 59 and 63 degrees. From October 13 to November 10 increase the storage temperature to 70 to 75 degrees. Perhaps you have a place in the basement for the cool period and a warm upstairs closet for the warm period. On November 10, repot those that were not potted the previous year and just top dress those that were. Then water the bulbs. Keep them on the dry side until growth is active, after which water them regularly.

If you are not interested in early flowers, start drying off the bulbs in October (instead of August) by withholding water. Let the leaves wilt and shrivel. Then store the bulbs at 50 degrees. These bulbs may be started into active growth any time from January to March.

Amaryllis can be increased by offsets which will develop into plants exactly like the parents. By using them you can increase your favorite varieties. The offsets form at the base of the mother bulb. They should not be removed from the parent bulb until they are almost ready to separate of their own accord. Remove the offsets during the dormant period and pot them, taking care not to injure the roots.

If you raise amaryllis from seed, and this is not difficult, you can expect considerable variety among the offspring. Perhaps a few will be particularly outstanding. Seeds are best sown singly in 2-inch pots plunged in a flat of moist peat moss to keep them from drying out. Seeds germinate in about two weeks. When the roots crowd the pots, shift the plants into 3-inch pots, taking care not to injure the roots. From these pots the young plants may be shifted into 4- or 5-inch ones. With good culture, some of them will flower when they are two years old, others at three. During the entire period from seed-sowing to flowering, keep the plants in active growth. Do not dry them off during the autumn as with mature bulbs.

Fig. 21–1. Potting an amaryllis bulb. Add drainage to the pot, then some soil. Mound the soil and place the bulb on the mound with the roots spreading. Fill the pot with soil and firm; one-third of the bulb should be in the soil. Keep the soil on the dry side until the shoot appears, then water more frequently.

Clivia

Of the three species in this genus, all native of South Africa, *Clivia miniata* is the most popular. There are several varieties of this species; in addition there are choice hybrids resulting from crossings with the other two species, *Clivia nobilis* and *C. gardenii*. Clivias grow and flower without effort and are very satisfying plants. The bulbs give handsome, evergreen, amaryllis-like leaves, about two feet long, and bear showy, lilylike flowers in shades of orange, yellow, and scarlet, at the summit of a stiff stem about 2 feet tall. The plants flower in the winter or spring.

Established plants may be grown for several years in the same pots if they are fed during their growing period, which begins in February and continues until about November. When in active growth they should be kept well watered and at a night temperature of 60 to 65 degrees. In November and December, when they are resting, keeping them on the dry side and in the cooler end of the 60-degree house. When the plants outgrow their containers, they should be repotted. This is best done in February. You can shift them into large pots or divide them and plant the divisions in smaller ones. It is difficult to divide plants without considerable injury to the thick fleshy roots. Hence, you may expect some retardation of growth after dividing. Clivias grow best and flower well under light shade. Provide them with shade except during the dark months of December, January, and February.

Clivias can be propagated from seed. Seedlings are moved from the seed pans into flats and then into pots, shifting them into larger pots as necessary. Keep the seedlings growing throughout the year.

Eucharis

The name *Eucharis* comes from the Greek word for *very graceful*, which describes these plants perfectly. They have handsome oval, evergreen leaves 8 to 12 inches long. The delightfully scented flowers are of purest white, borne on a cluster a foot tall. The plants flower freely. The blooms are attractive in bouquets and excellent for corsages.

Eucharis grandiflora, sometimes sold as *E. amazonica*, is native to Colombia and is the desired species for greenhouse culture. It is

Fig. 21–2. Beautiful members of the Amaryllis family. Upper left, Clivia. Upper right, Amaryllis. Lower left, Zephyranthes.

known as the Amazon Lily. The ideal night temperature is 65 degrees, but it will come along nicely at temperatures as low as 60 degrees. During the bright months of the year, usually from April to October, they require shade. In most localities they can stand full sun from fall to spring. The plant develops from a large bulb, some 2 or 3 inches in diameter, which should be planted in a 5-inch pot. The bulb should be about half in the soil and half out. Bulbs are usually potted in May or June. Water sparingly after potting until growth begins, when ample water is called for. During the growing period the plants benefit from occasional feedings. After the leaves have fully developed move the plants to the cooler end of the 60-degree house, and keep them somewhat on the dry side for about one month, but don't let the leaves wilt. After keeping the plants on the dry side for a month, move them to a warmer part of the house and water freely. Flowers will soon appear, and, somewhat later, new leaves.

Shift the plants into larger pots as necessary. When they have become very large, it will be necessary to divide them, which is best done in May or June. Turn the plant out of the pot and wash the soil from the roots, taking care to avoid injuring them. Separate the offsets, pot them singly in 3-inch pots, and shift into larger pots as required. Water sparingly until growth begins, after which increase the frequency.

Red spiders, thrips, green fly, and mealy bugs are pests to look out for.

Haemanthus—Blood Lily

The genus *Haemanthus* includes about sixty species of bulbous plants from South Africa. *Haemanthus multiflorus, H. Katherinae,* and *H. coccineus* are the species most frequently grown. *Haemanthus multiflorus* has leaves 6 to 8 inches long and flowers borne at the top of a naked stem which is 1 to 3 feet high. The flower cluster is ball-shaped, about six inches in diameter, and bears thirty to one hundred blood-red flowers. This species generally flowers in the spring, usually before the leaves appear. *Haemanthus Katherinae* has three to five leaves about a foot long. The flowers are bright red and occur in a spherical cluster which is about 9 inches across. This species flowers in the spring after the foliage has developed. The leaves of *H. coccineus* are about 2 feet long and the

Fig. 21-3. Anemone, left, and the Persian buttercup, right, are easily grown plants that make the greenhouse colorful in the spring. (Bodger Seeds Ltd.)

flower stalk 6 to 10 inches high. The flowers are red and arranged in a spherical cluster at the top of the stem. Flowers generally appear in August or September, before the foliage comes out.

The bulbs of the species mentioned are about 2 to 3 inches across, or even up to 6 inches. They should be potted with the neck of the bulb just protruding from the soil. Haemanthus prefers a night temperature of 50 to 55 degrees. After potting, water the plants sparingly until they are in active growth, then more frequently. During the summer months, provide shade. When the plants of *H. multiflorus* and *H. coccineus* show signs of going to rest, gradually withhold water but don't let the soil become bone dry or allow the bulb to shrivel. *H. multiflorus* generally has a rest period during winter and *H. coccineus* during late spring and early summer. After the rest period is over start them into growth by applying water. *H. Katherinae* is nearly evergreen and does not need to be dried off. The bulbs do not need to be repotted every year; repotting every third year is usually sufficient. The plants flower much better when the roots are not disturbed. When the plants are potbound, they will benefit from biweekly applications of dilute fertilizer.

Polianthes—Tuberose

There are about twelve species in the genus *Polianthes*. Only one, *Polianthes tuberosa*, commonly called *tuberose*, is a favorite greenhouse plant. This species grows to a height of about 3 feet, has leaves 1 to 1½ feet long and bears sweetly scented, waxy-white flowers about 1½ to 2½ inches long.

The plants grow well with a night temperature of 55 to 60 degrees. The bulbs may be potted at intervals of three or four weeks from January on for flowers in April, May, and June. You may pot one bulb in a 4-inch pot or three or four in a 6-inch one. Water after potting and then keep the plants on the dry side until growth begins, after which they should be given ample water until they are through flowering. After the plants have flowered, the growths will gradually die down. Gradually withhold water during this period. After the growths have died down, rest the bulbs at a temperature of 55 to 60 degrees. Repot the bulbs the following year.

Sprekelia—Jacobean Lily or Mexican Fire Lily

This fantastically beautiful flower (*Sprekelia formosissima*), 4 inches across, of glowing scarlet and velvety texture, comes from Mexico and Guatemala. The plant has narrow leaves about 1 foot long and bears a single flower at the top of a leafless stem. Bulbs are available from January through June and they are planted like amaryllis. Often flowers will be open one month after the bulbs are planted. When the leaves begin to turn yellow, gradually withhold water. After the leaves have dried store the pots in a dry place. When growth begins again repot if necessary or just replace the top inch of soil with fresh soil. During this period keep the soil moist.

Vallota—Scarborough Lily

Vallota purpurea comes from South Africa. The plant is evergreen and hence ornamental throughout the year. The scarlet flowers are funnel-shaped and about 3 to 4 inches long. The bulbs should be potted as soon as received, kept on the dry side until growth begins, and thereafter the soil should be moist.

Zephyranthes—Zephyr Lily

The delicate Zephyr lilies have grasslike leaves, often appearing with the flowers. The flowers are borne singly on thin bare stems, 6 to 12 inches long. Among the species are *Z. candida*, which has white flowers, *Z. grandiflora*, with rosy flowers, and *Z. citrina*, a yellow-flowered species.

Zephyranthes grows best at a night temperature of 50 degrees. The bulbs are small, about an inch in diameter. Plant four or five bulbs, with the necks protruding, in a 6-inch pot. During growth and flowering give the plants ample water. When the leaves begin to shrivel keep the bulbs on the dry side until growth is again active.

Buttercup Family (Ranunculaceae)

Two members, *Anemone coronaria* and *Ranunculus asiaticus*, of this large family are wonderful plants that thrive in a cool greenhouse, one maintained at a night temperature of 50 degrees. Both thrive when potted in an even mixture of loam, peat moss, and sand.

Anemone

Anemone coronaria (Southern Europe to Central Asia) makes a grand display from January through May. The beautiful flowers superficially resemble poppies and come in dazzling shades of white, blue, rose, scarlet, and purple. They are delightful as cut flowers and attract attention at flower shows. The tuberous roots are planted in September or October. When flowering is finished, let the pots remain dry until you wish to start them into new growth. Then begin watering either with or without repotting.

Ranunculus—Persian Buttercup or Turban Flower

The so-called Victoria hybrids of *Ranunculus asiaticus* are vigorous plants with large double camellia-type flowers. The color range embraces pink, yellow, orange, scarlet, apricot, and others. The flowers are long-lasting and excellent for cutting. The clawlike tubers should be planted about 2 inches deep in the fall, with the claws downward. Three or four tubers may be planted in a 6-inch pot. They may be grown in a greenhouse at 45 to 50 degrees or in a cold frame until February, after which they are grown in the greenhouse at 50 degrees, flowering in March and April. When flowering is finished, let the foliage dry down and then store the tubers in a cool dry place until the following autumn.

Iris Family *(Iridaceae)*

Freesia, gladiolus, and Dutch iris are beautiful, easily grown plants. They thrive when potted in an even mixture of loam, peat moss, and sand. As with other bulbs, water sparingly until growth begins and later keep the soil moist. These members of the iris family grow well in a bright, cool greenhouse.

Freesia

Freesias, natives of South Africa, produce graceful sprays of delightfully fragrant flowers during winter and early spring. The color range includes blue, yellow, rose, purple, red, white, and pink. The bulbs, really corms, should be planted in August in pots, flats, or directly in the bench. The corms are quite small; about fifteen can be planted in a 6-inch pot. A flat 4 by 12 by 25 inches will hold about one hundred corms. In the bench the corms should be planted about 3 inches apart each way. The tops of the corms should be about an inch below the surface of the soil. You can pot corms at intervals of three to four weeks for a succession of blooms. The plants will flower in about twelve to fourteen weeks. The stems are weak and require supports.

The corms can be saved and forced a second year, but the percentage which will flower may be reduced. If you wish to save the corms, keep the plants watered after the flowers are cut. When the foliage begins to wither, withhold water and let the foliage dry up, after which remove the corms and store them until August.

Freesias may be quickly grown from seeds sown in May. Soak the seeds for twenty-four hours and then sow them an eighth of an inch deep. They germinate in about a month's time. Keep the seedlings growing in the seed flat or pan without disturbance until September. Then withhold water until the tops have died down completely. Remove the small corms and plant them in a flat or bench with a spacing of 2 by 2 inches. They will bear excellent flowers in January and February.

Gladiolus

For a beautiful display of gladiolus in May plant corms 2 inches deep in a bench during January; space them 2 inches apart in rows 8 inches apart. If the soil is kept at a temperature of 65 to 70 degrees by means of electric heating cables under the soil, the plants will flower earlier, in late April.

Iris

A number of varieties of the Dutch iris do well in the greenhouse, among them Wedgewood, a beautiful blue; Imperator, a deep blue; White Excelsior, a pure white; and Golden Harvest, a splendid yellow. These varieties may be planted directly in a bench in the greenhouse in late October, November, or December and grown at a temperature of 50 to 55 degrees. They will flower in late winter or early spring.

They may also be grown in pots or flats which are stored at a low temperature in the same manner as tulips. With this method plant the bulbs in September or October. Space the bulbs 3 inches apart and plant them so that the nose of each bulb is 1 inch below the surface of the soil. Water thoroughly and then store the pots or flats in a cellar at 50 degrees or in a trench outside. The bulbs may be brought in at intervals from the middle of December on. At a temperature of 56 degrees the plants will flower six to eight weeks after they are brought in. They will flower nicely in a 50-degree greenhouse, but a longer time is required for blooming. Never let the pots or flats dry out. If the flats dry out once, you are not likely to get flowers.

If the largest Wedgewood iris bulbs (10 centimeters and up) are used, and if the bulbs have been precooled by the supplier, it is possible to have this iris flower for Christmas. The precooled bulbs are planted in 4-inch-deep flats in September or early October and then they are stored at a temperature of 50 degrees. The flats are brought into the greenhouse November 15 and grown at a temperature of 54 to 56 degrees. After they have been grown at this temperature for three weeks, the temperature may be increased to 58 degrees and later to 60 degrees to speed up growth. If grown above 60 degrees many of the plants will not flower.

Lily Family (Liliaceae)

The gloriosa lily, the many species of lily (Lilium), and the lily of the valley are magnificent plants. The bulbs may be potted in an even mixture of loam, peat moss, and sand.

Gloriosa—Climbing Lily of South Africa

Gloriosa rothschildiana, the national flower of Rhodesia, is a climbing lily that produces beautiful flowers with gracefully recurved, wavy, yellow and red petals. The flowers make splendid corsages. The long, slender, green leaves bear tendrils at their tips which should be provided with supports.

The plants are started from dahlia-like tubers which are placed horizontally on the soil surface and then covered with two inches of soil. Tubers are generally available in the fall and in the spring. After flowering is through, the foliage will begin to die, a signal to diminish the water supply. When the tops are shriveled remove them and store the tubers in a cool place until potting time in February. Gloriosa is increased by small tuberous roots which develop at the base of the stem. In dividing a large tuber make sure that an eye is present on each piece.

Lilies

There are at least a hundred species of lilies from which you can select. All of them have magnificent, large flowers, and many are pleasingly fragrant. If you select varieties thoughtfully and plant the bulbs at intervals, you can have lilies in flower during all months.

Lilies do well in a porous soil enriched with superphosphate at a rate of a 4-inch potful per wheelbarrow. When planting use pots appropriate to the size of the bulbs. Large bulbs can be potted singly in 6-inch pots, or three bulbs may be planted in a 10-inch one. Bulbs in 6-inch pots should have an inch of soil below them, those in 10-inch pots about an inch of soil above them. After potting, water thoroughly and then keep the bulbs somewhat on the dry side until growth begins, when the plants can stand more frequent watering. If bench space is limited, the potted bulbs may be kept under a bench until growth begins, after which they should be given full sun. Lilies are spindly if they are grown with weak light and if they are crowded. After growth is well along, lilies benefit from weekly application of a dilute solution of fertilizer. A solution made up of 2 ounces of 8–8–8 soluble fertilizer dissolved in 10 gallons of water is suitable. Tall plants should be staked to keep the stem straight.

Lily bulbs can be grown in the greenhouse year after year. When flowering is through, keep the soil watered until the foliage dies down. Even when the shoots are gone, water the soil occasionally. Avoid letting the soil become dust dry. Repot the old bulbs at the usual time. Remove the old soil, but do not injure the living roots.

Lilies are readily propagated from offsets and from bulb scales. Offsets are separated from the parent bulb and planted. The stock can be increased rapidly by plucking off the scales of a bulb and planting the lower 1-inch portion of each in moist sand. In time a small bulb will develop at the base of each scale. Separate the bulb and plant it in soil.

Lilies can also be started from seeds. About two years are required to get blooming plants from seed. Seeds are sown in rows (2 inches apart) on a firmed mixture of equal parts of sand, loam, and leaf mold. Then they are covered with a half inch layer of screened sphagnum moss. The seeds of *Lilium regale, L. candidum,* and certain others germinate within a few weeks by sending up leaves. Seeds of *Lilium auratum, L. superbum, L. callosum,* and others germinate by producing a minute bulb below the soil surface. The tiny bulbs form leaves only after they have been exposed to a cool temperature. Generally, the small bulbs are ready for a cool treatment three months after the seeds are sown. Then the seed pans should be stored for three months in a moderately damp place where the temperature is between 34 and 50 degrees. They are then returned to the greenhouse, where the bulbs will develop. When the plants become crowded, transplant them to fresh soil. Some species bloom the second year but others require three, four, or five years.

Aphids frequently attack lilies, but they may be controlled with a nicotine spray. Nicotine smoke should not be used, because it often burns the tips of the leaves. A virus disease, mosaic, causes the leaves to become mottled with irregular, elongated light-colored streaks. Control of aphids which spread this disease will help minimize the damage, as will selecting disease-free bulbs and discarding diseased plants. Botrytis blight, a fungus disease, appears as small reddish-brown circular spots on the foliage. This disease may be controlled with a Micronized Copper spray.

Varieties of Lily

Lilium auratum. Golden-banded Lily. Queen of Lilies. This is a gorgeous lily, 3 to 5 feet tall, that grows well in pots in a greenhouse. The flowers are white, dotted crimson, with a golden band running through the center of each petal. They are deliciously fragrant. Use fresh bulbs, not cold-storage ones, which do not force well. If the bulbs are potted singly in 5-inch pots about the middle of May, the plants will flower in August or September.

Lilium candidum. Madonna Lily. The Madonna lily, an old favorite, grows to about 4 feet and has beautiful, white, waxy flowers about 3 inches long. Bulbs are potted in August or September, grown at 45 to 50 degrees until March, and then at 55 degrees. With this schedule, the plants flower in May.

Lilium gigantium. The is an immense lily that may grow up to 12 feet high. The flowers are fragrant, about 6 inches long, white with reddish purple stripes inside. The bulbs may be planted during any month, and the plants flower in about three months. Bulbs potted on August 1 will flower in October and November, those on September 1 in December and January, on October 1 in January and February, and so on. The plants grow well at a temperature between 60 and 70 degrees.

Lilium krameri. This beautiful lily with its white and pink flowers is potted in December, grown at 45 to 50 degrees until March 1 and then at 55 to 60 degrees. With this procedure the plants blossom in May.

Lilium longiflorum. White Trumpet Lily. Easter Lily. The Croft, Ace, or #44 variety of this species may be grown as an Easter lily. These varieties have attractive foliage, a medium height, and beautiful, well-shaped flowers. Pretreated Croft bulbs as well as regular ones are available. Pretreated bulbs are those that have been stored at 31 to 40 degrees for five weeks. If the following schedule is followed, pretreated bulbs will flower in 120 days and regular ones in about 180 days. If you wish the Croft lilies to flower at Easter count backward the appropriate number of days and pot the bulbs at that time. If possible, try to use pretreated bulbs and get them from a company that caters to florists. The stock from such companies is generally reliable. If it is necessary to store the bulbs, keep them in moist peat at a temperature of 50 degrees. The bulbs are potted in 6-inch pots, then if you wish to time them for Easter, grow them at a temperature of 60 degrees, day and night. (If you aren't timing them, the day temperature can run 10° higher.) Six weeks before Easter measure the length of the flower buds. If the buds are an inch long continue growing the plants at 60 degrees. If the buds are longer than an inch decrease the temperature gradually. If the buds are not quite visible raise the temperature somewhat, but not over 75 degrees. At 75 degrees the plants will flower four weeks after the buds are first visible. The flower buds should be just turning down two weeks before Easter.

If they are more advanced than this lower the temperature; if less advanced, increase it. Never grow above 75 degrees. The best-quality blooms of Croft lilies are secured when the plants are raised cool during the last week. Throughout the whole growing period use water at the temperature of the greenhouse. After the plants are 2 inches high, they should be watered weekly with a solution made up of 3 ounces of an 8–8–8 soluble fertilizer dissolved in 10 gallons of water. The fertilizer should be applied at night. Throughout the growing period the plants should be well spaced.

Lilium speciosum. Showy Lily. This delightfully fragrant and beautiful lily can be highly recommended for growing in pots in the greenhouse. Varieties *album* and *rubrum* are available. *Lilium speciosum* var. *album* has nearly white flowers, whereas those of variety *rubrum* are white or blush, spotted with carmine. Both grow to a height of about 4 feet. The plants grow well at a temperature of 55 degrees. Plants flower about five or six months after the bulbs are planted. For flowers at Christmas, bulbs should be potted in July. For later flowering the bulbs may be planted in August, September, October, November, or any other month. After receiving the bulbs you may wish to plant some and set aside others for later plantings. Those which are not planted promptly should be stored in moist peat at a temperature of 34 to 40 degrees. Incidentally, all lily bulbs should be stored in moist peat to keep them from drying out.

Lilium tenuifolium. Coral Lily. This lily grows to a height of 1 to 2 feet and bears many brilliant scarlet flowers about 2 inches in diameter. The bulbs should be potted in October, about five in a 6-inch pot, then placed outdoors in a cold frame. If the plants are brought into the greenhouse in February and grown at 55 degrees, they will bloom for Easter. They may be brought in later for flowering at later dates.

Lilium tigrinum. Tiger Lily. The orange-red or salmon-red, black-spotted flowers of this lily are always admired. Bulbs potted in June and grown at 55 degrees will flower in October, those planted in July, at Thanksgiving.

Lily of the Valley

The lily of the valley, *Convallaria majalis*, with its dainty white scalloped bells, adds beauty and fragrance to the greenhouse and is

Fig. 21–4. *Lilium speciosum* is easily grown. (Romaine B. Ware)

a choice cut flower. The lily of the valley has a horizontal rootstock from which arises a small upright portion made up of a bud and many roots. These upright portions are called pips and are used for propagation. Use pips that have been stored at a temperature of about 28 degrees for three months. These pips can be obtained from supply houses. The pips may be grown in flats or pots, planting about twenty-five in a 7-inch pot. The potting medium may be sphagnum moss, peat, or sand. Sand is generally used. Plant the pips close together, with the crown of each about half an inch above the surface. Pack the sand firmly and then water thoroughly. Pips flower in 19–21 days if grown with a bottom temperature of 80 degrees and a top temperature of 75 degrees. A closed propagating case is a good place to grow them. For the first two weeks grow the plants in darkness and keep the atmosphere humid. Then increase the light gradually and give the plants more air. The temperatures indicated above are those used by the specialists. However, they will flower nicely even if grown at a lower temperature. The planted pips may be kept in the dark at 60 degrees until the leaves and spikes make good growth, after which the plants are gradually given light and the temperature increased to 70 degrees. Lilies of the valley may be had in bloom from January through May by successive plantings. Once the pips have been forced they are useless for subsequent forcing. However, they may be planted in a shady place in the garden where they will naturalize and flower in June year after year.

22

Greenhouse and Outdoor Garden

The greenhouse can be a wonderful adjunct to your outdoor garden, enabling you to beautify the yard and to raise a variety of delicious vegetables. To have early flowers and vegetables in the garden it is necessary to sow seeds in the greenhouse long before outdoor planting is possible. By starting flowers and vegetables in the greenhouse you can get earlier maturity outdoors, even allowing you to raise some plants which, if started outdoors, would be nipped by frost before they matured. The use of plants from the greenhouse enables one to make fuller use of outdoor garden space and eliminates the uncertainty that comes from the erratic germination of seeds under outdoor conditions. The young seedlings can be given better care and protection in the greenhouse than they can outdoors. Furthermore, it is a chore to weed stands of seedlings outdoors, whereas, if transplants are used, early weeds can be eliminated before the plants are set out. If you raise your own plants, your choice is not limited to the standard varieties that are available at garden supply houses.

In nearly all communities flower and vegetable plants are in strong demand in late spring and sell for a good price. If you want your hobby to pay its way, you might consider raising plants for sale to gardeners. You can raise superior plants and better meet the desires of gardeners in your community.

Plans should be made about the first of the year by obtaining catalogs from various seed companies. Study them carefully and select the varieties which appeal to you. Each year new varieties are introduced and the adventurous gardener generally experiments with a few new kinds. The kinds and numbers of each to raise may be based on your own likes and dislikes as well as those of prospective buyers. Certainly you should secure varieties that do well in the climate and soil of your area. For your own garden, you will probably want to plan for a sequence of flowers and vegetables throughout the summer. This succession may be achieved by starting some seeds in the greenhouse, others at appropriate times outdoors, and by the selection of early, midseason, and late varieties.

The time for sowing seeds varies from region to region and according to the date the product is wanted. If you want extreme earliness you must start the plants sooner than for flowers and vegetables later in the season. The amount of space available in the greenhouse during the spring months will also determine to some extent the time of sowing.

The tables on pages 362–63 show the approximate dates for starting various annual flowers and vegetables in the greenhouse. These dates are based on having moderate-size plants ready for planting in the garden in late May.

Plants that are sturdy and have several pairs of leaves transplant to the garden better than larger ones. However, if you prefer larger plants and have ample greenhouse space, sow the seeds two, three, or more weeks earlier. For example, if you want petunias to be in flower for Memorial Day sow the seeds in early January and then prick off into flats or small pots before moving them into 3-inch pots in which they will flower. If frosts occur in late May in your locality, the seeds may be started proportionately later. In localities with long growing seasons the seeds may be planted earlier than indicated in the tables.

Seeds are generally sown in flats provided with good drainage and filled with a finely screened mixture of equal parts of loam, peat moss, and sand. The soil surface is leveled and firmed. Sow the seeds in rows, thereby providing better air circulation and more space for the seedlings. Large seeds are covered whereas small seeds are left uncovered. After sowing, water the soil and cover the container with glass or place it in a polyethylene bag. Seeds of plants which are set back by transplanting (for example, cucumber,

Time To Sow Seeds and To Transplant Annuals To Have Plants
Ready To Set in the Garden the Last Week in May *

Plant	Sow seed	Transplant to pots or to flat
Ageratum	March, third week	April, third week
Amaranthus	April, third week	May, first week
Baby's breath	April, fourth week	May, second week
Bachelor's button	April, third week	May, first week
Balsam	April, third week	May, second week
Calendula	April, third week	May, first week
China Aster	April, third week	May, first week
Chrysanthemum	April, third week	May, first week
Clarkia	April, fourth week	May, second week
Cockscomb	April, third week	May, first week
Cosmos	April, fourth week	May, second week
Dianthus	April, first week	April, fourth week
Gaillardia	April, third week	May, first week
Larkspur	April, first week	April, fourth week
Marigold	April, third week	May, first week
Mignonette	April, third week	May, first week
Morning-glory	April, third week	May, first week
Nicotiana	April second week	May, first week
Petunia	March, first week	March, fourth week
Phlox	April, second week	April, fourth week
Salpiglossis	April, first week	April, third week
Schizanthus	April, third week	May, first week
Snapdragon	March, second week	April, first week
Verbena	March, third week	April, third week
Zinnia	April, fourth week	May, second week

squash, melon) should be sown in pots, from which they can be moved to the garden. Sow three or four seeds to a 4-inch pot and later remove all but one seedling.

Seeds of many species will germinate in about two weeks when maintained at a temperature of 70 degrees. Keep the soil moist during the germination period.

After the seeds germinate, the seedlings thrive with full sunlight, good air circulation, and a night temperature of 55 to 60 degrees. As with other plants, careful attention should be given to watering.

When the first true leaves are developed, the seedlings should be transplanted to pots or to other flats where they may be spaced two

APPROXIMATE DATES FOR SOWING VEGETABLE SEEDS UNDER GLASS
AND RANGES OF DAY TEMPERATURES *

Vegetable	Date of sowing	Approximate temperatures (day)
Beets	March 1–15	60–65
Broccoli	February 20–28	60–65
Cabbage, early	February 20–28	60–65
Cauliflower	February 20–28	60–65
Celery	February 20–28	60–65
Eggplant	March 15–25	70–75
Endive	February 20–28	60–65
Kohlrabi	February 20–28	60–65
Leeks	February 20–28	60–65
Lettuce	February 20–28	60–65
Melons	April 15–25	70–75
Onions, sweet Spanish	February 1–10	60–65
Peppers	March 15–25	70–75
Squash	April 15–25	65–70
Tomatoes	March 15–25	65–70

* From *Cornell Extension Bulletin 448*

by two inches. Transplanting into pots is superseding the use of flats. Square plastic or peat pots which are joined along their upper edges are favorites. They can be filled with soil all at the same time. Plants can be removed from the plastic containers without injury to the roots. When peat pots are used the plant is not removed; instead, pot and all are planted. To transplant from the seed flat remove the seedlings in groups with their surrounding soil using a small trowel. Pick up each seedling by its leaves and insert its roots in the hole dibbled in the soil of the new flat or pot. With the thumb and forefingers of both hands firm the soil around the roots. After the seedlings are transplanted, water them and keep them in a shady place until the plants have recovered from the shock of transplanting. Then provide them with full sun and good air circulation.

Do not let the plants become crowded and starved. It is important that ample supplies of water and nutrients be available at all times. Liquid feeding is desirable to keep the plants growing. If the plants become too large before it is time to set them in the garden, they can be transplanted a second time into larger pots.

Fig. 22–1. Growing plants for the outdoor garden. Petunias, front flat, and snapdragons in the flat behind.

Most seedlings of flowers should be pinched when the plants are 4 or 5 inches tall in order to develop bushy specimens. Among those which are improved by pinching are ageratums, branching stocks, lobelias, dahlias, phlox, petunias, and snapdragons.

A cold frame is a good intermediary between the greenhouse and the garden, enabling one to harden plants. One to three weeks before the plants are to be set out in the garden move them into the cold frame to inure them to outdoor conditions. Lift the sash during bright days to keep the frame from becoming too hot, but during the first period close the frame at night. Later, open the sash slightly at night and then gradually increase the ventilation. If you do not have a cold frame and if conditions permit, give the plants in the greenhouse more ventilation and a lower temperature for a week prior to planting outdoors. Also keep them somewhat on the dry side. These techniques result in hardier plants that are better able to withstand the shock of transplanting. For outdoor planting do not try to rush the season; wait until danger of freezing is over at least for the most sensitive plants, such as ageratum, balsam, celosia, dahlia, clarkia, zinnia, and the china aster. Among the half-hardy plants that can survive a light frost are calendula, cosmos, phlox, stock, verbena, and snapdragon.

Plants are easily removed from plastic pots. If joined peat pots have been used the individual pots are separated from the adjoining ones and then pot and plant are set in the garden with little or no checking of root growth. If the seedlings have been grown in flats, a practice known as *blocking* is desirable. Blocking consists of cutting the soil between the plants with a knife, as you would cut fudge, about a week or ten days before the plants are to be planted in the garden. Cutting back the roots stimulates the formation of a compact system of branch roots which holds a good ball of soil. Before transplanting, dampen the soil in the boxes in which the plants have been grown, and let it become uniformly moist. This will make it easier to lift each plant with a good ball of soil around its roots. If it is necessary to remove a lot of plants at a time and carry them some distance, wrap wet cloth or newspaper around them.

The soil in the garden should be moist and in good tilth. Make a hole large enough for the root system, set in place, draw in the soil, and firm it around the roots. Then water the plant with water or, better, with a dilute fertilizer solution.

You may wish to start some garden plants from cuttings. Cuttings of a number of plants may be made beginning in January and continuing until April—among them ageratum, fuchsia, geranium, heliotrope, lantana, and verbena.

Don't forget that the garden can be an adjunct to the greenhouse as well as the reverse. Before frost you may wish to take cuttings from geraniums, heliotropes, fuchsias, and others. Perhaps you will want to lift plants from the garden and pot them, or plant them in a bench in the greenhouse.

Perennials

Perennials are started from seeds, cuttings, or by dividing plants. Seeds of many perennials may be sown in flats or pots in the greenhouse during February and March. The seedlings are transplanted to flats or pots, and then, when the weather is settled, they are planted in the garden. During the first summer they will make sturdy growth, and during the second season they will produce excellent flowers.

If you prefer you can sow the seeds of many perennials in a cold frame during July. After the soil in the frame has been finely worked and is in good tilth, sow the seeds sparsely in rows. Then cover them with soil. Keep the seed bed watered, weeded, and shaded. Give the young plants protection during the winter. The following spring they can be moved into the garden, where many will flower during the summer.

Most perennials can be propagated from cuttings rooted in sand in the greenhouse. The best time to make cuttings of various perennials is given below. Unless indicated otherwise, stem cuttings are used.

Plant	*Make cuttings in*
Achillea millefolium	July and August
Anchusa italica	February and March (root cuttings)
Anemone japonica	March and April (root cuttings)
Asters	May
Campanulas	June and July
Chrysanthemum	May
Coreopsis grandiflora	May
Delphinium	June and July
Dicentra spectabilis	September
Eupatorium aromaticum	June and July
Gypsophila paniculata	June and July
Helenium autumnale	May
Heuchera sanguinea	May
Papaver orientale	March (root cuttings)
Phlox paniculata	May

Of course, practically all large perennials can be divided. This is best done in the spring.

Propagating Trees and Shrubs

Many deciduous shrubs may be propagated from cuttings made in June and July when the new wood is neither too soft nor too hard. The stems are in the proper stage if they snap clean when broken. The cuttings are made about 3 to 6 inches long from the new growth just below a node. Remove the lower leaf or leaves, but allow the terminal ones to remain. Keep the newly made cuttings from wilting by wrapping them in moss or moist cloth. Insert the cuttings in a flat or propagating bench containing sand or an even mixture of sand and peat moss. With a knife, make a slit in the rooting medium and insert the cuttings. Firm with the hand and then water thoroughly. The cuttings should be shaded by stretching cloth 3 or 4 feet above them. Keep the atmosphere moist and syringe the cuttings several times each day. When the cuttings have rooted, pot them in 2½-inch pots. If the climate in your region is mild, the young plants may be planted outdoors later in the season. However, in most regions, they should be carried over the first winter in a cool greenhouse or in a cold frame and planted outdoors in the spring.

Among the many plants that can be propagated from cuttings made in June and July, so-called softwood cuttings, are kerria, viburnum, abelia, azalea, deutzia, forsythia, hydrangea, rose, spirea, lilac, caragana, kolkwitzia, weigela.

Cuttings of conifers are best made in November. Make the cuttings 4 to 6 inches long, remove the foliage from the lower portion of the stem, and treat them with a rooting powder. Then insert the basal end of each cutting in sand. A bottom temperature of 65 degrees speeds rooting. As with softwood cuttings, provide shade and a moist atmosphere, and syringe the cuttings. Yew, chamaecyparis, juniper, and thuya root quite rapidly, sometimes in three weeks. Others, such as firs, spruces, hemlocks, and pines, root more slowly, requiring two or three months or even longer. Many conifers lose part of their needles during the rooting period. These dead needles should be removed. The rooted cuttings are potted and grown for the first season in a greenhouse or cold frame.

Such broad-leaved evergreens as aucuba, box, daphne, euonymous, vinca, and holly can be propagated by making cuttings in late August or September. The cuttings are planted in the greenhouse in sand or in a mixture of sand and peat moss.

23

Vegetables

Greenhouse-grown vegetables are tastier than those purchased at the store. They can be harvested at the peak of their color and flavor, and they can be prepared before any of their high quality is lost. Some hobbyists raise only vegetables, but many raise some vegetables along with their flowers—a few tomato plants and perhaps some lettuce, onions, and radishes, raised in pots, flats, or in a bench.

You can plan for a supply of vegetables throughout the year. Or you can raise vegetables only during the summer when the greenhouse may be empty of flowering plants and when the cost of heating will be slight. Cucumbers and tomatoes are excellent summer crops.

Your own likes and dislikes will influence your selection. If chives, cress, mustard, and other hard-to-obtain greens appeal to you, by all means raise a few. Vegetables which mature quickly and give a high yield in a limited space are most suitable for the small greenhouse. Lettuce, onions, beets, carrots, parsley, and radishes require comparatively little space and some of them can be intercropped with young flowering plants. On the other hand, a considerable area of peas, beans, sweet corn, melons, spinach, and potatoes would be required for just one meal, and these are not well suited to a small greenhouse.

Vegetables grow well in an even mixture of loam, peat moss, and sand. Good light is essential, as is an even supply of water. Don't let the growth become hard from lack of water. Periodic applications of fertilizer make for rapid growth and succulence in many vegetables. The ideal temperature varies with the vegetable; some kinds prefer a night temperature of 50 degrees, others 60 degrees, and a few 65 degrees.

The greenhouse is of great value in starting vegetable plants to be set out in the garden. For a discussion of this topic see Chapter 22.

Vegetables for the 50-Degree Greenhouse

A great many vegetables can be grown in a greenhouse maintained at a night temperature of 50 degrees—among them asparagus, beet, carrot, cauliflower, celery, chard, chive, cress, lettuce, mustard, parsley, radish, and spinach. Beets, carrots, and radishes at times may be planted between the rows of slow-growing plants, to make more effective use of your greenhouse space.

Beets

For fresh beets in late winter and early spring, seeds are sown about the middle of January directly in the bench 1 inch apart in rows 8 inches apart. When the roots begin to make globes, thin the plants so that they are 3 inches apart. Of course, the removed plants can be used as greens. An early variety, such as Improved Early Egyptian, is good for forcing.

Carrots

Seeds of carrots may be sown in January for a crop in the spring. The seeds are best sown in rows 6 inches apart. Later, thin the plants so that they are 2 inches apart in the rows. A light sandy soil favors the formation of straight roots. Early Nantes is a good variety.

Cauliflower

Cauliflower will grow well and produce choice heads in a humid greenhouse maintained at a night temperature of 45 to 50 degrees with a 10-degree rise on bright days. Plants grown from seeds sown in the middle of September will mature in late December or January. Sow the seeds in a pot or flat. The seedlings may be transplanted 15 inches apart in a bench, or they may be moved into 3-inch pots and later planted in the bench. Cauliflower should be furnished an even supply of water. When the cauliflower head is about the size of an egg, it should be covered to protect it from bright light, which will turn the head brown. The head may be covered by lifting the surrounding leaves up and tying them above the head. Be careful not to injure the leaves, and do not tie them together too tightly. They are still needed for food manufacture. Snowball is an excellent variety that produces compact, uniform, solid white heads.

Herbs

The gourmet delights in using herbs to impart interesting flavor and tang to many foods. Many of the herbs are beautiful and fragrant. Among the favorites are anise, basil, borage, coriander, dill, mint, oregano, parsley, rosemary, sage, and thyme. Mint, rosemary, sage, and thyme are propagated by stem cuttings whereas the others are started from seeds. The plants are spaced about 8 by 8 inches in a bench or they may be grown in pots.

Lettuce

If you have bench space available for two or three months you might want to use it for lettuce, a satisfactory and easily grown vegetable for the 50-degree house. If you want a continuous supply of lettuce, plant seeds about the middle of August and at monthly intervals thereafter. You can sow them in pots, or directly in the bench. For sowing in the bench sow two or three seeds at 8-inch intervals in rows 8 inches apart. When the seedlings are up, remove the surplus plants, leaving one at each spot. You can start radishes in the space between the young lettuce plants, for they will mature before the lettuce covers the area.

If you prefer, the seeds may be broadcast in a pot of soil. From the seed pot the plants may be set 8 by 8 inches in the bench, or if bench space is not available at the time, you can move them into flats with a spacing of 2 by 2 inches. When the plants in the flat begin to crowd each other, set them in the bench, or move them on into 2½-inch or 3-inch pots. If there is room between the rows of lettuce previously benched, you can plunge the pots in this space temporarily and later plant them in another part of the bench. Frequent transplantings do not make for better plants but provide more effective use of bench space.

Throughout the whole growing period the plants should be kept actively growing. Never let the soil become dry. It is best to water early in the day so that the leaves will not be wet during the night. Provide good ventilation and control aphids and cabbage worms—two of the more usual pests of lettuce.

There are many varieties of head lettuce and of leaf lettuce that grow well in a greenhouse. Among the good head varieties are White Boston, May King, and Boston Market. Grand Rapids Forcing and Salad Bowl are good leaf varieties, and Matchless is a choice Romaine or Cos lettuce.

Mustard

The leaves of such varieties of mustard as Tendergreen, Florida Broadleaf, and Improved Ostrich are useful in salads or can be boiled like spinach. The plants mature in a month or two. A spacing of 6 inches in rows a foot apart is ample for most varieties.

Radishes

Radishes are easy to grow. Because they mature in about a month, they are suitable for intercropping between slower-growing plants. For a succession, sow seeds at two-week or four-week intervals from October on. Seeds are sown in rows 4 inches apart. Sow at the rate of about twenty seeds per foot of row and later thin, leaving eight plants to a foot. A light sandy soil, 5 to 6 inches deep, is suitable for radishes, as is a night temperature of 45 degrees. The soil should be kept moist but not wet.

The globe varieties are preferred for growing in the greenhouse —among them Early Scarlet, Globe Select, Crimson Giant, Cardinal Globe, and Colonial Forcing.

Vegetables Suitable for Growing in a
60-Degree Greenhouse

Bean, cucumber, eggplant, onion, pepper, and tomato grow well in a greenhouse maintained at 60 degrees during the night. If you have plenty of space you may want to grow them all. Of the group, onions, cucumbers, and tomatoes are favorites for greenhouse culture.

Cucumbers

Cucumbers require a greenhouse that does not go below 60 degrees at night, and will do their best in one maintained at 65 degrees, with a rise of 10 degrees during the day, even more when the days are bright. If you want to raise cucumbers as an early summer crop in the greenhouse, plant two to four seeds in each pot or plant band about March 1, and later thin, leaving one vigorous seedling to each pot. Plant in a bench about April 1, spacing them about 2 feet apart each way. Cucumbers require an abundance of water, especially when they are in fruit. Never let the soil become dry.

The plants should be trained to stakes or to vertical strings, either of which should be anchored to horizontal wires strung above the rows and fastened to the greenhouse roof. The lateral branches should be cut back, leaving one to three female flowers on each branch. Flowers must be pollinated if cucumbers are to develop. Perhaps bees will enter the greenhouse and do the work for you, but rather than count on this it is better to hand pollinate. With a brush, transfer pollen from the anthers of the male flowers to the stigmas of the female ones. The male flowers occur in clusters and the female flowers generally occur singly, or occasionally in groups of two or more. The ovary of the female flower is evident back of the petals, and after pollination it rapidly enlarges and develops into the "cucumber."

Onions

If green onions are a favorite of yours, sow seeds at monthly intervals from fall on. A fall sowing will produce green onions early in the spring. One good variety is White Lisbon, which produces tender, long white onions. Onions grow best with a night temperature of 60 degrees. Seeds are sown half an inch deep and about an inch apart, in rows 6 inches apart. A sandy but rich soil is desirable.

Tomatoes

For tomatoes in spring and early summer, sow seeds in January. For a supply of tomatoes from September until January, sow seeds in June. Seeds are best sown in flats in rows 2 inches apart. After sowing, cover the flat with glass, paper, or burlap until the seeds germinate; then remove the cover. When the seedlings are large enough to handle, transplant them into flats, spacing the plants 2 by 2 inches. The plants may be transplanted from the flats directly to a ground bed or to a bench, or they can be moved into 4-inch pots. If you wish just a few plants, you may grow them satisfactorily in 8- or 10-inch pots, or wooden boxes of about equivalent volume, transplanting them from the 4-inch pots. Plants in benches or ground beds should be spaced about 2 by 2 feet or 1½ by 3 feet. It is best to have the soil 8 to 10 inches deep.

In greenhouse culture, plants are grown erect and usually with only one main stem. Remove the side shoots from the axils of the leaves as soon as they develop. Each plant may be supported with a perpendicular string. The string is anchored to a wire at the base of the plant and extends vertically to an overhead wire. As the plant grows, twist the vine around the supporting string. A wooden stake can also be used for support.

Tomatoes should be grown with a night temperature of 60 to 65 degrees and with a day temperature about 10 degrees higher—and even higher when the days are bright.

Tomatoes require an ample supply of moisture. Lack of moisture stunts growth and may cause the flowers to fall off. The plants benefit from overhead syringings on bright days. A complete fertilizer should be applied at intervals. When the foliage shows a paling of color, it is time to fertilize.

Flowers must either be pollinated or treated with a fruit-setting hormone if tomatoes are to develop. You can facilitate pollination by jarring the plants at intervals, or you can use a camel's hair brush to transfer pollen from the pollen sacs to the stigmas of the flowers. Hormones have been discovered to take the place of pollen, and the resulting fruit is seedless. Apply the hormone according to the manufacturer's directions.

Varieties which have been developed especially for greenhouse culture should be selected. Among those that force well are Livingston's Globe Strain A, Livingston's Globe Wilt Resistant No. 3, Michigan State Forcing, Waltham Forcing, and Tuckcross O.

Index

propagation of, 85
Streptosolen, 182
Subirrigation, 61–62
Succulent geraniums, 175
Succulents, 4, 6
   culture of, 314–15
   features of, 313
   in the fig-marigold family, 323–26
   insects attacking, 110
   in the lily family, 326–27
   main discussion of, 313–29
   in the milkweed family, 327–28
   in the spurge family, 328
   in the stonecrop family, 328–29
Sulfur, 54, 55, 57
Sultana, 201–2
Sundews, 157–158
Superphosphate, 55, 58–59
Supports for plants, 93, 95, 97
Swainsona, 182
Swan orchid, 311
Sweet pea, 63, 67, 68, 69, 96
   diseases of, 115, 125, 149
   main discussion of, 148–49
   pests of, 110, 111, 149
Symbegonia, 224
Sympodial orchids, 282, 284–85
Syringing plants, 38–39, 75
Systemic insecticides, 106

Taxonomy, 11
Tagetes erecta, 150
Tedlar, 21
Temperature, 4, 43–46
   control of, 21–23, 25
   and development of bulbs, 90
   and flowering, 102–3
   requirements for various plants, 43–45
   for rooting cuttings, 81–82
   for seed germination, 66
   in the tropics, 210
Temperature alarm, 26, 47
Temple bells, 275–76
Tersan, 118
Theaceae, 154
Thielavia basicola, 125
Thielaviopsis, 237
Thrips, 111, 112, 115
Thuya, cuttings of, 367
Thyme, 370
Ti plant, 208
Tiger aloe, 326
Tiger lily, 358
Tiger's-jaw, 324
Tillandsia, 244, 247–48
Titanopsis, 324
Tomato, 40, 61, 101, 363
   culture of, 373–74

Trace elements, 54–55
Transpiration, 38
Transplanting seedlings, 69–73, 362–63
Transvaal daisy, 143
Trees, propagation of, 85, 366–67
Trench, for storage of bulbs, 331
Trichocereus, 320
Trichoceros, 307
Trichosporum, 261
Tropics, varied climates of, 9, 210
Trumpet narcissus, 335
Tuberose, 350
Tuberous begonias, 89, 90
   day length and growth, 104
   diseases of, 233
   growing from seed, 230, 232
   in hanging baskets, 228
   main discussion of, 226–33
   pests of, 233
   propagation of, 228–30, 232
Tubers, 35–36, 90
Tulip, 4, 90
   diseases of, 119, 125
   flowering of, 332
   main discussion of, 337–38
   potting of, 330–31, 333
   varieties of, 337–38
Turban flower, 349, 352
Two-spotted spider mites, 111

Umbelliferae, 143
Uromyces caryophyllinus, 121
Urticaceae, 205

Vallota, 351
Vanda
   main discussion of, 310
   potting of, 292–93
   structure of, 285
Vapam, 60, 113, 119
Vascular wilt, 120
Vegetables
   culture in greenhouse, 368–74
   for garden, 363
Vegetative propagation, advantages of, 80; *see also* Cuttings, Leaf cuttings, Stem cuttings, Bulbs, Tubers
Ventilation of greenhouse, 21–23, 25, 39–40
Ventilators, 39–40
   automatic control of, 40
   screening of, 40
Venus flytrap, 4, 157, 158–59
Verbena, for garden, 362
Verbenaceae, 188
Vermiculite, 50, 64
Verticillium, 120, 122
Verticillium wilt, 119, 122